Margaret Tafoya

A Tewa Potter's Heritage and Legacy

Margaret Tafoya

A Tewa Potter's Heritage and Legacy

Mary Ellen and Laurence R. Blair

West Chester, Pennsylvania 19380

Frontispiece photograph:
Margaret and Alcario Tafoya in front of old house,
Santa Clara Pueblo, 1951—52. Clarence and Donald
Fulton photo, Albuquerque, New Mexico.
Front and back cover photographs by Mary Fredenburgh

Library of Congress Catalog Number: 86-62249.

All quotations from Margaret Tafoya unless otherwise noted.

All photographs by Joanne Blair unless otherwise noted.

Printed in the United States of America.
ISBN: 0-88740-080-9
Published by Schiffer Publishing Ltd.
1469 Morstein Road
West Chester, Pennsylvania 19380

This book may be purchased from the publisher.
Please include $1.50 postage.
Try your bookstore first.

Table of Contents

Margaret's hands

Forword

The name of Margaret Tafoya has long been synonymous with the best in Tewa Pueblo pottery. She has admirably adhered to the traditions of her pueblo both in lifestyle and in her pottery. These two areas of Margaret's life have come together through vast research by the authors. They have visited churches, collectors, archives and libraries in addition to numerous other services, to sort through old certificates, historical documents and scraps of papers to assemble the necessary information to complete this book. The most time consuming yet probably the most rewarding aspect of the research was the hours spent in interviewing the family to fill in where the history books could not. With new information on pueblo pottery available in recent publications, a volume on this most influential potter is welcome. The reader will be able to read and study the pre-history and history of the southwest, New Mexico and specifically Santa Clara Pueblo and then assemble the story of Margaret Tafoya and her family in historical, artistic and humanistic contexts.

Margaret Tafoya has long shunned the "spotlight" for herself. Three exhibitions have brought Margaret's pottery to the public through the importance and quality of the work of the family rather than herself as an individual. In 1974 I curated an exhibition for the Maxwell Museum of Anthropology in Albuquerque entitled *Seven Families in Pueblo Pottery.* This was the first exhibition with majority of the Tafoya family shown together. I assembled the main collection of Margaret's work along with that of her mother Sara Fina, for *The Red and The Black,* a retrospective exhibition for the Wheelwright Museum in Santa Fe in 1983. This exhibition looked at the work of Sara Fina and Margaret and opened the viewer's eye to the heritage of Margaret's craft. Also in 1983 at the Denver Museum of Natural History and later at the Colorado Springs Fine Arts Center, the authors curated a major exhibition, *MARGARET TAFOYA, A Potter's Heritage and her Legacy,* which concerned itself with the family through seven generations. This exhibition showed, in detail, the atmosphere of the work and the tremendous diversity within the tradition.

The authors have taken great care in presenting the Santa Clara traditions and the philosophies of the Tafoya family, and also their personal contributions to pottery and art. The pueblo peoples have a way of absorbing what is around them and assimilating and adapting this information to existing ways. The Tafoyas have done this beautifully in their pottery by using historical references to create pottery for a contemporary society. The family has become a focal point in the carrying of tradition in pottery making. With many short cuts being developed by potters to meet the demand for their work, it is refreshing to see the Tafoyas take the added time and extra effort to create an object of exquisite workmanship and honesty.

It has been a privilege to know Margaret Tafoya and her talented family over the past 15 years and a pleasure to discuss with them their processes in pottery making and all that is involved from digging the clay to presenting the finished piece. This, however, is the more mechanical aspect of the total. The other side is a very personal odyssey with the clay; giving and co-operating before the pot is brought from the fire. With pottery all through my background as a potter and collector, we found a comfortable vehicle with which to become acquainted. Margaret has been a major catalyst for my interest in pottery in general and I'm sure I can say that of the authors whose years of exploration are a tribute to Margaret Tafoya and her timeless, classic statement in clay.

Rick Dillingham
Santa Fe, Feb. 1985

Margaret Tafoya, Santa Clara Pueblo, 1951-52.
Clarence and Donald Fulton photo, Albuquerque, N.M.

Preface
"MOTHER CLAY"

It is almost impossible to admire and/or collect any art form without also being curious about the people who created it, their history, and the materials and techniques used to produce it. This is particularly true for Tewa pottery art forms. We attended pottery shows, studied all the specimens available, read the literature on the subject and met and talked with potters and other knowledgable people in a quest to satisfy our curiosity. When all of this was completed, it became evident that the research that has been done in the field of Tewa pottery and, in particular, Santa Clara pottery, is for the most part prehistoric and historical in focus. The need to preserve the native American potter's "living anthropology" was apparent and motivating.

Having known members of the Tafoya family for a period of years, we felt that Margaret Tafoya was the logical choice for such a study. She is not only the matriarch of a talented and famous Santa Clara family, she is also the matriarch of all of the traditional Tewa potters and probably one of the finest native American ceramic artists of her time. Well-known, she had been approached on several occasions concerning publications and television documentaries, but never had the inclination or the time to devote to such projects. Not one to seek publicity, Margaret has always gone about her work as a matter of course; it has simply been part of her way of life. It has only been recently that she could be convinced that her pottery and knowledge of the past should be preserved in written form.

The need to record this information is urgent. The Santa Clara Pueblo, in spite of its people's effort to resist transformation and accommodation of an outside culture, is undergoing change at a rapidly accelerating rate. Traditional Spanish surnames such as Naranjo, Tafoya, and Gutiérrez, given to the native people in the past by Spanish Catholic priests, are being replaced by such Anglo-sounding names as Ebelacker, Folwell, Nichols, Singer, and Swentzell. Within the past century, the common language of the pueblo has evolved from Tewa and some Spanish to English; today, some residents cannot speak or understand their native Tewa tongue. And even more regretably, those who lived through important segments of Tewa history are passing without having had their memories and lives documented. A case point: within a period of two months during the summer of 1980, three renowned Tewa potters passed away. With the exception of Mariá Martinez (Tewa/San Ildefonso), little was recorded about the other two: Grace Chapella (Tewa/Hopi) and Christina Naranjo (Tewa/Santa Clara). Rapid change is quickly dispersing and diluting Tewa heritage.

Margaret Tafoya's first priorty, according to her family, is just that—her family. The state of their well-being is prime concern, and she concentrates her will and stamina on this purpose, whether through ceremonial activities, agricultural pursuits, domestic responsibilities, or her abilities as a potter. A knowledgeable person in many areas, she prefers to stay close to home and to live in a traditional Santa Claran manner. Of her home she says, "This is an old house and I don't want to have any gas [heat] in here. Maybe some day I leave this world. Whoever gets this place can do what they want, but as long as I'm living, I want to keep it the old way" [referring affectionately to her efficient beehive fireplace].

Margaret's approach to pottery making also reflects traditional values. "I don't know if this young generation respect the Mother Clay or not. In our days, that's the first thing our parents tell us. Whenever you go and get the pottery clay, you take your corn meal [for prayers]. You can't go to Mother Clay without the corn meal and ask her permission to come to touch her. Talk to Mother Clay. She has a lot of respect and she will hear your word and she will answer the prayer."

When asked what she would like to have published regarding her contribution to native American pottery, Margaret replied, "I think it should be written that I'm the only one doing these large pieces. At the time when I was young, my mother is the only one, and my Aunt Santana." She refers to the extraordinarily large storage jars, some with the bear paw imprint, and the rainbow—banded water jars that have been made since the latter half of the nineteenth century and for which Santa Clara is famous. She sometimes resents the fact that others have been credited for work created by her and her mother; she considers it the Tafoya right to be recognized as the makers of these traditional and outstanding pieces. In addition, since her children have become independent, she now has the time to devote to putting her memories on tape and answering the questions used for the development of the following text. She seeks recognition not only for her family and herself, but also for her Tewa heritage.

We thought that we were knowledgable about the art of native American pottery when this publication was proposed, but we found that there was far more to be learned. What started as a biography of one Santa Clara lady developed into a many-faceted study. Time after time, we had to restrain ourselves from pursuing interesting side paths and concentrate our research and writing on our subject.

We have deliberately structured the text to follow the prehistory and history of the Tewa and the Santa Clara people and then to concentrate on Margaret Tafoya herself. Other Tewa people and their pottery are mentioned only as they have had an effect on the subject or for the purposes of comparison. It is not our intent to recapitulate the writings of others who have covered the subject of Pueblo potters and their work. Rather, this book is written for the benefit of the historian and the collector interested in Tewa culture and its effect on an outstanding artist. The historical, environmental, and family influences that have contributed to her work and differences between her techniques and those of other potters are emphasized with the hope that some insight will be gained into the way in which her masterpieces have come to be.

A comprehensive presentation of the work of some outstanding scholars may be found in volume nine of *The Handbook of North American Indians,* published in 1979 by the Smithsonian Institution. A Tewa born and raised in the pueblo of San Juan, volume editor Alfonso Ortiz was also responsible for one of the first well-recognized publications to focus on the skill and artistry of Margaret Tafoya. (Ortiz 1974: 170-173)

No Tewa is willing to divulge much information about either his/her prehistory or ceremonial life and since there is no written language, it is often difficult to separate fact from folklore and beliefs. Bitter experience taught the people not to share their tenets and religious culture with outsiders; there was a time when they were willing to do so, but as a result were ridiculed and persecuted. This betrayal drove them to underground religious practices and extreme secrecy. As a result, Tewa and other pueblo cultures have been preserved to a greater degree than many other native American civilizations in the United States. By mutual agreement, we avoided discussion of any sacred or private Tewa subject with Margaret. With rare exception, historical information presented was obtained from a review of available literature; occasional verification was obtained from Tewa aquaintances other than Margaret.

We have attempted to look through the eyes of a Santa Claran to view the history of the pueblo and its people, and have been given the rare opportunity to look into the past, to share her memories, to see the adaptation of her culture, and to study the evolution of her traditions. Little did we realize when we began our research that it would involve travel from coast to coast and as far south as Mexico City . We have endeavored to make our research as complete as time allowed. Although sometimes difficult, we tried to remove personal prejudices from the text and to remain unbiased. If we are in error, either through misinformation or misunderstanding, we apologize and trust that the reader is tolerant. All quotations are Margaret Tafoya's as tape recorded unless otherwise noted.

Our thanks are due to the many individuals and institutions who contributed to our research or who encouraged us. While too numerous to include in its entirely, the list of those who have lent outstanding support is as follows:

CREDITS (alphabetically)

American Museum of Natural History, New York, N.Y.
Archuleta, Mary E., San Juan, N.M.
Becker, Mr. and Mrs. Joe, Española, N.M.
Bonnell, Jon Scottsdale, AZ
Cain, Mary, Santa Clara Pueblo, N.M.
Colorado Railroad Museum, Golden, CO
Colorado Springs Fine Arts Center and Taylor Museum, Colorado Springs, CO
Cubells, Fr. José, Santa Cruz, N.M.
Cutler, Nancy Youngblood, Kansas City, KS
Denver Art Museum and Douglas Library, Denver, CO
Denver Museum of Natural History, Denver, CO
Denver Public Library, Denver, CO
Dillingham, Rick, Santa Fe, N.M.
Ebelacker, Virginia, Santa Clara Pueblo, N.M.
Ebelacker, Richard, Santa Clara Pueblo, N.M.
Enchanted Mesa, Albuquerque, N.M.
Fredenburgh, Mary, Santa Fe, N.M.
Fulton, Donald, Albuquerque, N.M.
Grammer, Maurine, Albuquerque, N.M.
Heard Museum, Phoenix, AZ
Holy Cross Roman Catholic Church, Santa Cruz, N.M.
Jobe, Mrs. J.B., Denver, CO
Lowie Museum of Anthropology, University of California, Berkeley, CA
Martinez, Rowena Meyers, Taos, N.M.
Maxwell Museum of Anthropology, University of New Mexico, Albuquerque, N.M.

Medecine Flower, Grace, Santa Clara Pueblo, N.M.
Millicent Rogers Museum, Taos, N.M.
Museo Regional de Guadalajara, Jalisco, Mexico
Museum of New Mexico, Laboratory of Anthopology, Santa Fe, N.M.
Museum of New Meixco, Photo Archives and Library, Santa Fe, N.M.
Museum of Northern Arizona, Flagstaff, AZ
Museum of the American Indian, Heye Foundation, New York, N.Y.
Naranjo, Nicolasa, Santa Clara Pueblo, N.M.
Naranjo, Teresita, Santa Clara Pueblo, N.M.
National Museum of Anthropology, Mexico City, Mexico
New Mexico State Records Center and Archives, Santa Fe, N.M.
New Mexico Tourism and Travel Div., Commerce and Industry Dept., Santa Fe, N.M.
Norton, Edna, Albuquerque, N.M.
Peabody Museum of Archaeology and Ethnology, Cambridge, MA.
Philbrook Art Center, Tulsa, OK

Reyna, Tony, Taos, N.M.
Rio Grande Sun, Española, N.M.
Roller, Toni, Santa Clara Pueblo, N.M.
Saint Francis Church, Lumberton, CO
Schlosser, Carl, Taos, N.M.
School of American Research, Santa Fe, N.M.
Smithsonian Institution, Washington, D.C.
Stanislawski, Barbara, Santa Fe, N.M.
Stevens, Michael, Taos, N.M.
Street, Hilda, Santa Fe, N.M.
Sunwest Bank of Rio Arriba, Española, N.M.
Tafoya, Lu Ann, Colorado Springs, CO
Tafoya, Shirley, Santa Clara Pueblo, N.M.
Tucker, Mr. and Mrs. Hugh, Española, N.M.
University of Colorado, Boulder, CO
Wilkins, Grant, Denver, CO
Woodard, Tom, Santa Fe, N.M.
Young, Webb, Phoenix, AZ
Youngblood, Mela, Santa Clara Pueblo, N.M.
Youngblood, Nathan, Santa Fe, N.M.
Youngblood, Walton, Santa Fe, N.M.

FIG. 1-1 POSSIBLE, PROBABLE AND ESTABLISHED TEWA MIGRATION ROUTES

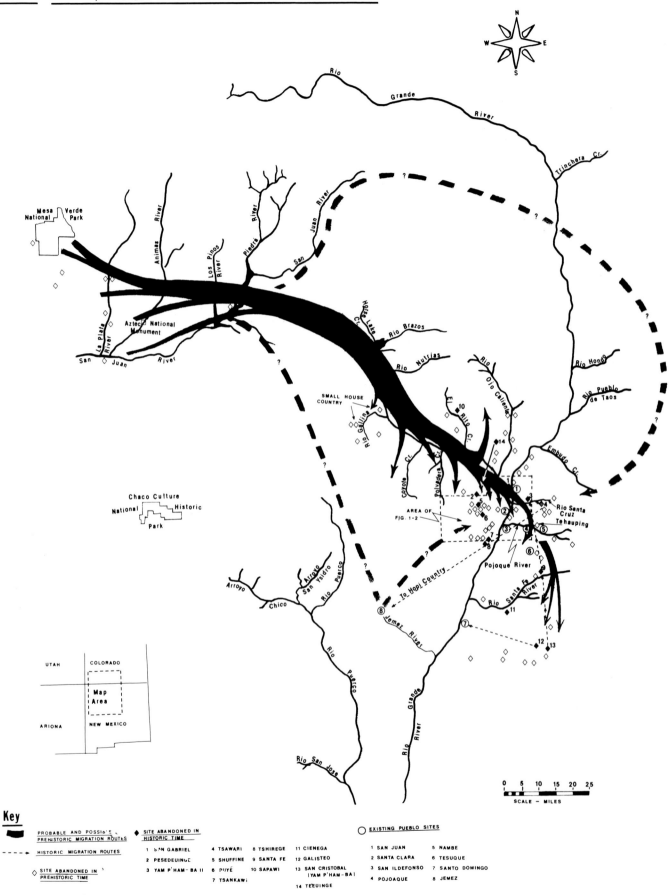

Fig. 1-1 Migratory Map

Chapter 1
History

In the beginning we were one people. Then we divided into Summer and Winter people; in the end, we came together again as we are today. But you can see that we are still Summer people and Winter people.

Tewa Myth (Ortiz 1969:16)

Dawn to the Days of the Knotted Rope
(? B.C. to 1694 A.D.)

Margaret Tafoya and her husband Alcario reside in Santa Clara, one of seven geographically separated pueblos. While all speak the Tewa language, there is no individual leader who has control over both religious or political matters for the group. Each of these villages is a distinct political entity, governed to a large extent by its own internally generated laws. The ties between villages are primarily those of language; however, there are also ties of social and religious customs. Six of the pueblos—San Juan, Santa Clara, San Ildefonso, Pojoaque, Nambe, and Tesuque—are located in the Rio Grande Valley north of Santa Fe, New Mexico. A seventh splinter group makes its home in the pueblo of Hano, atop First Mesa on the Hopi Reservation of northern Arizona.

Through the efforts of archeologists, anthopologists, and other scientists, knowledge of the prehistory, history, cultural development, and customs of the Tewa has been developed. Such findings lead to an understanding of how today's beautiful Tewa pottery art forms have emerged from the past.

How did the Tewa come to settle in their present locations? Anthopologists are divided in their theories on the matter. A widely accepted explanation postulates that most of the Tewas' ancestors were an ancient people known as the Eastern Anasazi, whose principal prehistoric domain was the Four Corners area of the southwestern United States (Cordell 1979: 142-146). However, there are others who favor the idea that the Tewas' primary roots extend from a people who already inhabited the area when the Anasazi migration began. Pottery recovered from many prehistoric sites seem to favor the first theory, but crude ceramics found in other excavations indicate that earlier inhabitants of the area had some primitive knowledge of the craft. It is certain that there were many influences responsible for the development of present Tewa pottery forms besides those attributed to the Anasazi.

Specimens of prehistoric pottery in the Smithsonian Institution's collections strongly indicate that the Indians of the southeastern United States were responsible for the development and ulitmate introduction of the art of incised pottery to the Tewa. While simultaneous invention has been suggested as a possibility, this art form seems more likely to have arrived in the Rio Grande area as a result of trade and population migration. There is also substantial evidence that other prehistoric people living to the east, south, and west of the Rio Grande Valley contributed to Tewa pottery art.

The beginning of the Anasazi culture occured and matured in the southwestern portion of the North American continent. For thousands of years before the birth of Christ, man had lived in this area in small wandering groups driven by the pursuit of food. These people followed the seasons and animal herds or moved about to harvest wild plants and hunt game. They had no need for acquiring stable, non—transportable possessions such as pottery.

About 2000 B.C., human living patterns began to change. Agricultural techniques developed by the peoples of Meso-America spread northward, and North American Indians learned well—digging skills; they then had cause to develop the ability to create vessels that retained water. This required cooperative work, and people began to band together in other than simple family groups. By A.D. 500, village systems were common in the Southwest and other advances followed. For example, the development of more efficient weapons and traps meant that less effort was required for hunting (Woodbury and Zubrow 1979:43-46). Thus, changes took place that dictated the need first, for baskets and later, for pottery. James in 1903 (1970: 17-21) explains how pottery making evolved from basket making in addition to pottery and baskets, large making. In addition to pottery and baskets, large abundant foods were developed.

As sedentary agricultural cultures were developed, these early people found that areas in the northern reaches of the Southwest had more rainfall and richer soils to support their crops. Game was more plentiful in these regions, as well. Agricultural work and hunting could be simplified, and so the population began shifting northward, toward the Four Corners area. As new communities

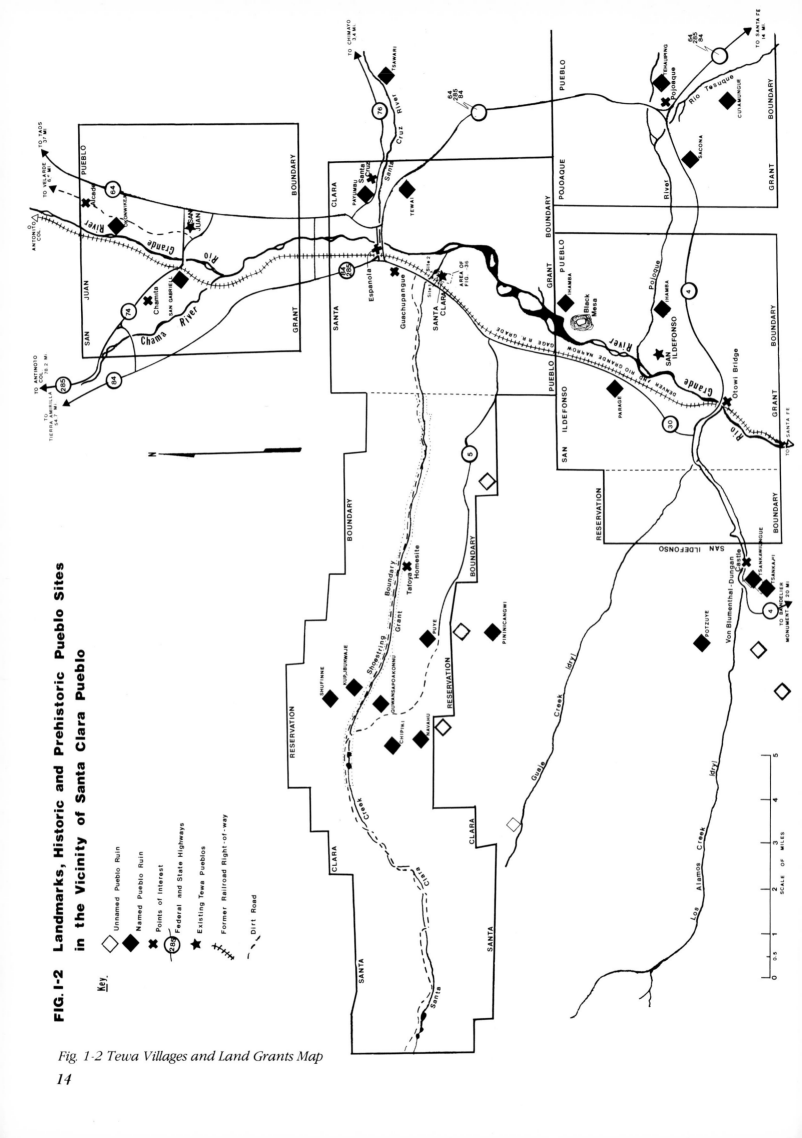

FIG. 1-2 Landmarks, Historic and Prehistoric Pueblo Sites in the Vicinity of Santa Clara Pueblo

Fig. 1-2 Tewa Villages and Land Grants Map

14

Fig. 1-3 Puyé Ruins, ca. 1920. Museum of New Mexico Photo Archives, Neg. No. 42030. Photographer unknown. Since this photograph was taken much of the area has been restored. The Santa Clarans continue to hold ceremonials in the plazas of the old ruins on the mesa above the caves. For location see Figure 1-2.

became more organized and people had free time, they were able to specialize in different types of craft production, and basket and pottery decoration improved. In addition to basket making (pueblo men's work) and pottery making (pueblo women's work), (Herold 1981:3), trades and skills developed that included weapon, trap and snare, tool, and textile production. Thus, a distinct culture, known as the Anasazi, formed, one whose influence eventually extended from the present—day eastern boundary of Nevada on the west to the eastern boundaries of Taos Pueblo on the east, and from Silverton, Colorado, on the north to Socorro, New Mexico, on the south—an area of roughly 150,000 square miles.

It was during the Basketmaker II period (ca. A.D. 1-500) that ceramic ware first appeared in the Anasazi area. From evidence available, it is not logical to assume that pottery was independently developed by these people. It appears to have come to them through exchange with those native Americans who developed the art centuries earlier in Central and South America and the southeastern United States. Once learned, it was elevated to a fine and beautiful state.

For reasons much debated by scholars, a great shift in North American Indian population centers began to ocur during the early part of the twelfth century and continued into the middle of the thirteenth century (fig. 1-1). The great settlements at Chaco, Mesa Verde, and other centers in the Four Corners area were gradually abandoned.

Gradually moving southward from Mesa Verde, the San Juan River basin, and the Aztec Monument areas of southern Colorado and northwest New Mexico, the native people followed the watercourses of the San Juan and Chama rivers southward toward the Rio Grande Valley (Cordell 1985: 39). As they arrived at confluences of various streams that feed the Chama, such as the Rio Ojo Caliente and the Rio del Oso, portions of the population moved upstream and established several large villages. These sites were later abandoned as the migration southward continued down the Rio Grande Valley and onto the Pajarito Plateau. The movement of the Tewa was ever southward because it was felt that those who moved north from a permanent location would not meet with good fortune, a tradition still observed by most conservative Tewas.

During the time of this great migratory movement, an event occurred at the village of Tehauiping (fig. 1-2) that was of great historical significance to the Tewa. According to accounts given to Adolf Bandelier (1892:84), it was there that the tribe divided into two branches, the northern branch elected to remain in the Española Valley and its envrions, while the southern branch moved out to settle an area some 40 miles due south of Tehauiping. Part of the northern Tewa, the Santa Clarans, claim that their ancestors inhabited the now-abandoned Puyé and Shufinne sites on the Pajarito Plateau prior to settling in their present riverside location. (Figure 1-2) According to Douglas (1917:3), "Old men of Ka'po (Tewa for Santa Clara) will tell strange and wonderful stories of their forefathers, when they lived in the great cliff cities of Puyé (fig. 1-3). That was more than a thousand years ago...What came before Puyé, you ask. The old men shrug their shoulders and hesitate. 'Our fathers told us that they lived in the small house country of the north, for by the laws of the Tewas, a people who would prosper would move ever south'."[1]

After moving southward again, the Tewa built small villages on the plateau, but inhabited them for only a short period of time. It is thought that the Tewa of Santa Clara abandoned the large cliff city of Puyé (fig. 1-3) for the plentiful water and fertile soil of the west bank of the Rio Grande in Española Valley at almost the same time that the first European set foot in the southwestern United States in 1539.

At a point due south of the present-day pueblo of Zuni, an impressive Moor named Estevancio, Esteban, or Estevan, arrived with a party of three hundred Mexican Indians (Terrell 1968). The group served as an advance scouting party for the main expedition headed by a Spanish priest, Fray Marcos de Niza.[2] Estevan collected a large contingent on his way north through Mexico, not to assist as guides but to act as his servants and concubines. The manner in which Estevan traveled, as well as the fact that he continually disregarded orders, displeased Fray Marcos enormously.

The first European to set eyes on a pueblo, Estevan approached the Zuni village of Hawikuh with great confidence. He had bluffed, intimidated, and eventually subjugated all of the other native Americans with whom he had made contact on his trip west along the coast of the Gulf of Mexico; why should these people who lived in this impressive village of stone be any different? Thus Estevan committed a grave error in judgement, one that would cost him his life.

As he approached the pueblo, the spectacle he presented was offensive rather than intimidating. Two greyhound dogs running before him, he strode forward to demand homage. His body was bedecked with tinkling bells, feathers, and turquoise and coral ornaments. Most outstanding was his talisman, a prayer gourd rattle with which he threatened those around him. Upset with his appearance and infuriated at his use of the rattle, the Zunis gave Estevan a cold reception. Not heeding the warning, he pressed on and was stoned to death.[3]

It is probable that news of this strange intruder and the manner of his death reached the Tewa at Santa Clara. Many historians have commented on the excellence of communication between the far-flung pueblo groups; messages were carried by runners capable of covering great distances in short periods of time. Word spread rapidly from pueblo to pueblo in spite of the fact that, in many instances, they spoke widely differing dialects. The Eastern Pueblo people probably felt that the intruder had committed offenses for which he was justly executed, and that was the end of it. Surely no other strangers of his type would dare to follow. Unfortunately for the Tewa and other puebloans, even more dangerous newcomers would follow in short order.

The first of these was Fray Marcos, who only dared approach the Zunis from a distance after learning of the death of Estevan. It is thought that he returned in terror to Mexico, where he spread the story that there were only three survivors of the Estevan party. Worse still for the puebloans, he told stories of the great wealth that was to be had from the country to the north; the legend of the Seven Cities of Cibola was born.

Spurred on by Marcos's lies and hoping for riches, the Spanish equipped a large military and exploratory expedition under the command of Francisco Vásquez de Coronado. To ensure safe passage, Coronado thought it prudent to send an advance scouting party led by Melchior Díaz, not only to investigate the enemy but also check Marcos's information. Díaz, because of the unusually cold weather, was unable to proceed as far north as had Estevan. He was, however, successful in gathering facts that indicated the Marcos was not the most reliable reporter; for example, he found that almost all of Estevan's party had survived the attack by the Zunis rather than the three reported.

In spite of Díaz's discouraging reports, Coronado marched northward out of Mexico toward the pueblos. He stopped at Hawikuh where he, too, received a hostile reception, but did not make the mistake of approaching the pueblo alone. A brief battle erupted, during which Coronado was seriously wounded and twenty Zunis were killed. The Zunis were subdued but Coronado was unable to proceed and delegated leadership of various exploration parties to others while he recuperated.

One of these expeditions was led by Captain Hernando de Alvarado, whose chaplain planted crosses in some of the pueblos; the Santa Clarans escaped attention, however, because Alvarado's route took him up the east bank of the Rio Grande, opposite their west—bank settlement.

The languages of the area must have dumbfounded Alvarado. Each of the approximately one hundred pueblos through which he passed used only one of eight different languages. Further complicating matters was the political and military independence possessed by each pueblo. Later colonizing and proselytizing efforts of Spanish military, religious, and political officials were severly hampered by their inability to take these factors into account; the Europeans refused to learn the languages or understand the governments of the natives. Rather, they expected the Indians to learn Spanish, a task for which the pueblos had little incentive and even less inclination.[4]

The explorations and military feats of Coronado and his men were remarkable but implanted nothing but fear, mistrust, and hatred in the minds of the natives. While the people must have realized that other invaders would come, it was almost forty years after Coronado's departure before other Spanish expeditions would enter the Rio Grande region. Then the region experienced four incursions; the first three did not come near Santa Clara, but the fourth was an expedition that would have great impact on this particular pueblo.

In September 1590, Gaspar Castaño de Sosa, faithfully following all the rules for good colonization set down by King Philip II of Spain in 1573, entered New Mexico with the thought of establishing a colony and permanently settling as its governor. These rules set a pattern of conformity for Spanish leaders that almost devastated the Tewa and other pueblo people. While lip service was given to the rights of the natives, the rest of the rules reflected the monarchly's financial concerns by establishing priorities that drained an area's wealth without returning anything to it. To encourage colonization without expense to the Crown, leaders who governed the colonies did so without charging the Spanish treasury. In return, they were granted extensive privileges that included rights to Indian lands, rights to collect tribute from the Indians, and also rights of indenture. The overall effect of these edicts was to encourage entrepreneurs to compete for office, rather than to put in place those who would rule with the objectives of enhancing colonial growth and prosperity. Following these royally established procedures only alienated the Indian people, the source of what little wealth there was in the land.

Castaño de Sosa's expedition included one hundred seventy people, a long supply train, and two brass field pieces (Horgan 1954: 157). His path took him northward along the Pecos River, to Pecos Pueblo, and from there through southern Tewa country, past the site of present—day Santa Fe, and then north to the pueblo of San Juan, where he headquartered. After several days of side explorations, he crossed the Rio Grande and followed the west bank in a southerly direction. In due time, he contacted the people of the pueblo of Santa Clara, making him the first European to do so.

Little is mentioned in his journal about his brief stay at Santa Clara; even the exact day of his visit is obscure. Depending upon interpretation, it either the fifteenth or sixteenth of January, 1591 (Hull 1916: 325; Shroeder and Matson 1965: 132-134). Of his stay, Castaño wrote: "They gave their obedience to His Majesty; a governor, *alcaldes* (councilmen), and *alguacil* (constable) were appointed; a high cross was set with the ceremonies previously mentioned." These ceremonies consisted of setting up a cross, several soundings of trumpets, firing arquebuses, and lecturing (mostly by gesture) on the significance of the cross.

The tremendous problem of communication between the Spaniards and the Indians must have left the Santa Clarans in a state of confusion. With an almost complete lack of verbal exchange, it is difficult to understand how they learned anything about either the complexities of the new Christian religion or of the political structure that they were apparently expected to adopt and superimpose on their centuries—old habits, especially when the contact was limited to a few short hours. It is also interesting to speculate on what basis the selection of individuals to fill the various offices was made. It is doubtful that the Santa Clarans placed much importance on the seriousness of the entire affair.

Both the Spanish colony and Castaño de Sosa faced a short and bleak future. Following his departure from Santa Clara, he crossed the Rio Grande at a point south of the village and proceeded toward the pueblo of Santo Domingo by a rather complicated route. During this portion of his travels, he visited the Tano, or southern Tewa people, whose ancestors had separated from the northern group at Tehauiping and settled in the Galisteo Basin. Thanks to Castaño's journal we have a little information about these southern Tewa, who eventually returned northward and exerted an influence on Hopi pottery and possibly on the pottery of Santa Clara as well.

At the conclusion of this visit to the Tano pueblos, the expedition made its way to the vicinity of Santo Domingo, where Castaño endeavored to establish a capital. He was convinced that his position with the Spanish throne was firm; he had followed almost to the letter the royal rules for colonization, even though it raised dissention within his command. An additional reason for his feeling of security was that he had discovered evidence of mineral wealth, though admittedly minor. He continued to send requests to the viceroy in Mexico City for more soldiers, colonists, and supplies so that his colony could grow and prosper.

The reply to these requests was a detachment of soldiers carrying orders from the viceroy for Castaño's arrest. It was said that he submitted meekly and returned to Mexico in irons. There he was tried, found guilty on all charges, and sentenced to six years in exile in the Philippines without wages (John 1975: 35, 36). Though his case was eventually revirewed and the verdict overthrown, it came too late for Castaño. He had been killed during the revolt of galley slaves aboard the vessel on which he was serving.

Castaño's journals provide little information about the pottery of the period. The most significant direct reference concerned the ware in use during the time of his visit to Pecos. He remarked on the presence of "much earthenware, red and mottled and black: dishes, bowls, salt containers, (*salteros*), basins (*almofias*), cups (*jicarillas*)—very elegant. Some of the earthenware is glazed." (Schroeder and Matson 1965: 100).[5]

Castaño's journal is poor in describing distances and directions travelled but he does mention visiting several active Tewa villages which are no longer in existence. From recent pottery—dating of vessels and shards recovered from various ruins, a list of now abandoned candidate villages can be made. For example, Castaño states: "On the 15th (January, 1591) of the aforesaid, we went to a pueblo which was on the other side of the deep river ..... and we were in it for about two hours."

"And so we then went to another pueblo, a league from this one and we slept in it." (Schroeder and Matson 1965: 129).

It is probable that the first pueblo mentioned was Yuqueyunque, later named San Gabriel — but what was the second pueblo where Castaño spent the night? Study and dating of pottery shards indicate that the village might have been Te'euinge. (Fig. 1-1) It is ironic that a people with no written language should provide firm evidence which would supply possible missing information to fill in the gaps in the history of an expedition of people who had the advantage of writing.

During the period that brackets the arrival of Coronado's party in Tewa territory and the time shortly following Castaño's departure, the Tewa people moved and consolidated their villages. No new sites seem to have been established, but the abandonment of large pueblos such as Puyé, and others was completed. Several reasons have been proposed for the evacuation of these Chama River basin and Pajarito Plateau settlements: sixteenth—century droughts and violence are the most frequently mentioned causes (Shulman 1956: 45-53; Wendorf 1953: 46). It was during this time that a group of Tewa moved from Puyé to the first of two sites located very near the present village of Santa Clara.[6] Other pueblos were established near Santa Clara, but on the east side of the Rio Grande; they were built and then deserted during this period. Sites such as Payumbu, (fig. 1-2) were completely destroyed and only an occasional pottery shard marked its location (fig. 1-4). Fragmentation of Tewa lands and property began in earnest on April

Fig. 1-4 Payumbu Pottery Shards. Shards located on the site of Payumbu or "Winnowing Basket Corner" ruins. For location see Figure 1-2. This pottery, much of which contained black on white painted designs, is typical of that produced by the Tewas of the area during the 16th century. The maximum dimension of the largest shard in this photograph is 5 inches.

30, 1598, when a Spanish colonizing party crossed the border near the present-day city of El Paso, Texas. This party was led by Don Juan de Oñate y Salazar and was so large that it extended for four miles on the trail. The caravan consisted of four hundred soldiers, one hundred thirty of whom had families travelling with them, ten Franciscan priests, thousands of cattle, and at least twenty lumbering wagons carrying provisions and personal belongings. The procession moved slowly northward, halting finally on July 11 near the two Tewa pueblos of Yuqueyungque and Ojke (later San Juan Pueblo), which faced each other on opposite banks of the Rio Grande. Following the tradition his predecessors had established, Oñate simply moved the inhabitants of Yuqueyunque into the village of Ojke, and renamed the former San Francisco de los Españoles; a year later, he changed the name again to San Gabriel. Because the people of Ojke received their Tewa neighbors and the Spanish so graciously, that pueblo's name was altered to San Juan de los Caballeros (San Juan of the Gentlemen).

The Spanish started work almost immediately on a church, the first to be built in Tewa country. The first mass was sung on September 8, 1598, and the initial steps toward the firm and permanent implantation of Christianity were taken. The Tewa proved to be less than cooperative, however; they isolated the church building and eventually moved away from San Gabriel to San Juan. According to Spicer (1981:157), this evacuation was voluntary, probably prompted by a gradual buildup of dislike and mistrust of the Spanish.

It is difficult to imagine any benefits derived by the Tewa or other pueblo populations during the period of Oñate's control. The people were treated cruelly; if they showed any signs of hostility, wholesale confiscation of their lands and property was their punishment. Practicing Christianity was almost a complete failure. Depending upon the account accepted, somewhere between sixty and six hundred Indians were baptized; this was not enough to maintain the interest of the Spanish clergy in view of the area's poverty. The colony was saved, however, by the seemingly miraculous effort of the clergy; within six months, more than seven thousand souls had come into the fold, and the colony was preserved!

Oñate was discretely recalled by Philip III who replaced him with Don Pedro de Peralta. Governor Peralta, acting under strict orders from the king not to conduct costly explorations and not to expropriate the homes of the Indians, moved the capital from San Gabriel to a location further south, naming the new city Santa Fe. This relocation was the source of some pleasure to the Santa Clarans the new center of Spanish activity was now twenty-one rather than six miles away.[7]

None of the approximately twenty-two Spanish governors who followed Oñate was a distinguished administrator. All except one engaged in bitter rivalries with the Church, rivalries that caught the pueblo people in the middle. Claiming to have the interests of the native Americans at heart, each confisticated property and made strong attempts to destroy pueblo cultures and religious values. From the time of Oñate until 1680, the lot of the pueblo people grew steadily worse.

What of the local forms of governments imposed on the pueblos by the Spanish? The pueblos very cleverly managed to use the newly appointed officials inflicted by the Spanish to handle only their external affairs. The true internal leadership which was so vital in maintaining their centuries old way of life continued in a secret but unchanged manner. The government pattern established by the intruder was made subordinate to the ancient ways.

For Santa Clara, as for the other pueblos, this was a time of great change. Tribute was demanded by both the Spanish politicians and the Church. At first, levies were imposed according to buildings; to ease the high taxes, the Indians consolidated, forming larger households. Spanish governors soon realized that legal tax avoidance was taking place and changed the system, requiring assessments on individuals rather than on living quarters.

A second change was the inauguration in 1617 of regular supply-wagon service between Mexico and Santa Fe. This had a profound effect on the lives of all, not only because it brought men and provisions, but also because it supplied the mechanism needed to move traded and expropriated products of the Rio Grande pueblo people to markets in Mexico and Spain. The caravans left Mexico once every three years. It took them eighteen months to complete their circular route, with an eighteen-month break in the journey to service and re-load their wagons in Mexico.

The caravan consisted of approximately thrity-two large, four-wheeled wagons, the first to be seen in New Mexico (Kessel 1979: 144-149). Divided into two equal squadrons, each was headed by a lead wagon that resembled a fleet flagship. Banners displayed the royal coat of arms, and the eight-mule teams were bedecked with special ornamental coverings and bells. These trains were supply lines to the colonists of New Mexico, providing the only regular mail, freight, and passenger service between Santa Fe and the south.

On its way north, the train was attended by Franciscan priests; a military escort; hundreds of mules and horses; various passengers, ranging from royal governors and merchants, to penniless soldiers of fortune. On the return trip, a similar conglomerate was assembled. With the train's establishment, civil authorities had reason to demand more tribute than their needs required, because the excess could now be shipped out of the area and sold in profitable markets.

The Franciscans were the most active representatives of the Church among the pueblos. By far its most ambitious was Fray Alonzo de Benavides, Father President of the river province who came to the area in 1626. Although his writings were as forceful as fanciful they do provide one of the few records which contribute to our knowledge of those times. Fray Alonzo believed that the people of the pueblo had provoked the raiding "Apache of Navaju" (Navajos) into taking hostile actions against them. When he established the mission at Ka'po (which he renamed Santa Clara), his purpose was to minister to both the Pueblo and the Navajo and to convince the two groups to come to an accommodation with one another. After much discussion between the delegations, a nominal peace was established, one which lasted for several years but one which had the ultimate effect of inviting the fox into the chicken coop.

Fray Alonzo was proud of his church at Santa Clara. Saint Claire was the founder of an order of Franciscan nuns who spent much of their time in the choir. As later noted by Fray Francisco Atanasio Dominguez (Adams and Chavez 1956: 114), the mission had no choir loft. Of his church Fray Alonzo wrote, "The church of the pueblo of Santa Clara I founded myself and, as I am the commissary of the Inquisition, these Tewa Indians prided themselves on the fact that I lived among them and painted the coast of arms of the Inquisition in the church of the pueblo of Santa Clara where I lived, since they do not wish any other church to have it" (Hammod and Agapito 1945: 64).

Neither the Navajo nor the Tewa were deeply impregnated with the religion of Fray Alonzo. Within a few years of his departure from New Mexico in 1629, there is little evidence that there were many converts among either people. The Tewa certainly did not seem to be much impressed with the new religion feeling that it often set a poor example at best. There are two classic examples of this.

Strangely, the first of these is provided by Fray Alonzo who claimed much personal success in teaching the Indian Christian ways (Henderson 1977: 8). In his writings, he relates the contents of a discussion he had with one Indian priest who had been converted to the new faith and then became disgusted with its practices, particularly with the actions of the Penitentes. Upon observing their rites, the new convert railed at Fray Benavides; "....'You Spaniards and Christians, how crazy you are! And you live like crazy folks! You want to teach us that we be crazy also!' ....I [Fray Alonzo] asked him wherein we were crazy. And he must have seen some procession of penance during Holy Week in some pueblo of Christians and so he said: 'You

Christians are so crazy that you go all together, flogging yourselves like crazy people in the streets, shedding your blood. And thus you must wish that this pueblo also be crazy!' And with this, greatly angered and yelling (dando vioces) he went forth from the pueblo saying the *he* did not wish to be crazy."

Applegate (1977: 46-48) provides the second example of the San Juan Tewa feelings toward the benefits of Christianity. This tale is similar to ones told at Santa Clara.

"Soon there arose a desperate need for the Indians to call on the new gods for help, for a terrible drought descended on that part of New Mexico. The growing corn of the Indians began to turn yellow and dry, and the water in the river became too low to be led by the irrigation ditches to the new fields which the Indians had made on the higher bank across the river when they gave up their old fields to the Spaniards. Formerly, had such a situation arisen, these Indians would have had a great rain-making ceremonial dance and called on their old god to send them rain. Now, the chiefs of the clans went to the padre at the mission church and asked him to lend them the blessed image of the child Jesus. The padre inquired of them why they wished the image, and the chief of corn clan answered: 'We wish to carry the child Jesus around the cornfields, so that he can see in what a bad condition they now are, and maybe he will have pity on us and send us rain.

"The padre agreed that the Christ Child might go, and the Indians carried it with ceremony over all the fields, chanting and pleading with the little image for rain. Then they returned it to the padre at the mission and went home to await results.

"Now, as sometimes happens in New Mexico in summer, a great cloud-burst rose over the Jemez Mountains and swept up the Rio Grande Valley. It deluged the Indian fields and beat the corn to the ground, and worse still, hail followed the rain and completed utterly the destruction of the crops.

"When the Indians saw what had happened they were very much cast down, for corn was their main staple of diet. That evening the chiefs held a council and early the next morning they again presented themselves before the padre and this time asked that he lend them the image of Mother Mary. The padre was surprised and inquired the reason for this request. The chiefs hesitated, but on his refusal to lend them the image without explanation, one chief said: 'Padre, we wish to carry the Mother Mary around the fields this morning, so that she can see for herself what a mess her naughty little boy has made of our cornfields.'

"The Indians of San Juan say to this day that if you will look at the image of Saint Mary in the old mission church there, you can still see on her cheeks traces of the tears she shed from pity when she saw their ruined cornfields.

"Ever since that time the San Juan Indians have had respect for the Christian gods but they appeal to their own tribal nature gods when they want rain for their growing corn. Then they dress in the ceremonial costumes as in ancient times and paint themselves with ceremonial colors and carrying sprigs of green spruce they form in long lines and shake gourd rattles filled with seeds, to simulate rain falling on green corn leaves. So they dance from sunrise to sunset, to bring down the rain, while nearby a large drum made of a hollow cottonwood log, covered with rawhide, is beaten to imitate the thunder, and a chorus sings the ancient incantations."

Neither the Navajo nor the Tewa were deeply influenced by Fray Alonzo's religion. They were, however, profoundly affected by the churchman's position as a commisary of the infamous Inquisition. With the reading in 1626 of the first formal Edict of Faith to the Spanish of New Mexico, a force was released that would provide one of the prime motives for revolt.

For several decades, the pueblo were shielded from the Inquisition's harsher effects both by distance and by the Church's preoccupation with the edict's political ramifications. Finally, in 1661, an agent of the Inquisition, Custos Posada, began taking testimony. On May 22, he instructed the priests of the region to forbid the pueblo people to engage in the practice of their sacred and beloved ceremonial rites. Further, the priests were ordered to find and destory every sacred Indian ceremonial object, including masks, prayer sticks, and effigies. This action, probably more than any other, planted the seeds of revolt that flowered a little more than a decade later. By the time Inquisition officials were told in 1665 to refrain from interference in the affairs of the colony, irreversible damage had been done; Tewa religion was driven underground where it remains to this day.

The disputes between the civil and religious authorities were severe and excessive. Feeling that his share of the tribute was being unfairly reduced, one governor revived the practice of the *vale,* a small slip of paper which entitled the bearer to abduct Indian children to be used as servants in his household. Some priests commanded the Indians to weave greater quantities of mantas and hangings for the local mission and for export. Afraid that the Church was getting more than its share of tribute, Governor Luis de Rosas had one of his military captains raid the conventos of Nambe and Santa Clara and drive off their cattle. At the pueblo of San Ildefonso he converted the mission buildings in which the Indian was to be taught the benefits of Christian life into garrison quarters.

Considering the ever increasing demands for tribute, the severe religious suppression and the numerous cruelties inflicted on the Indian, revolt would probably have occurred by the middle of the 17th century had it not been for the weakened condition of the native people. Pestilence, famine, and what had become the almost unrestrained raids of the Apache and Navajo tribes had brought the Rio Grande peoples to the verge of extinction. Conditions of the times were described in a letter of Fray Juan Bernal who attempted to explain why he had been unable to deliver a prisoner to the authorities in Mexico (Kessell 1979: 212).

"Sending him at present is all but impossible, Most Illustrious Sir, because this kingdom is seriously afflicted, suffering from two calamities, cause enough to finish it off, as is happening in fact with the greatest speed.

"The first of these calamities is that the whole land is at war with the very numerous nation of the heathen Apache Indians, who kill all the Christian Indians they encounter. No road is safe. One travels them all at risk of life for the heathens are everywhere. They are a brave and bold people. They hurl themselves at danger like people who know not god, nor that there is a hell.

"The second calamity is that for three years no crop has been harvested. Last year, 1668, a great many Indians perished of hunger, lying dead along the roads, in the ravines, and in their hovels. There were pueblos like Las Humanas [Gran Quivera], where more than four hundred and fifty died of hunger. The same calamity still prevails, for, because there is no money, there is not a franega of maize or wheat in all the kingdom. As a result the Spaniards, men as well as women, have sustained themselves for two years on the cowhides they have in their houses to sit on. They roast them and eat them. And the greatest woe of all is that they can no longer find a bit of leather to eat, for their livestock is dying off."

From the east at Pecos to the west at Zuni, the Indians began to feel pressure to revolt. Pushed by drought and hunger, the western Apaches raided the pueblo of Zuni, killed the resident priest with arrows and then stoned and mutilated his body. In the eight-month period from November of 1668 through June of 1669, Apaches were credited with killing six Spanish soldiers and three hundred and seventy three Christian Indians. The pueblo people learned that not only were the Spanish incapable of defending the native people, they were not even capable of defending themselves. The peaceful Tewa people were driven to raiding their own conventos for food. This was not a daring feat, for often convents were not staffed, the priests being driven by fear to seek the relative safety of the church at Santa Domingo where they would be safe from the wrath of the governor and the raids of the nomads. This was a shattering experience for what few pueblo converts there were. Those few souls at Santa Clara were abandoned by their friar for over one year.

All of the pieces were in place for a bloody uprising in the pueblos. The only thing still required was a forceful, intelligent leader who could unite all of the villages. This leader was brought to the fore by the stupid and cruel actions of Governor Juan Francisco Treviño, in office from 1674 to 1677. Following the tenets of the Inquisitions, Treviño, hoping to heal the breach between the civil and ecclesiastical, had forty-seven pueblo religious leaders arrested, tried, and convicted for the crimes of witchcraft and sorcery. Three of these leaders were hanged and the others were whipped and sent to prison. Among them was Popé, a Tewa from the Pueblo of San Juan, a man destined for posterity not only as a zealous religious leader but also as a military genius (Ortiz 1980: 18-22). Simmons (1974: 26) describes the result of these arrests: "A large delegation of chiefs and warriors appeared in Santa Fe and confronted the Spanish governor, demanding the release of their sorcers and offering as ransom chickens, eggs, tobacco, and bales of hides. The governor was much taken aback by this show of force and he hastened to comply with their request by freeing the prisoners. His quick retreat in the face of this confrontation simply demonstrated that the Spanish hold on the province was fast deteriorating."

From the moment of his release, Popé plotted revolt and revenge. The planning took five years and the details were closely guarded secrets—the Tewa had been well taught by the Spanish in the art of keeping secrets. Popé went so far as to order the execution of his own brother-in-law, governor of Popé's home Pueblo of San Juan.[8] The Santa Clarans also provided leaders and assumed a major role in the planning of the rebellion.

The exact day of the revolt was set, and runners were dispatched to each of the pueblos to announce the time of the uprising. To avoid error, each carried a knotted rope; the number of knots signified the number of days before the uprising. To keep track of time, a knot was undone each day. On August 9, 1680, the uprising began and confused terror spread across the length and breadth of the colony.

The Santa Clara people, according to plan and under the leadership of Domingo Naranjo, joined the battle. Two Spanish soldiers and a civilian were killed and a woman and her child were carried off. Two divisions of Santa Clara fighters had been formed, and they mustered in the plaza and went about their assignments: they collected and destoryed any Spanish property upon which they could lay their hands, and continued with the destruction of the church. The hated seal of the Inquisition painted on the church wall was consumed by flame, never to be replaced. Leading the Santa Clara forces was not a Tewa but a *mestizo.* Naranjo's father was a freed Negro slave and his mother was a Tlascaltec Indian of New Spain, a servant who immigrated with a Spanish family to the Rio Grande Valley (Sando 1976: 55). (Naranjo is a very prominent name in the Santa Clara pueblo, borne by many capable potters; Margaret Tafoya's paternal grandmother was María Nestora Naranjo.)

The uprising was short and effective: only sixty-one days elapsed between the beginning and the day the last Spaniard fled deep into Mexico. The Spanish were completely driven from the territory and would not return for a period of twelve years.

During the ensuing twelve years, the region was controlled by a newly formed government of the federated pueblos, led for a year by Popé. Although a brilliant military strategist, he proved to be a despotic and poor peacetime leader; he frequently instituted oppressions as cruel as those of the Spaniards. Never successful in uniting the pueblos politically, his adminstration was plagued with climatic problems; drought severely curtailed food supplies. It was also a time of increased Navajo and Apache raids, since even the minimum deterrent of the Spanish presence was removed. Popé lost his office in 1681 and no strong or effective successor could be found to replace him.

It was during these hard years that the southern Tewa villages were targets of incessant Apache raids. The few survivors of Gallisteo Pueblo fled to Santo Domingo, where they were given refuge and a permanent home. The people of the largest southern pueblo of San Christobal left their village and moved north to Santa Fe, where they hoped to settle permanently. This desire was to be frustrated by future events forcing these people to move twice more before finding a permanent home.

During the eighty two year period of Spanish colonization, there was little influence or encouragement of Tewa arts by the Spanish. Reluctance to borrow or incorporate into Indian life anything Spanish is illustrated by the fact that rather than use a Spanish word which was not in the Indian vocabulary such as the words for some tools, religious practices or new foods, the Tewa would invent an alternate expression (Spicer 1962: 450-451). Dances, however did incorporate some Spanish influence, i.e. the female dance dress was adopted from the Spanish *manta,* a costume which survives to this day and the Matachina Dance with its frequent violin accompanyment are probably the only surviving Spanish influences on Rio Grande Indian music. Spanish carving and carpentry techniques were adopted by a few native people but the Indians received little encouragement to work in either of these areas or the area of painting. What little work was done in the churches was eradicated by the revolt. Weaving was almost eliminated

Fig. 1-5 Tsawari (Wide White Gap Ruin) 1986. site of the original home of the Tewa people in the Santa Cruz Valley, some of whom went to First Mesa at Hopi.

because of its popularity with the conquerors who found a profitable market for it outside of the territory. As a result, weaving became an unpleasant chore against which the Indians rebelled and all but stopped producing. Pottery, which was also subject to confiscation, was not as much in demand in foreign markets and was one of the few art forms done by the natives of the area which flourished.

Officially, the revolt was suppressed on September 13, 1692, when a newly appointed Spanish governor, Don Diego de Vargas Zapata Luján Ponce de León, drew up his troops in front of the entrance to Santa Fe. Amid much fanfare, he demanded and received the surrender of the natives occupying the city. However, for many of the pueblo people, especially the northern Tewa, hostilities continued for almost another four years.

De Vargas's reconquest was said to be peaceful, but was in fact ruthless. The southern Tewa living in Santa Fe submitted to de Vargas, believing his promise of fair treatment. Following the surrender, the people of this group were, for the most part, distributed among the Spaniards as slaves. The remainder were banished to the north to settlements such as Tsawari and YamP'ham-ba II (fig. 1-2) and forced to locate in the Santa Cruz Valley on the Santa Clara land grant.

After the official end of the revolt, the Tewa contiuned to resist Spanish domination. The people of Santa Clara joined their neighbors in armed resistance as de Vargas's promise proved to be worthless and oppression continued. From the Tewa viewpoint, the only alternative was to fight. The warriors of Santa Clara joined with their neighbors, including the newly arrived southern Tewa from Santa Fe, in renewal of the revolt. They fortified themselves on the summit of Black Mesa (fig. 1-2)—a spectacular volcanic formation that rises between Santa Clara and San Ildefonso—and hurled down rocks and arrows and verbal attacks on the enemy below. Dislodging them was not easy due to the mesa's impregnability. Four separate assults were made by de Vargas's army between January 28 and September 4, 1694. The final assult lasted five days and ended in a truce; the Indians were again promised fair treatment if they would return peacefully to their homes. And again, Spanish promises were soon broken.

In 1694, the Spanish took possession of land on the south bank of the Santa Cruz River immediately opposite the southern Tewa's new settlement. A year later, these people were forced to evacuate their new homes to make room for the present-day church and village of Santa Cruz. Driven eastward toward the settlement of Chimayo and their other pueblo of Tsawari (fig.1-5) (Wide White Gap Ruin), they were forced to abandon some of the region's most fertile land. Their fury at being driven from their homes three times in approximately ten years spilled over, and they vented their wrath by killing two priests; on the fourth of June, 1696, Fray José de Arvizu and Fray Antonio Carboneli of Taos were martyred.

Realizing the consequences of their act, they abandoned their homes for a fourth time and fled for their lives, eventually settling with the Hopis on First Mesa, over three hundred miles away.[9] Prior to their departure, the leaders of the pueblo called their people to a meeting and gave them their options. They could stay where they were and certainly be put to death by the Spaniards, they could take refuge in nearby Tewa pueblos such as Santa Clara, or they could migrate.

There was an almost equal division on the issue of remaining with their neighbors or moving to a new area; even clans and families were divided. Some members of the Corn Clan who left for the west were ancestors of the potter Nampeyo, while those who remained behind and settled at Santa Clara were the forebears of Margaret Tafoya.

Traces of the southern Tewa settlements in the Santa Cruz valley are all but obliterated. All that can be found are occasional pottery shards which mark the sites which these strong and proud people once occupied.

The Return of the Spanish Government
(1692 A.D.-1821 A.D.)

But in another image of life during the decades that bridged the eighteenth and nineteenth centuries along the New Mexico River there seemed to breathe the peace of a long ending. It was an image that presented much of Spain and modified all things Spanish with the ways of the river land and its earliest Indian people. It was the life of the haciendas in their riverside pastures and classic glades. Spain was far away and had to be imagined now, instead of remembered. But tradition was strong, even as with each generation it encountered slow change...

(Horgan 1954: 351, 352)

Following the revolt, the pueblo federation that had expelled the Spanish quickly disintegrated. Attacks on native people, their livestock, and their crops by the raiding Apache, Navajo, and Commanche (termed *barbaros* by the Spanish) increased at an alarming rate. Even the meager protection afforded by the Spanish garrisons was missed. To make matters worse, Tewa dressed in captured Spanish garb poached on Ute hunting grounds, thus creating a powerful enemy of a previously non-belligerent nation (John 1975: 120, 121). In spite of the need to unite against these hostile forces, the same pueblo people who formed such a powerful alliance against the Spanish began to quarrel among themselves. Both northern and southern Tewa developed serious differences with their new allies, the Tiwa, Towa, and Keresan peoples. To all of these problems were added those of crop failure, starvation, and the pestilences that periodically swept the Rio Grande Valley. Within twelve years, the great alliance was in shambles. The union became too weak to resist Spanish return, and it was probably true that many even welcomed its reimposition.[10]

In many ways, it was inevitable that the pueblo people were eventually overrun by Europeans; French, English, Spanish—the nationality was incidental to the cruelties inflicted. In a positive vein, the revolt, a natural consequence of these cruelties, realized substantial gains for the pueblo people. Although the law was often ignored, demands for material tribute or impressed servitude became illegal under the new rule. The Franciscan fathers slowly and reluctantly learned not to persecute the followers of pueblo ceremonial rites. A third benefit was the royal decree that set aside well-defined portions of land with adequate water supplies for the exclusive use of the pueblo. Finally, the use of the *encomienda,* a document issued to favored Spanish politicians and settlers that allowed them rights to the fruits of Indian labor, was all but eliminated in the colony after the revolt. De Vargas was one of the few to be issued an *encomienda* by the crown but he wisely refused to exercise his rights. Many forms of impressment were still practiced, but were never legally recognized; over the next one hundred thirty years, they were slowly eliminated.

Although it was widely recognized by the Church that their previous suppression of Indian religion was one of the prime causes for revolt, the Church officials were slow to learn. It was not until the small Tewa revolts of 1696 which resulted in further martyrdom of priests that they finally accepted the fact that some form of accommodation was necessary if both the Church and colony were to continue to exist. Gradually and grudgingly the friars who accompanied the Spanish on their return were forced into forms of religious coexistence which have been passed on to us today. For example, in return for the Indians agreeing to celebrate the Christian feast days, the priests allowed the Indian to celebrate by performing centuries old Indian dances and rituals.

The revolt's end also marked the end of the period that allowed the freedom to settle land and erect new pueblos. A time for limited cooperation with the Spanish settler had arrived. Indian land areas, through either force or necessity, were consolidated and finally restricted to the boundaries of the grants of 1698.[11] The population was thus limited to fewer and fewer village centers. In order to save what was left of their poor world, Indians and Spanish settlers were forced to tolerate each other. Military as well as religious accommodations were crucial to survival.

Also following the revolt, the Spanish crown, drained of much of its wealth by war, found itself in an even weaker position to support the river colony than they had been prior to the conflict. Religious art became unaffordable and could not be replaced; material comforts for the settlers became scarce; fewer professional soldiers could be provided for defense against the ever-increasing *barbaros* raids. pueblo people were captured, enslaved, or murdered; their crops were stolen or destroyed; and their livestock was driven off (Bruge 1979: 103-121).

Santa Clara's protection by San Juan to the north was not always dependable. The neighboring pueblo was not above conspiring with the Navajo. This constant state of turmoil existed throughout the time of Spanish reoccupation and continued until the United States took possession of the colony and forced the raiding nomads to occupy reservations.

To increase the effectiveness of the small professional colonial garrisons, Governor Francisco Cuervo y Valdés formed pueblo militias, trained and led by local Spanish military contingents. While

Fig. 1-6 Sunwest Bank of Rio Arriba, N.A., Española, N.M. Laminated copy of the original United States Land Grant to the Santa Clara Tribe. The Santa Clara Land Grant Survey was completed in 1856. It was not until 1858 that congress approved assignment of the land title to the Santa Clara people and 1864 when the document was signed by authority of President Abraham Lincoln. It bears the signature "D. Neill" who was thought to be Lincoln's personal secretary.

There are only three copies of the deed: one kept at the National Archives; one at the Library of Congress and the third—shown above—is the property of the Santa Clara Indians. To protect the third copy, the First National Bank of Rio Arriba had it laminated with protective plastic on April 27, 1976.

Receiving the encapsulated copy for the tribe are Walter Dasheno, Governor of the Santa Clara Tribal Council, Lt. Governor Alfred Naranjo and Pueblo Treasurer Calvin Tafoya.

not able to stop the raids, these forces probably held the colony together during these times. The Tewa, peaceful people in the past, proved themselves to be courageous fighters (Bruge 1979: 103-121).

The Santa Clara mission, like those of all of the pueblos, was completely destroyed during the revolt; improperly rebuilt, it collapsed shortly after its reconstruction. Scarcity of resources prevented further work until 1758, when it was resurrected under the guidance of Fray Mariano Rodriguez de la Torre, a man of seemingly unlimited strength and patience.

Father Domínguez, while conducting an inventory of Santa Clara Mission in 1776, offered the following remarks about the efforts of the poor dedicated Fray Mariano Rodriguez (Adams and Chavez 1956:114).

"Although the Indians and settlers assisted in this project, no levy was made for the purpose, since most of it was at the fathers expense, as is shown by the fact that he supplied twenty one yolk of oxen to cart the timbers and he fed the laborers gratis.—"

When the roof of the nave of the church was finished, the Indians and settlers left the rest up to the father and his resources. Therefore the funds necessary to roof the transept and sanctuary were taken from his alms. The carpenters, in addition to being well paid, ate, drank and lived in the convent at the fathers expense for a period of two months in the winter, when the days were very short in this region.

Concerning the behavior of the pueblo people toward the church he had nothing positive to record.

"Even at the end of so many years since their reconquest, the specious title or name of neophites is still applied to them. This is the reason their condition now is almost the same as it was in the beginning, for generally speaking they have preserved some very indecent, and perhaps superstitious customs. Of these I mention the following: As Christians, a Saint's name is given them in holy baptism as is the custom in our Holy Mother Church, but they value it so much that they do not mention it among themselves nor are they known by it, but rather by appellations according to the custom handed down by their ancestors.

"They use these to such an extent that most of them do not know their Saint's names, they usually have their joke among themselves, repeating their Saint's names to each other as if in ridicule.—

"Their repugnance and resistance to most Christian acts is evident, for they perform the duties pertaining to the Church under compulsion and there are usually many omissions. They are not in the habit of praying or crossing themselves when they rise or go to bed, and consequently they have no devotion for certain saints as is customary among us. And if they sometimes invoke God and His saints or pray or pay for masses, it is in a confused manner or to comply in their confusion with what the fathers teach and explain. For example, they pay the father for a mass, and he asks them what the intention is in terms adjusted to their understanding, and they reply: *You know, that saint what more good, more big, him you make mass. I not know, maby him Virgin, maby Saint Anthony, etc.,* not to weary ourselves by more. And the father applies it with good direct intention, as he knows he must do." (Adams and Chavez 1956: 254,255)

What Father Domínguez has done, in reality, is to provide almost classic examples of the traits developed by the people of Margaret Tafoya—secrecy, ridicule and rejection—to protect their heritage and culture.

During the years preceeding the beginning of construction on the new mission at Santa Clara, the name Tafoya makes its appearance in the Spanish archives. Tafoya was once spelled T-a-f-u-e-r in Catalan, a former autonomus republic in northeast Spain. (Woods and Alvarez-Olman 1978:133). This was to be the source of the surname bestowed on both Margaret and her husband Alcario as well as many other completely unrelated Spanish and Indian people. The first Tafoya which the authors could find in the records, apparently a complete scoundrel, went by the first name of Juan. In 1707, Juan de Tafolla, one of the different spellings of Tafoya, had suit brought against him relative to taking an Indian captive. The outcome of this action is unknown but apparently caused him little trouble, for only three years later it was recorded that he was engaged in another shady venture. At that time, it was charged that he had extorted large supplies of deer skin in return for obtaining permission from the viceroy for the Indians to retain their kivas. Since it was then illegal to destroy or harm the kivas on very high authority, the permission promised by Juan was meaningless.

Juan's name along with his brother Antonio next appears in the records when they filed a petition for a huge tract of land west of the original Santa Clara Pueblo grant. The boundaries of the land which they claimed were to begin on the east with the western boundary of the pueblo, "on the west as far as the high mountain range, on the north by a high wooded black hill which points toward the mountain, on the south a straight line from the little table land of San Ildefonso" [Black Mesa]. Governor Juan Domíngo de Bustamante approved the grant petition on June 8, 1724 (Twitchell 1914: 280).

The land given to the brothers was at least three times the size of that given to the entire Santa Clara tribe for their subsistence and provided and controlled the source of almost all of the usable water for the pueblo. Naturally the Santa Clara officials objected to losing control of their water supply. As a compromise the Indians were promised that the land would be used only for grazing and not for agriculture, and that only animal corrals would be erected on the property. The brothers were represented by their father Cristobal Tafoya in all of the claim transactions.

In 1733, Juan and his brother made a serious tactical blunder. They requested that the claim be again validated since they lost the original papers but had inhabited the property for eight years. They claimed essentially the same boundaries except for the one on the north which they better defined as running along the boundary of the land of Juan de Mestas. During the course of the proceedings, witnesses were produced and the brothers reaffirmed the fact that the land would be used only for grazing. That they planned permanent occupation was proven by the facts that they had cleared land, built houses and even erected a chapel (Figure 1-2). They closed out their petition by saying that they would have more to say on the matter.

More was said in the following year, when they requested permission to renege on their agreement to use the land only for grazing. They claimed that only water from a spring would be used for irrigation, and that no diversion of the waters flowing in the Santa Clara Creek would be made. Spanish officials looking into the merits of the request located the spring in question and found that it was directly related to stream flow. In addition, they learned that the Tafoyas had been engaged in illegally cultivating the land for a good period of time. The request for agricultural use was therefore denied (Twitchell 1914: 142, 280, 282-284).

According to the oral history of the Santa Clara people, the Tafoyas struck again. Finding their claim to have little value when it could not be used for agricultural purposes, the claim was abandoned, but not before a small strip of property bordering both sides of the creek was sold back to the Santa Clara people, property which formerly and rightfully belonged to the pueblo. This strip of land contained approximately five hundred acres, was five hundred feet wide, and followed the stream on both sides for a distance of roughly nine and a half miles. This was to be the last grant of land to the Santa Clara people under Spanish rule and is officially known as the Pueblo of Santa Clara Land Grant of 1763. To the Santa Clarans, it is known as the "shoestring grant". According to the people, not only did the Spanish Tafoyas receive money for land which was not theirs, they were also given the fastest horse in the pueblo as partial payment. The "shoestring grant" was officially recognized by the United States Government in 1894.

Ironically, after giving the people of Santa Clara land-problem headaches, these Tafoyas were faced with one of their own. They petitioned the governor to evict a family who had squatted on what they considered to be their property in Santa Cruz.

During Spanish rule, it was the custom for priests to bestow Spanish surnames on the Indians of their missions. These names were usually those of the Spaniards who either had the pueblo people as laborers on their farms or who sponsored the Indians when they were baptized. Thus, it is easy to see how completely unrelated people living within the same small community would have identical surnames. Thus, it is possible that both Margaret's and Alcario's ancestors, while unrelated, were either laborers for or were sponsored by Juan, Antonio or Cristobal Tafoya at the time of their baptism by Fray Mariano Rodriguez.

The land surrounding Santa Clara was also being altered by the influx of settlers and associated villages. Chimayo, for example, was established about six miles east of the Santa Clara grant for the alleged purpose of bringing weaving back into the colony, reestablishing the art. It has been noted that these settlers were not only of Spanish decent but included skilled Mayan artisans from Guatemala as well. The village was located on the site of a prehistoric ruin near a Tewa shrine, one at which the pueblo people had worshipped for centuries. A legend claims that this shrine was originally a place where fire and water came from the ground and gradually subsided into a pool that the ancient people called "Tsimayo", or "place of the flaking stone" (obsidian). From prehistoric days to the present, the Tewa people have made pilgrimages to this place to obtain earth, which, when eaten or rubbed on the body, is claimed to have healing powers.[12] Santa Cruz also prospered and was one of three towns in the colony whose population exceeded two thousand. Its location, astride the only road between Santa Fe and Taos resulted in it becoming an influential trading center and providing an important stop over for travelers of the time. Its church, Holy Cross, became the largest in New Mexico after an extended building period (Forrest 1929: 73). Due to its location and size, it became the mother church for various Tewa missions in the area, and its priests visited the missions to say Mass and administer sacramental rites.[13]

Other settlements were established for unfortunate groups of people known as *genizaros*, Indians captured by either the Spanish or a hostile tribe and Hispanicised and Christianized at an early age. This group was ultimately given legal rights and allowed to become landowners of the province. The men generally became soldiers who warded off attacks by hostiles (Young 1983: 2). The *genizaros* founded the town of Abiquiu; located on the south bank of the Chama River some nineteen miles northwest of Santa Clara, it was deliberately established on the invasion route followed by raiding Ute and Navajo from the north.

To prevent uprisings generated by displaced Indians who had taken refuge with the Hopi and other western pueblo people, the Spanish embarked on a pacification and relocation program which it was hoped would result in greater internal strength for the colony. In 1716, Governor Felix Martínez, after a series of unsuccessful attempts at persuasion, led an expedition to the land of the Hopi. The prime objective was to force the southern Tewa, who had been driven from the Santa Cruz area, back to a relocation area in the Rio Grande Valley (Spicer 1962: 193, 194). The mission began poorly. At first, the Spanish endeavored to get the Hopi people of the village of Walpi to force the Tewa residing on the same mesa to come down to negotiate with them. The Walpi people wisely decided that if the Spanish wanted the Tewa to come down, they should climb the mesa and force the descent directly rather than getting themselves involved. Nothing came of the whole affair since the Tewa refused to send a representative down to listen to the Spanish entreaties and propositions. Their main objective unaccomplished, Martínez returned eastward accompanied by less than 150 Indians who consisted of a few Tewa (not Santa Clara related), a few Santo Domingans, and 113 Jemez repatriates. The Tewa on First Mesa had demonstrated that they were there to stay. There they would not only instill new ideas into Hopi religion and pottery-making, but would become instrumental in maintaining the pottery art of the Hopi people themselves.

The civil and military branches of the Spanish empire continued with their shortsighted treatment. Commenting on the Tewa's situation in the Santa Clara-San Juan area in 1807, Lt. Zebulon Pike noted that they were not enslaved to an individual but were enslaved to the state. "...they were compelled to do military duty, drive mules, carry loads or, in fact, perform any other act of duty or bondage that the will of the commandant of the district or any military tyrant chooses to ordain." (Horgan 1954:409)

Pike was struck by the behavior of the Spanish authority and could see how its policies would eventually allow the takeover of the territory by a more benevolent power. His report continued, "I was myself eyewitness of a scene which made my heart bleed for these poor wretches, at the same time that it excited my indignation and contempt, that they would suffer themselves, with arms in their hands, to be beaten and knocked about by beings in no way their superiors, unless a small tint of complexion could be supposed to give that superiority." Pike noted these comments after observing an incident wherein two Tewas returned to their nearby homes without Spanish permission

and the remaining Tewa refused to reveal their names or the destination of the absent men. For their silence, Pike said, several were "knocked down from their horses by the Spanish dragoons with the butt of their lances. . . .The boiling indignation in their souls at the indignities offered by the wretch clothed with a little brief authority!. . The day of retribution will come in thunder and vengeance!" (Horgan 1954: 409). Although not ending as violently as Pike predicted, Spanish authority was to last for only fourteen more years.

During the second period of Spanish occupation, the settlers, not the politicians, the priests, or the military authorities, established good rapport with the native people, probably because their ways of life were quite similar. Though Pike showed contempt for Spanish military and civil authority, he developed a great deal of respect for the settler and Indian, who lived side by side in the northern Rio Grande area. He characterized them as "the bravest and most hardy subjects in New Spain, because constant warfare with Indians [*barbaros*] had toughened them and the lack of easy wealth from gold and silver had made them 'laborious.'" (Weber 1982: 278, 279).

In the international realm, the Spanish mother country was being brought to its knees by poverty and corruption, both from within and from its colonies. Its ability to donate goods and maintain both the Church and the military in its far-flung possessions became more and more taxed. In the Rio Grande Valley, this situation—the *barbaros'* increasing attacks, coupled with Spanish attention to frontiers beleaguered by French and American invasion—resulted in abandonment of the area. In one last show of military strength, the Spanish governor dispatched a mounted party of one hundred regular soldiers and mobilized five hundred militia to capture Pike and his handful of men. Since Pike, in pursuance of his mission to obtain information concerning conditions within the Spanish colony, was awaiting capture in a small stockade, the Spaniard's offensive was unnecessary.

The one hundred thirty-nine year era of the second Spanish occupation of New Mexico was marked by that territory's slow withdrawal not only from the mother country but also from the domination of rulers in Mexico City who had been so influential during the first period of occupation. It was an era when the locality developed a uniqueness of its own due to the strength and persistance of both the pueblo Indian and the Spanish settler. A strong, colorful, primitive art form developed which replaced the art destroyed during the holocaust of 1680 and provided religious art which was required in every colonist's home as well as the churches. The Fransiscan fathers who, according to Horgan (1954:384) "when necessary could do anything," filled the need.—— As the eighteenth century passed and the friars were gradually withdrawn, the work was left wholly with layman. Born in the river world, they knew no direct European influence.[14]

The Church of the Holy Cross of Santa Cruz became the cradle from which these new art forms developed. Fray Andrés García, while stationed at the Church of the Holy Cross in the 1760's, carved and painted many religious objects so badly needed by the church and its people. The work of this man demonstrated that he was an outstanding artist as well as a priest. He had a strong influence on many of the local parishoners who came in contact with him, although his influence on the Santa Clara people is not greatly in evidence. He is considered to be one of the founders of the Santa Cruz School of Art which contributed to the now famous Cordova style (Anon 1983: 97).

It was a time when the area developed a uniqueness of its own; the colony continued to recede into the remoteness of the north and soon reached the point where most, if not all, of the goods needed for survival were made locally.

In comparing the arts and crafts of Spanish and Indian, it becomes apparent that the Spanish borrowed more from the Indian than the Indian from the Spanish. The pigments used by the Spanish were undoubtedly derived from ancient native American mineral formulations used for painting kivas, masks, and kachinas. Spanish prayers to their saints took on an Indian character when accompanied by the sprinkling of salt or cornmeal on the icons. Weaving was revived by the Spanish population but the dyes used were of native derivation, developed long before. Spanish clothing came to resemble that of the Indian and the architecture of the area developed a quality all its own, inspired by the region's uniquely beautiful natural patterns. The Penitentes' holy morada developed a form and secrecy similar to that of the holy kiva.

Other locally produced art objects formed from the gifts of Mother Earth also appeared. Wooden crosses inlaid with straw were polished until they took on the luster of gold. Metal chalices, candle-sticks, and baptismal bowls were replaced by ceramic art pieces or wood carvings created by native people. Tewa clay ware appeared as religious art objects and utilitarian vessels.

Although not greatly influenced by the Spanish, Tewa pottery making improved tremendously during this period. The simple black-on-white decoration was abandoned in favor of more spectacular red and cream colors as potters located and learned to use nearby sources of pigments and slips. According to Harlow, the Tewa pueblos divided into two distinct pottery-producing areas, analogous to their geographic location: northern and southern. The northern group—San Juan and Santa Clara—focused their attention on highly finished unnpainted red and black ware in artistic shapes that perpetuated older forms. The southern group—Tesuque, Nambe, Pojoaque, and San Ildefonso—developed outstanding painted pottery (Chapman 1970: 48; Harlow 1973: 31; and Frank and Harlow 1974: 29).

Mexican Rule Under the Three Guarantees
(1812 A.D. — 1846 A.D.)

The chaotic years in Mexico following the end of the War of Independence saw the problem of Indian relationship to the new national unity emerge as a major concern for the new leaders. By the 1850's however, it was apparent that the policies adopted had resulted in creating not a solution but a most serious threat to the very existence as a unified nation.

Speicer (1962:334)

Despite a series of brief but bloody revolts and counter-revolts that swirled through the river province during the decade of 1810 to 1821, the transition from Spanish to Mexican rule was peaceful. When the new regime of Mexico assumed power, the attitude of the colonists was one of willing cooperation. Viewed in retrospect, however, the rule of the government of Mexico between 1821 and 1846 had little positive effect on either the welfare or future of the colonists; it had even less on the Tewa Indians. Well-meaning and high-sounding promises were made by the revolutionaries, but little thought was given as to how these could be implemented or what real effect they would have on the welfare of the new republic's people. These promises became known as the "Three Guarantees:" independence from Spain, recognition of Catholicism as the only religion, and the equality of all citizens, including native Americans, who were now considered to be Mexican citizens.

Independence from Spain meant little to the residents of the river province. The people had learned over the years to live with scant help from Spain; the financial or political assistance from Mexico was even more meager. They gradually developed their own form of economy and their own art types; each village slowly developed its own government, which worked well with almost no outside intervention. These units continued to operate virtually uninterrupted throughout Mexican rule. The Mexican governors, like most of their predecessors, remained within the confines of the capital at Santa Fe and concentrated their efforts on improving the welfare of the few wealthy colonists of the province, rather than the welfare of the general populace. Any hope the Tewa had of returning to the ways of life that existed before the arrival of the Spanish rapidly vanished.

Recognition of Catholicism as the sole form of religion could not have had much appeal to the Tewa. They had successfully resisted the complete substitution of the Catholic religion for their own ceremonial ways throughout centuries of Spanish rule, and tenaciously clung to their old religion during Mexican domination, adopting only those practices that suited their purposes.

The new government to the south was even less capable of providing any assistance to the Church than had been the old. Churches were required to find their own form of local support, which was usually obtained from two sources: enforced tithing and the collection of *arancles,* or stole fees (Weber 1982: 76). When tithing was abolished by law in 1832, the remaining form of involuntary church support, stole fees (charges by the priests for performing sacramental rites such as baptism, marriage, and burial) were highly unpopular and difficult to collect. It became common practice for the parishioners to avoid these rites rather than pay the necessary fees.

The new edicts and lack of government support had a devastating effect on the Church in general, but the church at Santa Cruz seemed to weather the period rather well. It appeared to have had excellent voluntary support from its faithful, and records indicate that the sacraments were performed at an undiminished rate throughout the period for both European and Indian populations.

Ultimately, the most damaging promise was that of equality. This pledge was given to the Indians without supplying them with either tools or training to properly manage their property under the new system. During Spanish times, Indian groups were restricted to limited parcels of land, which was the best available for agricultural purposes and had a good water supply. Once these restrictions were made, the Spanish government insured that, with few exceptions, Indian land would not become the property of the non-Indian. Under new Mexican law, pueblo people were given the right to either buy or sell land and other properties. As a result, they often sold or traded away, either deliberately or through coercion, more property than they were able to acquire. This proved to be a devastating freedom.

With little governmental protection, the pueblos became the more-frequent targets of intensified raids. To protect themselves, the Tewa encouraged Spanish colonists to move onto their land by giving them choice property to settle and farm; in so doing, they often relinquished their property rights forever. Good farmland was scarce, and with the population increases, pressure to sell became almost impossible for many Tewa to resist. With the "willing relinquishment" of portions of their land, the small Spanish land grant took on an irregular patchwork pattern within its formerly established boundaries. Land was often transferred by verbal agreement or a handshake.[15]

At the beginning of Mexican rule, there was little resentment expressed against the new system. Increasing evidence of mismanagement and corruption, however, inspired dissatisfaction and even rebellion once again. A full-scale revolt broke out in the river province in 1837. Short-lived and with little influence on the future of the citizens, the revolt, known as the "Chimayo Rebellion", deserves brief review, as some of the principal characters in this drama may have been ancestors of Margaret Tafoya, and the fighting took place both on and near Santa Clara land.

Albino Pérez, province governor from 1835 to 1837, was not warmly greeted by the local citizenry. Considered by many in the province to be an intruding outsider and spy, Pérez found Santa Fe to be the run-down capital of a province in a state of bankruptcy, with a small, poorly trained, and almost starving army. He was expected to keep order and at the same time protect the province against the *barbaros'* raids. Realizing that there would be little help from the central government at Mexico City, he felt compelled to institute the first general tax ever levied. He also initiated governmental changes designed to wrest power from the locally elected settlement officials and concentrate it at Santa Fe under his supervision (Sperling 1983: 62-67). What began as mistrust of Pérez soon turned to hatred.

The fuse of the powder keg of rebellion was lit when one of Pérez's henchmen took it upon himself to arrest the *alcalde* of Taos. Infuriated natives, both Indian and Spanish, immediately rescued their mayor and proclaimed their independence from both Pérez's rule and that of the government at Santa Fe. They unfurled their banner of freedom, marched south, and placed it in the village of Santa Cruz.

Upon receipt of the news of this uprising, Pérez foolishly took immediate action. He organized a force of one hundred fifty and sent them to the land of the Tewa to suppress the revolt. The two groups met just south of the Santa Clara boundary on August 8, 1834. Pérez's poorly equipped and trained forces were quickly and decisively defeated. Almost immediately, the rebels followed their victory by marching into the undefended capital of Santa Fe, where Pérez and his followers were rounded up and brutally executed. For the first time in the history of the province, an Indian was made governor and took up residence at Santa Fe; José Angel Gonzáles of Taos pueblo ruled for barely one month. (It is no wonder that few historians include his name in lists of province governors.)

Wealthy colonial families, fearful of a loss of status and privilege, and American merchants, fearful of a loss of wealth, wasted no time in plotting the overthrow of Gonzáles' government.

They conspired with ex-governor Manuel Armijo, who, with partial financing from the merchants, raised an army and marched on Sante Fe from his residence in Albuquerque. Poorly organized, the shaky rebel government was forced to retreat to Santa Cruz. The defense of this village was the responsibility of Pablo Montoya of Taos. Montoya was soon persuaded to abandon the cause of Armijo and to surrender a few of the insurrection's leaders, some of whom also bore the surname of Montoya.[16]

Unfortunately, the capitulation of the Montoyas did not end the hostilities, which continued to smolder until late January 1838. It was then that a battle erupted just east of the village of Santa Cruz in which remnants of the rebel army were severely beaten. The hapless governor Gonzales was captured and put to death in as cruel a manner as his predecessor Pérez had suffered.

Not included in the "guarantees" was the fact that the Mexican government relaxed the strict trade restrictions against the United States imposed by the Spanish. A trade route between the two countries known as the Santa Fe Trail, was opened in 1821. A new class of people, the merchants, began to ply their trade within the river province. Although not completely trusted by either the residents or the officials of the Mexican government, they prospered and became wealthy. They sold or traded anything to anyone who had cash or trade goods. This included the bartering of arms and ammunition to both the locals and the nomadic Indian raiders who were terrorizing these same locals. The descendants or imitators of the first "yankee traders" were to learn that the art and especially the pottery art of the Rio Grande pueblo people was a valuable commodity, and they eventually began to operate Indina curio shops which have provided some of the first public outlets for the ceramic art of Margaret and her ancestors.

All four of Margaret Tafoya's grandparents were born under Mexican rule. On her father's side, Juan Buenaventura Tafoya and María Nestora Naranjo were born circa 1830 and 1835, while her maternal grandparents, Desiderio Gutierrez and Filomena Cajete, were born circa 1838 and 1840. Desiderio's mother, Candelaria Tafoya Gutierrez, made the first piece of pottery that can be directly assigned to Margaret's forebears (fig. 1-7).[17]

Fig. 1-7 Clark Field Collection, Philbrook Art Center, Tulsa, OK. #P.O. 98. Plain black polished storage jar, ca. 1835. Made by Candelaria Tafoya Gutierrez. Unsigned. Identified by Margaret Tafoya, Christina Naranjo, Teresita Naranjo, and Mary Cain. 19¾" high, 21½" diameter. 3¼" high lid, 8½" diameter. The large patch appears to be unfired adobe, and the leather reinforcing is thought to have been done by Manuel Tafoya between 1928 and 1932.

The Yankee Fist with a Slight Taste of the Confederacy
(1846 A.D. — 1879 A.D.)

I am not particularly proud to be here to observe this quatrocentennial. After all, you people are honoring those who brought disease to my country and my people, thereby reducing the Indian population. We have very little land left, but you continue to encroach on our villages. You strip our trees from the watersheds to produce lumber and floods; you plow up the earth to raise grain crops and sandstorms; you have turned a large section of land that used to be fertile. . .into outright desert.

You call us savages for dancing without our street clothes, although our costumes are very pretty, and then you show up at our dances with so little clothing on that we wonder who the real savages are.

Pablo Abieta — 1940 speech [paraphrased]
(Sandow 1976: 148-149)

Their distance from the outside world and their new government in Mexico insulated the citizens of the river province. They were not aware of how badly the relationship between the government of their country and that of the United States had deteriorated. It was summer 1846, when word was passed around that the United States Army was fast approaching the gates of their capital at Santa Fe, before they knew that a state of war existed.

Almost without warning, on April 18, General Stephen W. Kearney led his exhausted troops into the plaza at Santa Fe, raised the flag of the United States on a makeshift pole, and announced that the territory of New Mexico was now part of the United States. Initially, transition from Mexican to American control seemed peaceful, but a group of disgruntled Mexican officials, claiming that they had been promised favors in return for peaceful submission, lit the bonfire of rebellion once again. And again, the battles took place to a large extent on Santa Clara land.

Both Mexicans and Taos Indians, fueled by alcohol and goaded by dissidents, united in a violent uprising against newly appointed American officials, American settlers, and natives friendly to them. The revolt reached its height on January 19 and 20, 1847. The American governor, Charles Bent, was captured, tortured, murdered, and his body mutilated. As soon as Bent was disposed of, the mob moved against other officials and settlers and accorded them the same treatment.

Colonel Sterling Price, in charge of the American garrison at Santa Fe, hastily organized a force of three hundred fifty men who were not only well-armed but were also in possession of four twelve-pound howitzers. They quickly moved out toward Taos (Horgan 1954: 764-768). Simultaneously, the rebels, now two thousand strong, left Taos and made their way down the Rio Grande Canyon toward Santa Fe. The two groups met near the town of Santa Cruz on the land of the Santa Clara people. The rebels, in spite of their greater numerical advantage, were quickly defeated by the American's superior fire power and retreated northward up the frozen canyon. At one point, they made a stand near the small settlement of Embudo, but were routed. Their retreat toward the north continued, with Price's forces following in a pursuit slowed by deep snow drifts and foul weather.

On the morning of February 4, the American forces drew their big guns up to the walls of Taos Pueblo and fired almost point blank. Attention was concentrated on the wall of the church, where most of the Taos warriors and the Mexican rebels had taken shelter. By a combination of heavy shelling and hacking at the walls with axes and metal bars, a breach was achieved. At the same time, the roof of the church was set afire and burning powder fireballs were tossed through the opening. The church was never rebuilt; it stands to this day as a grim monument to the brief battle.

In the three short encounters, the rebels lost almost one hundred fifty men, with an equal number wounded. Compared to this, American losses numbered only ten, with an additional fifty-two wounded. The United States quickly demonstrated that it would not tolerate rebellion and this example served to keep the area under control.

For the Tewa, changes under centuries of Spanish rule and the short period of Mexican rule had often been either resisted successfully or slowly and reluctantly adopted. Over the centuries, Indian and Spanish residents of the river province had settled into a self-contained, and practically self-controlled, way of life. Such was not the case when the Tewa came under the rule of the United States of America. The new rulers were ruthless, had a high degree of vitality, seemingly unlimited resources, a well-organized, if erratic, political system, and a strong and well-organized military machine. Change could no longer be resisted.

It was quickly realized by the new government that the area's most urgent and pressing problem, one which required an immediate solution, was that of subjugating the raiding and pillaging Comanche, Apache, and Navajo tribes. The territory's resources were being depleted by their constant attacks. Between 1846 and 1850, it was estimated that the New Mexicans lost 423,000 sheep, 12,887 mules, 7,050 horses, and 31,581 horned animals to the raiders; the people's ability to resist was deteriorating. In 1851, Colonel E. V. Sumner came to Sante Fe to review the situation in New Mexico and was appalled by what he saw, especially in the province capital, which he termed "a sink of vice." For both "moral" and administrative reasons, he ordered that the army's departmental headquarters be moved from Santa Fe to Fort Union, on the other side of the Sangre de Cristo Mountains. Fort Union remained the headquarters and supply depot for the Army of New Mexico for the next thirty years (Horgan 1954: 811-813).

The relocation from Santa Fe to Fort Union was only a minor step in solving the army's problems. The drained and scattered Union Army of New Mexico was falling behind in their pay. The cavalry found itself almost without mounts, suffering a shortage of horses caused by theft of the stock and an eighteen months drought which severely curtailed the animals food supply.

The first attempt by the new government to contain the marauders came in the form of a notice to the chiefs, governors, and other officials of all the pueblos (including Santa Clara) issued by James S. Calhoun, first American civil governor of New Mexico. It stated that, "the savage Indians who are daily murdering and robbing the people of New Mexico in which I include your pueblo, must be exterminated or so chastised as to prevent their coming into or near your pueblo. For this purpose, you are directed to abstain from all friendly inter-course with the Navajo Indians and should they dare come into your neighborhood, you are authorized to make war upon them and to take their animals and such property as they may have with them, and to make divisions of the same according to your laws and customs" (Bailey 1964:

30). It would have been difficult for the pueblos to carry out Calhoun's orders, for between raids, the Navajo were peaceful traders who exchanged meat, livestock, and woven goods for pottery and agricultural products.

Although the civil governor could organize local militia and issue edicts concerning the pueblos' relations with the Navajo and other hostiles, he did not have the legal power either to arm the locals or control the army. To add to the problem, the Civil War was beginning in the eastern United States, and the army's efforts to subdue the hostiles were diverted.

The Pueblo of Santa Clara was particularly vulnerable to raids, especially by the Navajo. The pueblo, unlike other Tewa settlements, was located on the west bank of the Rio Grande, below the Parajito Plateau and near the Jémez and San Pedro Mountains. The raiders would hide in the mountains and swoop down across the plateau almost at will, secure in the knowledge that relief for the Santa Clara people would be slow in arriving since all roads were on the east side of the river and relief parties would be slowed down by having to ford the river.

It was during the height of these raids that at least one pair of Margaret's grandparents were married. On October 15th, 1855 Juan Buenaventura Tafoya (Long Cloud) and María Nestora Naranjo (Snowflakes on the Leaves) were married at the Santa Clara Pueblo by a visiting priest from San Ildefonso. Long Cloud would go on to become a *cacique,* a position of great prominence as a spiritual leader, and Snowflakes on the Leaves would bear his nine children and develop into an outstanding potter. The clay deposits were located in remote locations which were exposed to the raiders, making clay gathering a hazardous occupation. The same was true for the location of feul which was necessary for the firing process.

Margaret has very vivid recollections of her grandmother María Nestora and her pottery, both large and small pieces.

When considering reasons for eliminating raids in the province, the welfare of the pueblos was of low priority. It was considered much more important to maintain the safety of increasing numbers of settlers from the United States and its territories, and to protect the supply trains needed by Yankee settlers and merchants as well as by the military.

In the summer of 1861, following a punitive campaign against the Navajo in the fall and winter of 1860-61, Colonel Edward R. S. Canby announced his plan for pacification. A critical part of that plan involved the formation of a reinforced First New Mexican Volunteer fighting force under the command of Kit Carson (Kelly 1970: 1-4).

In May of 1862, just prior to the formation of the volunteer group, the campaign against the nomadic Indians was temporarily postponed. The Civil War had come to New Mexico.

The Civil War in the Southwest was waged sporadically, with the Union troops being generally victorious. It appeared for a time that the city of Santa Fe would be permanently lost to the confederates, but because of overextended supply lines and unfortunate breaks, the southern army withdrew from the remote and inhospitable territory. For the most part, the Confederates despised the land and its people, and felt that, (according to Brigadier General H. H. Sibley), "... except for its geographical position, the Territory of New Mexico is not worth a quarter of the blood and treasure expended in its conquest. . . .the indispensable element, food, cannot be relied on. During the last year, and pending recent operations, hundreds of thousands of sheep have been driven off by the Navajo Indians. Indeed, such were the complaints of the people in this respect that I had determined, as a good policy, to encourage private enterprise against that tribe and the Apaches, and. . .to legalize the enslaving of them." (Horgan 1954: 830)

Fortunately for the native Americans the Confederate threat was removed and there was no threat of enslavement. Occupancy by the Confederacy had no influence on the life or future of the Santa Clarans.

Once the Confederate threat was removed, the New Mexico Volunteers and the Union Army could finally give their undivided attention to the troublesome tribes. Brigadier General James H. Carleton, new to the area, enlarged on Canby's earlier plan and began to move against each of the offending tribes on an individual basis. The first step was to locate a site for a new installation, a combination of fort and concentration camp to be called Fort Sumner in an area of New Mexico known as the Bosque Redondo. From a strategic standpoint, this location (some one hundred fifty miles southeast of Santa Clara) was excellent. It also acted as a barrier to the movement of the Comanche and Kiowa nations, for it stood in the center of their rendezvous area. The military was thus able to block the plunder trail that led from the northern end of the territory deep into Mexico (Bailey 1964: 146-148).

The Mescalero Apache were the first to be dealt with; the campaign began on October 11, 1862. By mid-March 1863, the broken warrior nation was interned in Fort Sumner. Less than one quarter had eluded capture and this once proud nation of people were completely subdued. The Navajo were the next group to receive Carleton's attentions. Kit Carson was once again pressed into service, and his first action was to recruit one hundred Ute scouts with the promise that they could retain captured Navajos as slaves and keep their property as prizes of war. The story of the Long Walk, as this bleak period in Navajo history is known, is a dismal one. Eventually over eight thousand Navajo—small children, old people, women—were forced to march from their northern Arizona and New Mexico homes to Fort Sumner, where they were crowded in with the Mescaleros. The tribe was subdued, and their trade with the pueblo people stopped. (Dobyns and Euler 1972: 26-29). The army then to share with other tribes. (Cash and Wolff, 1974: to an Oklahoma reservation that they were forced to share with other tribes. (Cash and Wolff: 56, 59-66) The Utes were the last group to be dealt with; since they learned first-hand the folly of fighting the U.S. army, they peacefully agreed to accept a series of unfair and meaningless treaties.[18]

With the defeat and relegation of nomadic tribes to camps or reservations, the Santa Clarans should have been able to settle down to a life of peace with little interference from outsiders. Unfortunately for them, the shocks brought on by Yankee rule were severe and lasting.

The small land grants allotted to the Santa Clara and other pueblo people by the spanish during the closing years of the seventeenth century—boundaries that had been respected (for the most part) by both the Spanish and the Mexicans—were violated by the United States, in spite of treaty assurances. The land that had been managed so well over the centuries by the Santa Clarans was slowly and insidiously taken from them by erosion, encroachment and condemnation.

Americans in search of good farmland crowded into the territory, impinging upon the original Spanish settlers, who, in turn, pushed the Indians. Poor farming practices, overgrazing, and overcutting of timber laid bare the land, and it could no longer hold water from the rains. The floods which resulted scoured the land, and as the water rushed southward, carried away many thousands of tons of rich farm soil. Additional thousands of acres were taken from the pueblo, condemned for use by road and railroad rights-of-way.

Although the time after American subjugation was a period of difficulty for the Tewa, Juan Tafoya and his family not only survived but thrived. Records kept at Santa Cruz indicate that Margaret Tafoya's paternal grandparents maintained a long-lasting relationship with the Church. They had their nine children baptized as Roman Catholics, they acted as godparents to many pueblo babies, as best man and matron of honor at many pueblo weddings, and as witness at other church sacraments. Long Cloud, with the help of his wife and children, farmed one of the most productive plots in the land grant. As a *cacique*, he had unusually demanding ceremonial duties, but also found time to act as a

negotiator and interpreter for the federal government and business representatives. María Nestora was active in ceremonial affairs as well. Her fourth child, Margaret's father José Geronimo (White Flower), was born on April 17, 1863, just one month after the Mescalero Apache were banished to Fort Sumner.

In addition to Nestora, Margaret's maternal grandmother was also an excellent potter and they both made wares of simple and beautiful lines that foreshadowed much of their granddaughter's work (fig. 1-8, 3-49 and 3-54).

The year 1879 marked the beginning of a period during which the Santa Clarans suffered their greatest loss of land since the return of the Spanish in 1692. During the latter half of the nineteenth century, the United States was swept with a frenzy of railroad building. Fifteen to twenty valuable acres of Santa Clara land were condemned for use as a

for a terminal and the land for the accompanying railroad town of Española.

Realizing the extent of damage that the railroad would do to the pueblo's land, and the irreversible change it would bring to the lives of his people,

Fig. 1-8 Private collection. Plain black polished pitcher, ca. 1875. Probably by María Nestora Naranjo Tafoya. Unsigned. Identified by Margaret Tafoya. 5" height, 4" diameter. Typical of utilitarian vessels made at that time.

Juan Tafoya led a delegation to protest its construction. Although not completely successful, the group did manage to have the right-of-way realigned, avoiding encroachment on the best of the pueblo's farmland as well as land sacred to its people. The remains of the original unused right-of-way is still visible to the discerning observer.

Construction began at Santa Clara and brought not only profound change to the pueblo, but also a lasting effect on pottery styles and motivations for its creation.

The "Chili Line"
(1879 A.D. — 1941 A.D.)

All that you had to do to get the train to stop at Santa Clara was to stand by the track and wave a handkerchief.

Margaret Tafoya

On the continuum of recorded Tewa history, the Santa Fe branch of the Denver and Rio Grande Railroad was but a flashing moment. In spite of its brief life of only sixty-one years, however, this little railroad brought dramatic changes in the life of the Santa Clara people and their neighbors in the northern Rio Grande Valley. These people, who had resisted and repelled change throughout the centuries, would never overcome that brought on by the railroad's intrusion. Their economy changed, their trading habits changed, and they were exposed to the outside world and the investigations of archeologists and anthropologists.

It had long been realized that rail link between the major cities and agricultural centers of Colorado and the trade center and capital city of Santa Fe was desirable and could be profitable, but work on the roadbed was delayed for many reasons. Hostiles had to be removed, there were political blocks, there was a bitter railroad war going on to the north at Royal Gorge, and finally, many potential backers suffered financial reverses.

The "railroad war," a conflict between the Denver and Rio Grande and the Santa Fe, was concluded by a "treaty", one of the terms of which was that the D & RG would not push its track further than a point ninety miles south of the territorial line between New Mexico and Colorado. Nonetheless, D & RG management found a way to circumvent this agreement, and the line entered pueblo land in December 1879.

Almost simultaneously, a new company, the Texas, Santa Fe and Northern Railroad, was formed; it eventually completed a short line from Santa Fe to Santa Clara Pueblo, where it joined the Denver and Rio Grande Railroad in 1887. The two lines merged, with the D & RG in control. The famous "Chili Line" was a reality (Chappell 1969).

The construction of a rail line within their land—land to which President Lincoln granted them an exclusive right a mere fifteen years earlier (fig. 1-6)—made a mockery of U.S. guarantees. The pueblo was torn open and exposed to intrusions from the outside world and its alien culture. Field expeditions to Puyé other sacred Tewa shrines could be arranged for anyone who could afford the railroad fare. For $22.95, one could purchase a round-trip excursion to the pueblo from Denver; for an additional $3, saddle horses could be rented and room and board could be obtained at camps a few moments' walk from these sites. Special excursions were arranged from Santa Fe to Santa Clara and other pueblos so that tourists could watch the ceremonial dances. What was once a difficult and uncomfortable expedition could be economically accomplished with relative ease and comfort. By the time of Margaret's birth, such invasions had become commonplace (fig. 1-9).

Not only did the "Chili Line" provide the non-Indian with easy access to the Tewa's world, it also provided the Indian a means to explore the outside. Through the efforts of some Santa Clarans—chief among them Margaret's uncles Tomas (Lightning) and José M. (Red Bird)—the people began to venture from the pueblo for short periods during the summer to give exhibitions of Tewa dance at such resorts as Seven Falls and Manitou Springs in Colorado. As a result of the adventurous spirit of these two men, many other groups went out to entertain tourists; they found summer work both profitable and a welcome change from the routine of the pueblo. As part of these appearances, it was natural for the women that accompanied them to sell their pottery in formerly inaccessible areas. This led to wider cultural exchange and the establishment of a broader network of business relationships between the native American artist and the Anglo trader.[19]

The railroad had other influences on Santa Clarans. Different ethnic traditions were introduced to the pueblo through intermarriage of railroad workers with Tewa women. The railroad also provided a system of time-keeping; the northbound trains whistle as it passed the pueblo signified that noon was nearly at hand and that the people could cease their labors for a welcome rest and lunch break.[20] The pueblo's five o'clock quitting signal was the ringing of a bell on the small railroad handcar that passed from the south on its way toward its home base in Española (Sando 1975: 53-59). Spectacular wrecks provided dramatic news for the local citizens—in 1889, a train plummeted into an arroyo after failing to cross a burnt-out trestle; in 1891, an engine jumped the tracks at Otowi Bridge; in 1893, a train crashed through a trestle near Tesuque Pueblo; and in 1923, a wreck occurred just south of Española when the track gave

Fig. 1-9 "Indians Who Came to Meet the Train." Courtesy of the Museum of the American Indian, Heye Foundation, New York. Photographer George H. Pepper. Pepper was a frequent traveler in the Southwest and was in charge of the first expeditions which excavated the Chaco Ruins. He photographed the Santa Clara Feast Day activities on August 12th, 1903, the same day that this photograph was taken and approximately one year before Margaret's birth.

way and lost its mooring in a roadbed turned to soft mud by heavy rains.[21]

At the time of its operation, one of the most important functions of the railroad was to transport produce and livestock into and out of Española Valley. Thus, local apples, cherries, and piñon nuts (ten freight car loads in a good year, harvested primarily by Indians) were shipped to areas that had never experienced these delicacies before. It also moved refrigerated meat and live, squealing hogs from the San Luis Valley to Santa Fe for transport to waiting west coast markets.

In the context of pottery, the most lasting influence the railroad had was to de-emphasize the need to create utilitarian ware, to emphasize the tourist-curio pottery market and later, the market for fine art. Beginning in 1821, factory made pots, pans, food storage, and eating utensils began to reach New Mexico via the Santa Fe trail, but only a small number of these entered the northern pueblos. With the coming of the railroad and the establishment of Española as a trade center, these goods flooded the shelves of the markets in the newly created rail town and became readily available to the Santa Clara people. The need and incentive to make food- and water-containing vessels quickly disappeared; today, there are few who have the skill

to produce these beautiful objects—Juan Buenaventura Tafoya's descendants are among this select group. Accelerating this loss were the train passengers. They did not have room to carry the large pottery pieces home in their luggage and so sought out the souvenier or smaller ceramic piece. In doing so, they often purchased items that were quickly and poorly formed, polished, and fired.

Conversely, the railroad provided a safe, rapid means of transporting Santa Clara pottery to the homes of east coast collectors and museum archives. In 1879 and 1880, James Stevenson, under the direction of John Wesley Powell, gathered a huge collection of pottery representative of all of the southwestern pueblos (which is now buried in the archives of the Smithsonian Institution). Stevenson found the ware at Santa Clara so interesting that he spent two seasons there studying; at least one of Margaret's mother's pieces is represented in this group (fig. 2-8)

Shortly after the departure of Stevenson, Captain John Gregory Bourke arrived on the scene often travelling to the Santa Clara area via the "Chili Line". Bourke, who was working on a government assignment concerning Indian affairs, kept an interesting and well written diary about the country and its people and vividly reviewed his journeys on the narrow gauge rail line (Bloom 1936). On July 16, 1881, he hired Pablo Tafoya (relationship to either Margaret or Alcario Tafoya unknown), Francisco Naranjo and Rafael Vigil to act as guides and interpreters. "To put them in good humor, I not only hired these men as guides, but purchased freely of pottery, baskets and apricots ———". (Bloom 1936: 255). The pottery pieces were in his possession until his death when they were passed on to his daughter Sara Bourke James. In 1940, Mrs. James donated the pieces and other Indian art items which her father had collected to the Peabody Museum at Harvard University. Again, no record was kept of the makers of the pottery or art work. His papers, from which Bloom drew his information on Bourke's travels, she donated to the library at West Point.

Other collectors and recorders of Santa Clara history who rode the train and who deserve mention, are George H. Pepper and Mr. Frank C. Churchill. Both made photographic records of the Santa Clara pueblo, its people and surroundings about the time of Margaret's birth (Figures 1-9, 2-35). In addition to his photography, a pottery collection from unidentified makers which was much more extensive than that of Bourke, was put together by Pepper and donated to the New York Museum of Natural History.

The town of Española began expanding into the Santa Clara land grant as the railroad neared completion. It was a widely held opinion that this intrusion was unattractive, at the very least. It was "a nondescript collection of canvas tents and board shanties on a flat beside the river," according to Eleanor and Birge Harrison, who recorded their opinion in 1885. As the town spread out, it bit off more and more of the pueblo's land.

The end of the "Chili Line" and the abandonment of its right-of-way came swiftly after the fourth decade of the twentieth century. From the beginning, it had been a money-loser; the line was narrow-guage and ran on light-weight tracks which could not carry any significant volume of freight. When the trucking industry developed, the line was doomed. During its last days, it ran only one train a day in either direction, and these consisted of one passenger and one baggage car (fig. 2-23). The last train to run left Santa Fe on September 1, 1941 following Fiesta; it carried no paying passengers. The life of the little railroad ended on a characteristic note: it arrived at the end of the line, Antonito, Colorado, eighteen minutes late.

Coexistance and Accommodation
(1879 A.D. — 1904 A.D.)

This court has known the conduct and habit of these Indians for eighteen or twenty years, and we say without fear of successful contradiction, that you may pick out one thousand of the best Americans in New Mexico, and one thousand of the best Mexicans in New Mexico, and one thousand of the worst Pueblo Indians, and there will be found less, vastly less, murder, robery, theft, or other crimes among a thousand of the worst Pueblo Indians than among a thousand of the best Mexicans or Americans in New Mexico.

Chief Justice Watts. Case of U.S. vs. Lucero.
New Mexico Territorial Court
January, 1869: 1 N.M. 422. (Sandow 1976:72).

At the same time Judge Watts was writing these words, the decision that he was rendering denied the pueblo people federal protection against trespass on their land by outsiders (Sando 1976: 73). This was only one of many court decisions or government regulations which refused the Indian protection against land encroachment, denied them the right to vote and did not allow them religious freedom, all this at the same time as attempts were being made to force the Indians to pay taxes.

For centuries during the first occupation of the Spanish, the pueblo people had learned to protect their way of life by instituting a policy of peaceful withdrawal and non-communication concerning anything about their religion or folklore, both of which are closely interrelated. Under the more benevolent Church and political rulers during the second Spanish occupation and the occupation by Mexico, the Tewa people began to trust more and more the policies of their governors and to expose some of the secrets of their ways of life. Uninformed United States policies would change all of this.

The policies of the U.S. Government toward the pueblo Indian, while not as cruel as the early Spanish, were as severely intolerant as those in force before the Pueblo Revolt. The effect was to force the Indians to return to their secretive ways which had protected them so well in the past. As late as the second decade of the twentieth century, it was not uncommon for the white man to be invited to visit Indian kivas. In fact, in a few instances, Catholic priests were requested to participate in joint Christian-Indian kiva blessing ceremonies. As more and more of the United States Indian policies were put into effect, pueblo people found it increasingly necessary to return to their secretive ways. The access which the Anglo had to study Indian religion and other aspects of pueblo life, had again been blocked. Commenting on the effects of this development, Elsie Clews Parsons stated, "Of all the more visited Pueblo peoples the Tewa have been the least systematically described... I undertook in November, 1923, the unwelcome task of duplicating research among a people who are past masters at the art of defeating inquiry....The short-haired English-speaking young man I counted on as historian was one of the most tongue-tied Pueblos it has been my misfortune to meet." (Hill 1982: xxviii, xxix). It had taken almost one hundred eighty years for a trust to have been gradually built up, not only between two religions, but also between two political systems. Almost overnight, this trust was destroyed by shortsighted U.S.—Indian policies.

At a time when the Rio Grande natives were losing their rights by government edict, U.S. schools were being built for them, whose teachers were preaching the advantages of life under a democracy. In 1881, under the control of the Presbytarian Church, the Albuquerque Indian School was founded, and one at Santa Fe, which Margaret would be forced to attend, was soon to follow. In 1881, church control of the Albuquerque School was abolished. Day schools at or near the pueblos were being built, one of the first of which was at Santa Clara (Figure 2-35). The Santa Clara school accommodated children from the first to about the sixth or seventh grades, with those requiring further education being sent to boarding schools located at various distances outside of the pueblo's control.

During this period, the pueblo people were fluent in their Tewa tongue and Spanish. With the coming of the new government schools, a third and completely different language, English, was imposed on them. In view of the government's actions, there was resistance in adopting this new tongue. Some of the old-time residents of Santa Clara learned no English at the day school, but picked it up when they left the pueblo for a higher education or were forced to learn it to conduct business with the government or the new merchants whose businesses were springing up around the pueblo.

"The government boarding school became a principal tool in the destructive war waged against the traditional culture. Because they were taken great distances from their homes, it became increasingly difficult for children to maintain their cultural pride and ties. At first a few boys were released from the schools for short periods to be instructed by the tribal elders. Then the Commissioner, calling the Pueblos 'half animal', ordered the practice stopped, even though the elders pleaded that as a result the Pueblo religion would die. At the schools, the Indian students were compelled to receive the teachings of the Christian religion without the permission of parents or clans. Parents could not even select the denomination into which the child was being immersed." (Mails 1983: 342, 343).

Margaret's grandparents and parents were forced to adopt a policy of non-communication with the outside world and again began to place more and more emphasis on returning completely to their traditional ways. Government oppression continued even during Margaret's youth and she learned to respect and deeply believe in the traditional values of her people reflecting these ways in her pottery. Improve on, but remain with tradition. Always remember that by being traditional, one is striving to return to a way of life that had provided peace, plenty and tranquility. "Return to the old ways in your way of life, in your religion, your actions, your beliefs and your art."

At the same time that the white man was suppressing the ceremonial ways of the Indian, he was also attempting to learn more about them. While trying to eradicate the Tewa religion, anthropologists, archeologists, ethnographers, and ethnologists were invading the Tewa country by road and rail in an effort to learn more about their way of life and its history. It is easy to understand why reliable Indian informants were difficult to locate and one is tempted to speculate that much of the information given to these scholars was deliberately misleading and unreliable.

Margaret's father came in contact with J.A. Jeançon who was doing research on the Santa Clara Pueblo in 1911, but this is the only reference which could be located in which any of her relatives were mentioned as acting as a guide or interpreter for Anglo investigators. In this instance, he was one of six mentioned who verified the name of a prehistoric pueblo ruin located on the Santa Clara land grant (Harrington 1916: 291).

For twelve years (1880-1892) the famous anthropologist, Bandelier, studied the Santa Clara Pueblo. It is rumored that his continued inquiries were eventually unwelcome at the village and he finally settled with the people of the Cochiti where he completed his better known work (Bandelier 1971).

To further complicate the picture at Santa Clara, a bitter religious schism occurred in 1894. It resulted from the death of a young girl who, in spite of the fact that she was in poor health, had been ordered to participate in a dance by the *cacique*. The girl's family group removed themselves from the main body saying, in effect, that when their daughter was returned to them they would return to participating in community affairs. This would have a profound effect on the selection of pueblo governors, the conduct of religious affairs, personal relationships of the people, and even the conduct of agriculture at Santa Clara for the next 42 years. The division would even have an effect on the future relationship between the Tafoya family of Margaret and Alcario and their neighbors. As deep and bitter as the split was, in true Tewa fashion, the dirty linen was never washed outside of the pueblo, but was treated as an internal matter which was of no concern to the outside world.

Fig. 1-10 Smithsonian Institution, N.A.A., Washington, D.C. Neg. No. 1971. Photographer F. W. Rinehart. Santa Clara representatives at the 1898 Trans-Mississippi and the International Exposition, Omaha, NE.
Standing left to right: *Santiago (identified as Albino by Margaret Tafoya), Augustin, David Gercio Tafoya (Alcario's uncle) and Albino.* **Seated:** *Juan José Gutierrez (Santana Tafoya's husband and Margaret's uncle), Pedro Baca (interpreter for the group and Margaret's godfather), and Juan Diego.*

Geronimo and Sara Fina were married during the presidency of Chester A. Arthur. President Arthur took a personal interest in Indian affairs, promoting Indian education, while favoring the breaking up of the Indian tribal system.

The Rio Grande Valley was being made more and more accessible to the rest of the United States. The Atchison, Topeka and Santa Fe Railroad gave access between the river province and Kansas City to the east, and the Pacific Coast on the west. By 1888, the line had extended its tracks to Galveston on the Gulf of Mexico and northward to Chicago. In 1882, one could change from the Chili Line in Denver to the Chicago, Burlington and Quincy Line going east to Omaha, Nebraska, and Chicago. In 1898, a delegation of fifteen Santa Clara Indians traveled eastward on the C.B. and Q. Line to Omaha to participate in one of the first demonstrations of pueblo Indian life available to the world outside of the Rio Grande Valley.

The Trans-Mississippi Exposition was held at Omaha from June 1 through November 1, 1898. It is not known why representatives from the Santa Clara Pueblo were selected for the honor and how the fifteen representatives were chosen. However, Geronimo Tafoya, a few of his close friends, an in-law, an uncle of Sara Fina's and relatives of his future daughter Margaret's husband were included (Figure 1-10 and 1-11). At the time of his appearances in Omaha, Geronimo was 35 years old and was the father of five children, the latest of whom, Dolorita, was only 10 months old.

Fig. 1-11 Photo taken at same time as Fig. 1-10. Neg. No. 1970. **Standing left to right:** Pedro Cajete (Sarafina's uncle), José Guadalupe Naranjo (Geronimo's half brother), Bonifacio (identified by Margaret as Dolores Cajete), Geronimo Tafoya (Margaret's father), and Casimiro Tafoya (Alcario Tafoya's step father. **Seated:** Doloreo (identified as Diego Naranjo by Margaret), Gov. Santiago Naranjo, ex-Gov. Jose Jesus Naranjo.

Theodore Roosevelt (inaugurated in 1901) was immensely popular and his well publicized western travels made that area of the United States a desirable one for people of means to travel. Travel was to become much easier with the organization of the Ford Motor Company in 1903. The wonders of the West rapidly became available to a new tourist market which in the past could not afford the expenses of the trains and the room and board of most hotels. Santa Clara would forever be open to the visits of the curious tourist.

The Rio Grande Valley became increasingly exposed to the world outside. More productive farming techniques were introduced into the area and more aggressive merchandising methods increased the availability on many products which were new to the area. Indirectly all of this had a profound influence on the art of the valley, but not always in the direction in which one would expect. There would be more artistic influences exported from that area than would be imported. Forms of literature, weaving, ceramic art, and music spawned within the river province would eventually greatly influence the arts of the surrounding country well outside of New Mexico.

Tourism and immigration, encouraged by the United States government, influenced the ceramic art of the Santa Clara people. Some of this would be negative, but positive factors would eventually dominate.

New ceramic technologies, manufacturing equipment, and synthesized and mass-produced raw materials would have a negative effect on the quality of work and the degree of skill necessary to provide ware for the tourist market. A new type of buyer was willing to settle for purchasing curios rather than utilitarian pottery pieces or well-crafted works. Low prices were offered and this resulted in an emphasis on quantity rather than quality.

The last incentive for producing large, well formed utilitarian works was removed for Santa Clara potters as a water well system was developed for the pueblo. Santa Clara was one of the first of the pueblos to adopt a modern water conveying system. Very early in the twentieth century, the first wells were dug along the banks of the Santa Clara Creek. This occurred during the time of another schism, this one between the Summer and Winter peoples; each group having its own well some fifty feet away from the other (Hill 1982: 40, 41). It is easy to imagine that the women of these rival organizations would try to outdo the other in producing the finest examples of water jars, which could be displayed to their rivals at the wells and which would prove to the outside world that one society had within its membership the most outstanding ceramic artists. From the time of digging these first wells in 1900 to the piping of water to homes which was almost completed by 1938, the art of water-jar making reached its zenith. The production of large water-jars declined during the 1930's and only a few, such as Margaret and her mother, continued to produce the shape as a non-utilitarian art form. In fact, vessels produced after the thirties not only cannot hold water but are severely damaged by it. Other potters in the pueblo have continued with the form which is now commonly reproduced, but in much smaller dimensions.

Techniques of slipping and polishing greatly improved at Santa Clara in the early 1900's. Clays which could be converted into slips and finely stone-polished were discovered nearby, and techniques for smoothing the unfired vessels developed to better accept the new improved slips.

New forms were developed for sale to the tourist trade. *Animalitos* were produced in abundance, although these forms had been scarce before the middle of the nineteenth century. Shapes alien to Santa Clara potters were made in the hope that they would be easily marketable. These included such items as tea pots, ashtrays, dishes, candlesticks, cups, etc., some of which are still being produced.

Enlightened museum personnel and teachers in the area have encouraged and rewarded those artists who produce quality art according to their own traditions and designs. In general, the negative effects on quality resulting from the introduction of kilns, mass produced raw materials and materials such as rubber and plaster molds to replace skilled forming techniques have been greatly nullified by these teachers.

Recently Tewa artists have learned the techniques and styles of the white man and have become outstanding painters, sculptors, contemporary potters, writers, poets and musicians able to compete with any artist in the world. In recent years, Indians have been encouraged to teach both Indian and white students. So popular has the Indian art form become that there are now many non-Indian artists who masquerade as native Americans with the hope that they can obtain a share of the now lucrative Indian art market.

The rugged beauty of the Rio Grande Valley, as well as the strength and character of its inhabitants have attracted the attention of writers, artists, and scholars, all anxious to unlock its secrets and portray its exotic beauty.[22] It has also challenged bureaucratic authorities—Spanish, Mexican, American—to control its resources and its destiny. Mother Earth, that nourished Margaret Tafoya and her people for eons, is today much as it has ever been: for its native ceramic artists.

Fig. 2-1 Courtesy of Mary Fredenburgh, Santa Fe, N.M. Photographer and source unknown. José Geronimo and Sara Fina Gutierrez Tafoya ca. 1920-25. Note Geronimo's neatly bound and tied braids and Sara Fina's well pressed clothes and white wrap-around moccasins. The lighter colored necklace worn by Sara Fina may contain her dime wedding token, and the lower black necklace is the one now worn by Margaret on special occasions as in Figures 2-43 and 2-54.

Chapter 2
Margaret Tafoya's Life 1904

"I am an Indian and was baptised in my Indian way. How could I change it? How could I wash it off? I am an Indian and I was dedicated in my Indian way. I belong there."

Margaret Tafoya

On August 17, 1904, the last of eight children, a girl, was born to "White Flower" and "Autumn Leaf," better known to those outside of the Santa Clara Pueblo by their church given names as Geronimo and Sara Fina Gutierrez Tafoya (figure 2-1 and 2-2). Continuing the tradition of their ancestors, Geronimo and Sara Fina selected a person related to the immediate family, in this instance the child's paternal grandmother María Nestora Tafoya "Frosted Leaf" to name her on the fourth day after birth. Influenced by the season, the family clan affiliations and other factors known only to Nestora, the child was given the name that translates to "Corn Blossom" in English. This would be the only name by which she would be known until the fourth day of the following month, when a Roman Catholic priest, the Rev. Ghislain Haelterman, would journey to the Santa Clara Indian Mission Church from the mother church at Santa Cruz, New Mexico, and baptize her with the Spanish Christian name of María Margarita Tafoya (figure 2-3).[1]

Margaret's Christian godfather was Pedro Baca (figure 2-4), a life-long friend of her father's and her godmother was Pedro Baca's wife María Margarita Naranjo Baca after whom Margaret was named. From her early youth, Margaret was known to those outside of her pueblo first by Margarita and later by the Anglicized version of this name, Margaret. The later name is the one she has used to identify her pottery from the time when collectors began to require identification. In some instances, this form of identification of Margaret's work goes back to the late 1920's.

At the time of Margaret's birth, she had seven siblings, four girls and three boys. Five of these would become excellent potters. The parents of this very talented and unusually hard working family, Geronimo and Sara Fina Tafoya, were religious, industrious, well respected members of the Santa Clara community.

Geronimo Tafoya was born on April 17, 1863. In addition to his Tewa name of "White Flower", he was given the Christian name of José Geronimo.[2] He was the third oldest in a family of nine children. In many instances his siblings and their offspring made remarkable contributions to pueblo Indian art. Such an atmosphere surrounding a child with Margaret's talents could do nothing but contribute to her artistic skills.

Although his primary concern was in raising food for his family, Geronimo did make both utilitarian and art pottery as well as helping Sara Fina with other aspects of pottery production (figures 2-5 and 2-6). He is remembered as a quiet, pleasant, mild-mannered industrious person of small physical stature. Not only did he not sign his pottery, he was reticent about admitting it was his work. It was he who was the main marketer for the family's pottery. He was known to have loaded his burros with pottery and make selling trips lasting several weeks. These journeys could take him to places as far away as Durango and Silverton, Colorado, and covered distances of approximately five hundred miles.

Both of Margaret's parents instilled in their children not only a remarkable work habit, but also a highly developed drive for achievement which, in turn, has been passed on to grandchildren and great grandchildren. Sara Fina is remembered as a strict disciplinarian especially concerning pottery-making, and she would tolerate nothing but perfection from her children in their ceramic endeavors.

She had but one sibling, a younger sister named Pasqualita, "Yellow Macaw Feather", born in 1883. Their mother, Filomena Cajete Gutierrez, passed away before the younger child had reached her teens and Sara Fina assumed the responsibility of raising her adolescent sister. With this in mind it is understandable why Sara Fina was considered by others to be a no-nonsense person.[3] According to Margaret, Pasqualita's pottery production was limited. "She never made big pieces."

The wedding of Sara Fina and Geronimo probably took place in the year 1883. There can be no question but that they were married by a Catholic priest, and there are three explanations as to why the records have not been located. First, it is in the records and was simply overlooked by the reseachers. Next, they were not married within the jurisdiction of the Santa Cruz church—this is highly

Casado con Teofila Martinez, N.M., Agosto 1934. (W.C. Inferraro), N.M.

Dia 4 de Diciembre

M[a] M. Tafoya — Bautice a maria margarita nac. el dia 17 de Agosto en Santa Clara Santa Clara e Hija leg[a] de Geronimo tafoya, y de Celestina gutierez (Ind[ia]) (Ind[ia]) Padr[s]: Pedro Jose Baca y M[a] margarita Naranjo.

G. Haelterman

Opposite page:

Fig. 2-2 Smithsonian Institution, Bureau of American Ethnology Collection, Neg. No. 1951A. B.A.E. photographer Reinhardt at the Trans-Mississippi and International Exposition, Omaha, NE, 1898. Photographed at the same time as Figure 1-11, Geronimo later told his children that he was ill at the time, left his bed long enough for the photo session, and therefore is the only one of the Santa Clara delegation not elegantly dressed.

Top:

Fig. 2-3 Courtesy of the Holy Cross Roman Catholic Church, Santa Cruz, N.M. Margaret Tafoya's birth record, page 292 in the Baptismal Register from March 1894 to May 1915. "Ma. M. Tafoya, Santa Clara Indian. Maria Margarita born the 17th of August at Santa Clara, daughter of Geronimo Tafoya and Celestina Gutierrez. Godparents: Pedro José Baca and Maria Margarita Naranjo. G. Haelterman" (Translation from Spanish) Note: Sara Fina is mistakenly identified as Celestina. Errors such as this are common in the records and are undoubtedly due to language barriers.

Left:

Fig. 2-4 Courtesy Mary Fredenburgh. The Santa Clara delegation at the Trans-Mississippi and International Exposition, Omaha, NE, 1898. Pedro José Baca, Margaret Tafoya's godfather, was the official interpreter.

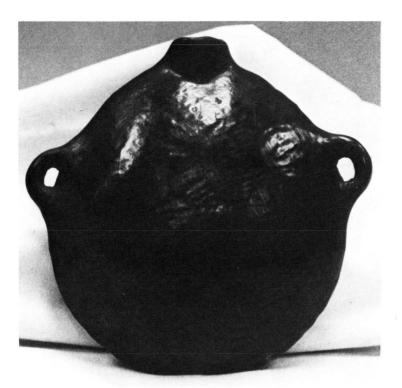

Fig. 2-5 Smithsonian Institution, Department of Anthropology #L-6003. Black micaseous canteen ca. 1880-1900 by Geronimo Tafoya. 8" diameter across handles, 7½" height, 3" wide. Unsigned, identification by Smithsonian and Teresita Naranjo. The clay deposit from which this was made was later destroyed by flood.

Fig. 2-6 Maurine Grammer collection. Black polished wall sconce, probably by Geronimo Tafoya, 1930's, 12 ⅝" height, 8⅞" width, 3⅛" depth. Unsigned, obtained by Mrs. Grammer from the maker. Pieces similar to this, made by Sara Fina or Margaret Tafoya, have been located in other collections. A difficult shape to form and fire because it is made from five separate clay pieces which are joined together while still plastic.

unlikely. The third possibility is supplied by Margaret. She remembers being told that the Santa Clara Mission Church (1628) had either been deliberately destroyed or had fallen into a state of disrepair, which necessitated several rebuildings. It was during one of these periods of decay that her parents were married. (The present church was not made habitable until 1918). At these times, visits by the priests were not conducted on a regular basis, and many of the sacraments of the Church were performed in people's homes. Under these conditions, the records could easily have been lost or simply not entered in the books when the priests returned to their base church. It was told to their children that in place of a ring, Geronimo presented Sara Fina with a wedding token of a dime. This was later made part of a rough turquoise necklace (figure 2-1). It is not known if this heirloom still exists.

The literature which mentions Sara Fina usually spells the name Serafina or Sarafina. Several pieces of her later work have been found which have been signed a plurality of ways including Serafina, Sara, Sera, and Sarafina. She was bilingual, speaking both Tewa and Spanish, though she could not speak English, nor could she read or write. The signatures on the pottery are attributed to her children,

particularly Manuel who assisted her. Margaret is adamant about the correctness of the double name used in this text, claiming Sara was the name given by the godmother and Fina by the godfather.

This was a lady of many talents who combined her gifts with a determined, hard-driving approach to life. She was skilled in the use of herbs and medicines for the healing of sickness. She was an accomplished practical nurse and her services as a midwife were much in demand among the Santa Clara people. She was a proficient seamstress, using this ability not only to clothe her family, but also as a means of securing outside income. During the planting, cultivating and harvesting seasons, she worked in the fields beside her husband and other family members. She was a mother not only to her sister, but also to a large family of her own.

In spite of her responsibilities, Sara Fina always had time for hospitality. As custom deemed, the Tafoya family home was opened to all on feast days. Before the automobile, this meant accommodating over-night guests who came from distant pueblos for the celebrations. Her efficiency is demonstrated by the fact that on these occasions she is remembered as wearing beautifully colored mantas with spotlessly clean, white, ruffled, blouses. The finishing touch of her holiday dress was a fine pair of white moccasins which she wore on her feet except when she was required to go outside when the weather was wet and muddy. At these times, she would carry her footwear on her head to prevent it from getting dirty. Margaret remembers, "Mother wore Indian dress and moccasins—all her life— always have a shawl on and tie it." (figures 2-7 and 2-1)

Sara Fina's amiability towards her good Anglo acquaintances was noted by the late Blanche Fulton of Albuquerque, New Mexico, a close friend of Margaret's family from 1931 until her death in 1970. In her notes written in 1949, Mrs. Fulton recorded, "How we hate to see our long-time Indian friends passing away. Margaret Tafoya's mother passed away in the summer of 1949. She was very old, but

such a kind person. She was always glad to see us, but could speak no English, but we could make each other understand pretty well."[4]

Sara Fina was undoubtedly the outstanding Tewa potter of her time. The variety, size and beauty of her work went unduplicated until Margaret began to apply herself seriously to her pottery endeavors. Sara Fina's early work was marked by the production of both small and large utilitarian pieces. Many of these were undecorated, while others had scalloped rims and various impressed designs including rainbow bands and bear paws. The shapes included water jars, dough bowls, storage jars, small bowls, dishes, canteens, candlesticks, and many more practical items (figures 2-8 through 2-14) including some made with micaceous clay (figure 2-15).

Margaret's Moccasins. Mary Fredenburgh photo.

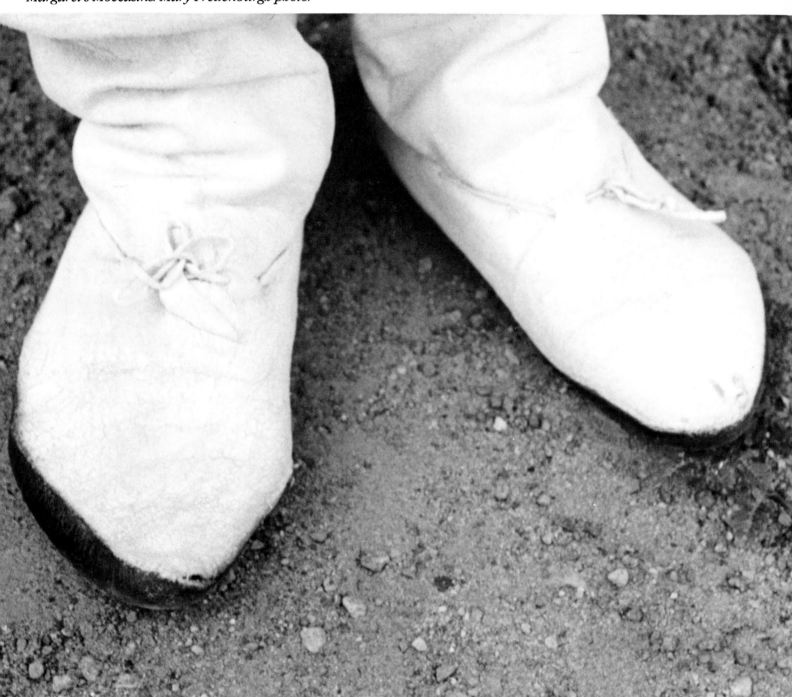

Fig. 2-7 University of New Mexico, Maxwell Museum of Anthropology, Albuquerque, N.M. Unlabelled snapshot, photographer unknown, probably taken around the turn of the century. Identified as Sara Fina by Margaret Tafoya, Grace Medecine Flower and Mary Cain. The firing of many large pieces at one time is a lost art at Santa Clara. Firing of small pieces simultaneously is common, but larger ware is now fired singly.

Fig. 2-8 Smithsonian Institution, Department of Anthropology #47023. Black polished water jar with impressed swirled neck by Sara Fina Tafoya. 13¾" height, 13⅛" diameter. Unsigned, Identification by Teresita Naranjo. Label reads: "47023, Santa Clara, N.M., Major J.W. Powell, J. Stevenson, 1880." The walls of this vessel are extremely thin and the impressions are sharp and uniform. This is one of the earliest documented pieces made by Sara Fina, when she was approximately seventeen years old.

Bottom left:
Fig. 2-9 Clark Field Collection. Philbrook Art Center, Tulsa, OK. #P459. Classic red polished storage jar by Sara Fina Tafoya, ca. 1900. 25" height, 21½" diameter. Unsigned, identified by Margaret Tafoya from a photograph. Firing smudges were common on red pottery made at that time. The four bold impressed bear paw designs are characteristic of Sara Fina's imprints.

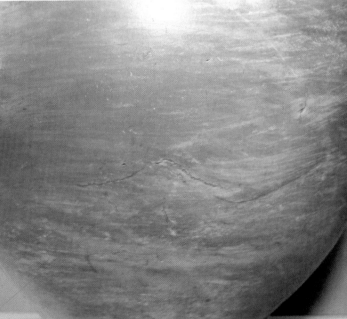

Fig. 2-10 Detail section of Fig. 2-9 storage jar. The cracks are characteristic of those produced from working with a dry, non-plastic clay-temper mix necessary to form very large vessels. They are surface cracks and may run in any direction depending on how the clay surface was smoothed.

Fig. 2-11 *Private collection. Black polished bread pot by Sara Fina, ca. 1890. 9" height, 12" diameter. Unsigned, identified by Margaret Tafoya. Slipped about one third of the way from the lip to the base and completely*

Fig. 2-12 *University of New Mexico, Maxwell Museum of Anthropology, Albuquerque, N.M. #73-26-1. Black polished storage jar, ca. 1930, with four impressed bear paws possibly by Sara Fina. 21" height, 15¼" diameter. Unsigned, tentative identification by Margaret Tafoya, but in question because of somewhat unfamiliar paw design.*

polished. The interior is slipped approximately two inches down from the rim. Thin walled—5/32". Made on a convex puki similar to the one in Margaret's possession.

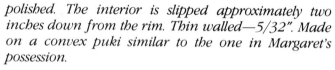

Fig. 2-13 *School of American Research, Santa Fe, N.M. #727. Black polished water jar with three impressed rainbow bands by Sara Fina Tafoya, ca. 1927. 11" height, 10" diameter. Unsigned, identification by Margaret Tafoya. Unusual and difficult to form for even a skilled potter.*

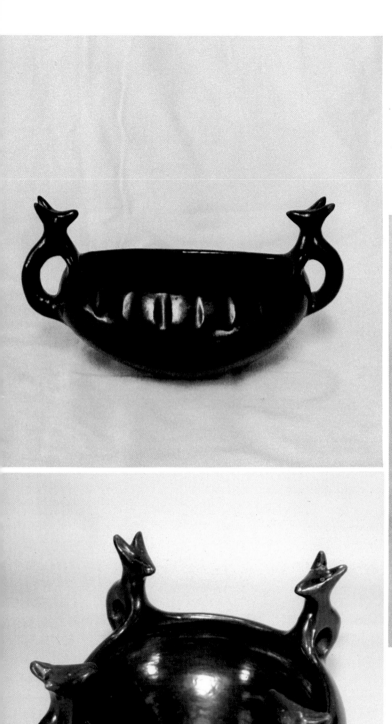

Fig. 2-15 Maurine Grammer collection. Micaceous pitcher by Sara Fina Tafoya, 1930's. 6½" height, 6½" diameter. Unsigned, obtained from the maker by Mrs. Grammer. Micaceous clays do not need sand additions to control drying and shrinkage. They are resistant to thermal shock and make excellent cooking utensils.

*Fig. 2-14 Maurine Grammer collection. **Top:** Black polished impressed bowl with two animal handles by Sara Fina Tafoya, ca. 1930. 10¾" diameter across handles, 5⅜" height. Unsigned, obtained by Mrs. Grammer from the maker. Note similarity of handles with those on bowl by Margaret Tafoya, **below,** which was made about the same time. 8½" diameter, 7" height. Four handles.*

The earliest form of carved pottery is attributed to Sara Fina (figure 2-16 and 2-17). Her later, deeper carved pieces which are signed, are said to have been carved by her son Manuel, although she formed the base pieces. The carving on his ware is remarkably similar to that which is attributed to his mother (compare figures 2-18 and 2-27). This is true also of Sara Fina's later bichrome and polychrome pottery designs (figures 2-19, 2-20 and 2-21).

When the sales of art pottery to tourists and Indian curio dealers, (the forerunners of the present-day Indian art dealers) became an important source of income for the family, the variety of her work was expanded to include non-utilitarian art forms. The diversity of her work included not only her traditional shapes, but also many new forms which pleased the public's taste and were therefore more salable (figure 2-22).

Fig. 2-16 Denver Art Museum, Denver, CO. #XSC124. Black polished jar by Sara Fina, ca. 1922. 10" height, 12¼" diameter. Unsigned, identification by Teresita Naranjo. The decoration is unusual for the slip which was applied to the interior of the design, and the design itself appears to be formed by a process that used both impressed and carved techniques.

Fig. 2-17 Denver Art Museum, Denver, CO. #XSC125. As in Figure 2-16 this is one of a series of twelve made by Sara Fina. 9" height, 10¾" diameter. Unsigned, identified by Teresita Naranjo. The design has been gouged, pressed in, and smoothed. One of the earliest Avanyu designs made at Santa Clara, located by the authors.

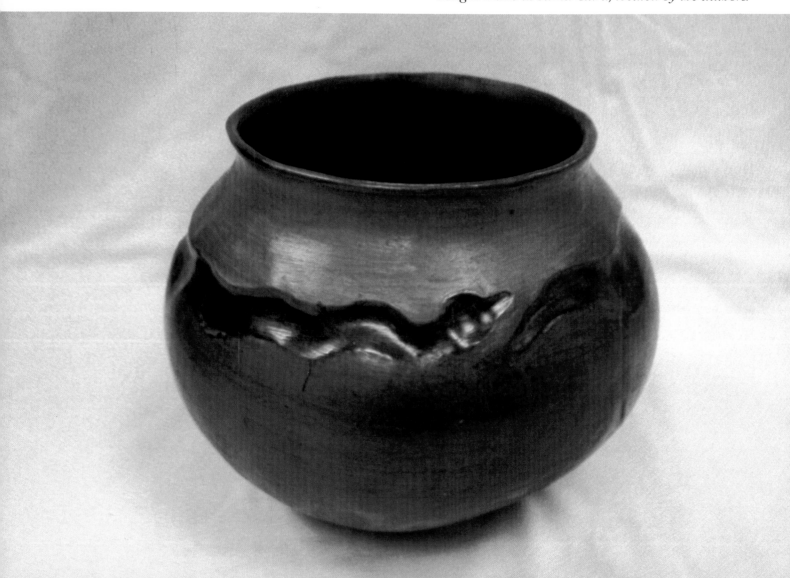

Fig. 2-18 Wheelwright Museum of the American Indian, Santa Fe, N.M. (No number) Red carved bowl, signed Sara Fina, ca. 1930. 10" diameter, 4⅛" height. The carving is exactly like her son Manuel's, and may have been done by him. See Figure 2-27.

Fig. 2-19 Denver Art Museum, Denver, CO. #XSC38P. Red-on-red bowl with design outlined in white by Sara Fina. 4⅛" diameter, 2⅛" height. Unsigned, but purchased from the maker in 1933 for the museum collection.

Fig. 2-20 Private collection. Polychrome wedding vase, signed Sara, ca. 1930. 10¼" height, 7" diameter. The intricate decoration is shown in detail in Figure 3-57 (17). The variation in earth colors is remarkable.

Fig. 2-21 Denver Art Museum, Denver, CO. #XSC73G. Polychrome plate signed Serafina, ca. 1930's. 11" diameter. A rare example because there are few verified Sara Fina plates, and there are two Avanyus in the design probably painted by Manuel.

Fig. 2-22 Walton Youngblood collection. Black polished vase with distinctive claw handles, ca. 1925-30 by Sara Fina Tafoya. 11½" height, 8" diameter. Unsigned, formerly of the Blanche Fulton collection. Note the similarity of handles on Margaret Tafoya's piece in Figure 3-15.

The high degree of polish on much of Sara Fina's work is remarkable considering that it was applied over surfaces smoothed with corn cobs rather than sandpaper, a tool which she disdained. It should be noted, however, that her later work is very smooth, there is no ridged appearance of the surface, and so was probably sanded by another member of the family. In spite of the fact that she did not sign her pottery, others did so for her, and an occasional piece continues to surface from private collections and museum archives which is signed or can be identified and authenticated by family members.

Margaret's earliest memories include those of being exposed to her mother's pottery-making.

"When I was small, like all pueblo children, we sit around Mother's side when she is making pottery. We get a piece of her clay and try to make animals or maybe bowls. We make these just for fun. Sometimes Mother fix it for us, and that is the way we started, putting our hands in the clay and whether we know it or not, through our playing with clay we learned pottery-making. We were brought up that way. We learned that we could live better working on pottery. Every one of my sisters they know how to make pottery and even the brothers like Manuel."

Particularly vivid are the memories of observing her mother work on the large and beautiful storage

and water jars, few of which are being made today. "At times she make big, squatty ones, but not too high, Took her two or three days just to make the bottom part, and it took about a week to finish it because she have to let it stand. She make a lot of them squatty ones—very pretty." (figure 2-7)

Naturally, Sara Fina had the greatest influence on Margaret's development into a great Tewa potter, but there were also others who contibuted. There are memories of her grandmother, Nestora Naranjo Tafoya, not only making candlesticks, but also the candles to go in them. Two others often mentioned by Margaret were her aunt, Santana, and her oldest sister, Tomacita.

Santana Tafoya Gutierrez known to the family as "Aunt Tana", must have been a unique character and was well known in the pueblo. She bore her husband Juan José at least seven children before she could no longer tolerate his ways and instituted a pueblo divorce. In its most elementary form in those times, this consisted of simply not allowing him back in the house. When it was finally decided by the village officials that she would have to share their joint property, she complied in the strictest sense of the word. She divided his shoes in half giving him one from each pair. His clothes were similarly divided. These actions proved to Geronimo that she was not quite right in her mind. As

Fig. 2-25 **Left:** *Museum of New Mexico, Anthropology Laboratory, Santa Fe, N.M. #46226/12. Black polished impressed vase by Tomacita Tafoya Naranjo, ca. 1916. 7¼" height, 5" diameter. Unsigned as was all pottery produced in Tomacita's time, and identified by Margaret Tafoya. Long delicate necks were characteristic of many of Tomacita's works.*

Figure 2-25 **Right:** *#12433. Black polished, impressed pitcher by Tomacita Tafoya Naranjo, ca. 1910. 6½" height, 3¾" diameter. Tomacita was a master of impression and was known in her time for graceful handled vessels.*

2-26 *Private collection. Black polished candlestick with animal figure at base by Manuel Tafoya, ca. 1940. 8½" height, 4" diameter base. Unsigned and identified by Margaret Tafoya and Teresita Naranjo. Note the animal's blunt nose.*

Margaret remembers, "My dad got so mad. He said, 'that lady is crazy.' I felt so bad for my aunt. 'She is not crazy,' I told my dad, 'they mistreated her, that's why'."

Santana, with Sara Fina, was one of the first to develop an eye for the tourist pottery trade. She made not only old forms, but also unique, non-utilitarian pieces which she sold on the platform of the Española railroad station to tourists whose trains passed through twice a day on their way to and from Santa Fe (figure 2-23). Margaret remembers admiring the large, thin-walled pottery made by Santana and she still maintains a great respect for her aunt's work (figure 2-24). Apparently, this respect was mutual as Santana, before her death, insured that Margaret would eventually inherit her prized "puki". (Full explanation of puki in Chapter 3.)

The puki was first passed on to Santana's daughter, Nestora Gutierrez Naranjo Silva. Nestora apparently was a very outgoing person, being one of the most widely photographed people of the Santa Clara Pueblo. She was also a fine potter who produced ceramic pieces until she passed away in 1980 at the age of one hundred one. Remembering her mother's respect for Margaret's ability, she passed her precious inheritance on to Margaret. This event Margaret recalls vividly. "One of my pukis came from my grandmother on my daddy's side and it went to my aunt [Santana], my daddy's sister. From there the puki was passed to cousin

Fig. 2-27 Private collection. Red carved bowl by Manuel Tafoya, ca. 1945. 6½" diameter, 3½" height. Unsigned and identified by Teresita Naranjo. This shallowly carved design is characteristic of Manuel's work and may be found on some pieces bearing Sara Fina's signature. Compare with Figure 2-18.

Nestora. One time she came over and she said, 'Corn Blossom, I brought this puki to you. My mother told me whoever making these large pieces, it must go to her, this puki. It have to go on to the family, and neither of my daughters has interest in making these large pieces, so what is the use of my leaving it to them? It will be sitting there and not make use. You doing this work so here it is from my mother.' Today I still have it." The origin of this puki is not known, but Margaret remembers it as being in the possession of someone in her family for generations.

The oldest of Geronimo's and Sara Fina's children was Tomacita, "Yellow Aspen". She was twenty years of age, married and with child, at the time of Margaret's arrival. Within the Santa Clara Pueblo, Tomacita was already established as a fine potter capable of producing artistic pieces. It is unfortunate that she and her offspring have been completely overlooked in the many writings covering Santa Clara potters or members of the Tafoya family. This oversite is understandable since she died at an early age and signed none of her work. The identification of most of her pieces can only be made by a few of the older, knowledgeable Santa Clara people. (figure 2-25)

The second oldest in the family was Manuel, "Falling Leaves", some nineteen years Margaret's senior. The records show that he married in 1910 and again in 1916 after the death of his first wife, but no record of children by these marriages was found, nor does anyone interviewed at Santa Clara remember his wives or any offspring. Manuel assisted the family with all of their many chores and all facets of pottery-making. It is known that he was a good potter on his own, one of his specialities being the creation of unique animal forms with blunt noses which were often attached to bases of candlesticks (figure 2-26). He also carved (figure 2-27) and was an excellent decorator of traditionally-shaped ware with some of his decoration resembling the polychromes of Lela and Van Gutierrez (figure 2-28). He dug colored clays in the foothills surrounding the Española Valley and experimented with different colors. In many instances, he painted or carved pottery formed by other family members (figure 2-29). As far a can be determined, his work was never signed and can only be identified by some family members. In spite of his excellent pottery-making abilities, his main interests remained in farming and he is best remembered as a farmer.

Although not clear from the church records, the next oldest in the family was probably "White Weasel", baptized with the Spanish name of Juan Isidro. No one remembers his producing any ceramic ware. He married a woman from San Juan Pueblo, and for a time made his home in that Tewa village to the north. Following the death of his wife, Juan Isidro returned to Santa Clara and for the remainder of his life worked land near the mouth of the Santa Clara Canyon. With typical Tewa humor,

Fig. 2-28 **Left:** *Walton Youngblood collection. Poly-chrome box with lid by Manuel Tafoya, ca. 1930. 4¾" height, 4¼" length, 3¼" width. Unsigned, collected by Blanche Fulton, and identified by Margaret Tafoya. Note the unique handle and intricate painted design. Manuel was very particular as to the proportions of his boxes.* **Right:** *Red-on-red box signed Margaret Tafoya, ca. 1930. 4½" x 3¼" x 4". Originally made to hold corn meal, these are now collector's items.*

Fig. 2-29 *Denver Art Museum, Denver, CO. #XSC46P. Polychrome bowl formed and signed by Christina Naranjo. Purchased by Frederick H. Douglas for the museum from the Old Santa Fe Trading Post in 1938. 6½" height, 7¾" diameter. The painted serpent design is thought by members of the Tafoya family to have been done by Manuel Tafoya for Christina.*

Fig. 2-30 *Private collection. Black carved vase signed Christina Naranjo, ca. 1960's. 14½" height, 10¼" diameter. One of Christina's larger pieces and typical of the fine quality of her work.*

he is remembered as "Uncle Joe Weedy" because his house was located in an unkempt field.

The fourth child and second oldest girl was "Lightning Basket" or María Christina. Christina was known as a fun-loving, generous, extroverted person. In addition to becoming a famous potter, she was also recognized as the maker of pottery for others, including María Martinez of San Ildefonso, according to Margaret. Christina signed most of her work which she sold directly to dealers or the public (figures 2-29 and 2-30). In 1915, she married José Victor Naranjo and bore him nine children, some of whom were and are producers of fine traditional Santa Clara ware. In her later years, she worked with her daughter Mary Cain, and both signatures can be found on these creations (figure 2-31).

Six years after the arrival of Christina, the family was joined by Dolorita, first given the Tewa name "Raining". Dolorita married Albert Padilla in 1916, and records indicate that they had eleven children. Dolorita, like all woman in her family, was a potter. While no one can remember her signing her work, a few signed pieces do exist. (One such was located in the archives of the Philbrook Art Center in Tulsa, Oklahoma, which, except for the color, is almost an exact replica of a piece made by Sara Fina (figure 2-32). Margaret commented, "She made all kinds [of pottery] just like we do. She never made big ones, not more than twelve to fourteen inches. Her bowls kind of come out in a little neck. I can't say that she signed her pottery or she didn't."

The next child in the Tafoya family was Pauline (misnamed Paula in the church records, according to Margaret) who was first named "Little Fish". She died between thirteen and fourteen years of age, and it is doubted that she ever produced anything but a child's version of pottery.

Fig. 2-32 **Top:** *Maurine Grammer collection. Black bird bowl by Sara Fina Tafoya, 1920's. 10¾" length, 5" height. Unsigned, acquired by Mrs. Grammer from the maker. The form of this piece is almost identical to that made by her daughter, Dolorita.* **Bottom:** *Philbrook Art Center, Tulsa, OK. #75.39. Red smudged bird bowl signed Dolorita Tafoya, ca. 1954. 5⅝" height, 11¾" length. Rare example by Margaret Tafoya's sister Dolorita Tafoya Padilla who seldom signed her pieces. (She is not to be confused with her cousin, Dolorita Tafoya Gutierrez, who is 25 years her junior and signs her first name only.)*

Fig. 2-31 Private collection. Black carved vase signed Christina Naranjo and Mary Cain, 1974. 7" height, 6½" diameter. Probably formed by Christina and carved and polished by Mary Cain. During Christina's later years, her daughter Mary did Christina's carving as well as assisting her mother in all other phases of pottery making.

Fig. 2-34 Walton Youngblood collection. Black polished horse figure by Camilio Tafoya, ca. 1945. 5¾" height, 6" length. Unsigned, originally collected by Blanche Fulton. Camilio has made many pottery horses.

The youngest boy in the family was given the Tewa name "Sun Flower" and later baptized José Camilio. He preceded Margaret by two years. Margaret remembers that in his youth Camilio's main interest was agriculture, and it was not until his later years that he worked at and became recognized as a potter. At first, he produced large, massive, carved traditional pieces (figure 2-33) and sculptured horses (figure 2-34). Later, working with two of his children, Grace Medicine Flower and Joseph Lonewolf, he became famous along with them for nontraditional, delicately incised pottery, sometimes called graffito.

With the exception of her mother Sara Fina, Tomacita is credited by Margaret as having the greatest and most direct influence on her pottery making. This influence was even greater than that of her aunt Santana. The Santa Clara primary school was very close to Tomacita's home (within 100 yards) and so it was natural that the child would spend much time there with her older sister, for whom she felt much love and admiration. Margaret feels that she learned much more here watching a master potter work, than in the classroom.

Fig. 2-33 Private collection. Black polished and carved wedding vase, signed Camilio Tafoya, ca. 1955. 16½" height, 9" diameter. Massive thick walled piece, deeply carved, is typical of Camilio's earlier work.

Fig. 2-43 Private collection. Mary Fredenburgh photographer. 1983. Margaret Tafoya poses with her trader friend Tony Reyna of Taos Pueblo and his collection of her pottery. Margaret knew Tony as a boy and his parents were also her friends. Reyna is now a well known Indian art dealer. The blanket he is wearing was given to him when he was governor of his pueblo in 1982. It is to his credit that this remarkable collection remains intact.

Fig. 2-44 Streets of Taos, Santa Fe, NM. Mary Fredenburgh photographer. Black polished swirled melon bowl by Margaret Tafoya which was converted to a lamp, ca. 1954. Mrs. Street has an excellent collection of this type of Margaret's work.

Fig. 2-50 Private collection. L. Blair photographer. 1984. Margaret Tafoya exhibits the Pendelton blanket that was the first award she was given for her pottery at the Santa Fe Fiesta in the early 1920's.

63

Fig. 2-54 Walton Youngblood collection. Mary Fredenburgh photographer. Margaret and Alcario Tafoya at the 1979 wedding of their grand-daughter Nancy Youngblood to Paul Cutler, United Methodist Church, Santa Cruz, NM. Margaret is wearing the black bead necklace she inherited from Sara Fina. (Figure 2-1)

The school was a converted adobe building with a floor space of approximately 1,100 square feet (figure 2-35). It was located just outside the north corner of the old pueblo near the plaza which housed the kiva of the Winter people (figure 2-36). The distance between the school and the Tafoya home was about one hundred forty yards. This small structure, near the center of many of the pueblo's activities, accommodated all of the Santa Clara children from about ages five through twelve. Margaret does not remember much about her school days except that she learned next to nothing that would be of use to her in later life. She learned little of the English language, and to this day does not feel comfortable with it in spite of the fact that she expresses herself well, is quick to understand the slightest spoken or written detail, and is particularly fast at exchanging quips.

Fig. 2-35 **Top:** *Museum of the American Indian, Heye Foundation, New York, NY. Neg. No. 27035, Churchill collection. Photographer unknown. View of Santa Clara Day School taken in 1904, the year of Margaret Tafoya's birth. It was located in the north corner of the older part of the pueblo. Santa Clara was the first pueblo to establish an educational program under United States occupation.* **Bottom:** *Museum of the American Indian, Heye Foundation, New York, NY. Neg. No. 27031, Churchill collection, 1904. Photographer unknown. Left to right: Superintendent of Schools Crandall; Mrs. Crandall; Mrs. True, mother of Clara True and school housekeeper; Clara True, Margaret Tafoya's elementary school teacher and long time family friend; and Col. Frank C. Churchill, U.S.I.S. Inspector.*

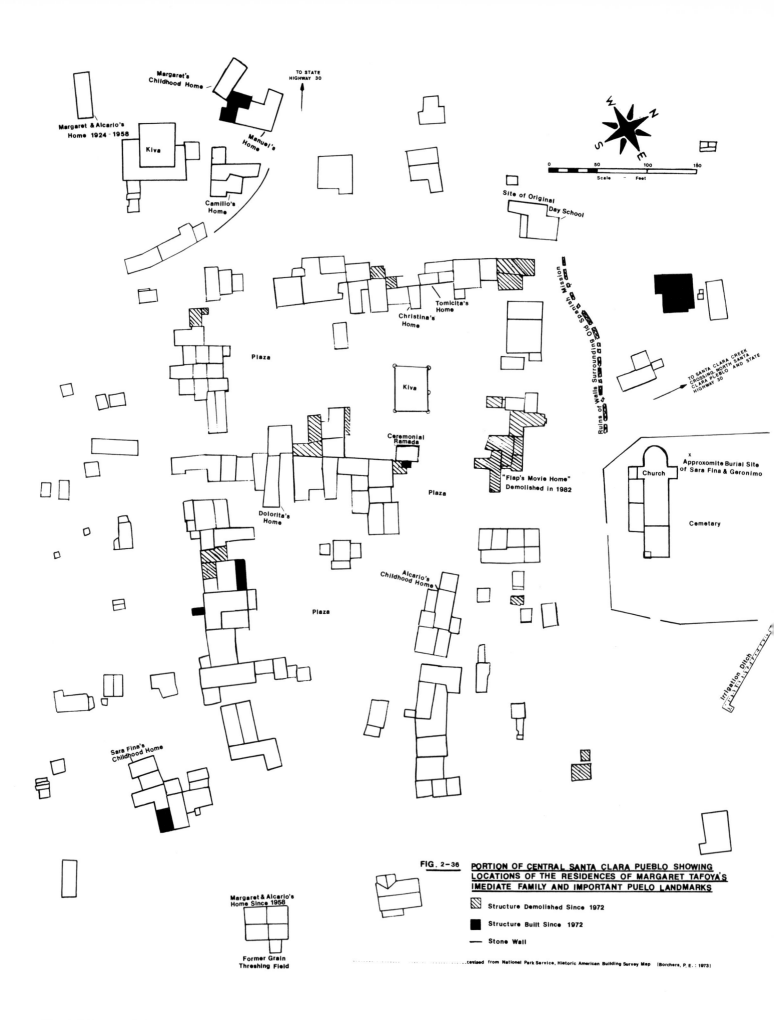

Margaret's
Childhood Home

TO STATE
HIGHWAY 30

Margaret & Alcario's
Home 1924-1958

Kiva

Manuel's
Home

Camilio's
Home

Site of Original
Day School

Tomicita's
Home

Christina's
Home

Plaza

Kiva

Ceremonial
Ramada

"Flap's Movie Home"
Demolished in 1982

Plaza

Dolorita's
Home

Plaza

Alcario's
Childhood Home

Sara Fina's
Childhood Home

TO SANTA CLARA CREEK
CROSSING, NORTH SANTA
CLARA PUEBLO, AND STATE
HIGHWAY 30

Church

Approxomite Burial Site
of Sara Fina & Geronimo

Cemetary

Ruins of Walls Surrounding Old Spanish Mission

Irrigation Ditch

FIG. 2-36   PORTION OF CENTRAL SANTA CLARA PUEBLO SHOWING
LOCATIONS OF THE RESIDENCES OF MARGARET TAFOYA'S
IMEDIATE FAMILY AND IMPORTANT PUEBLO LANDMARKS

Structure Demolished Since 1972

Structure Built Since 1972

Stone Wall

Margaret & Alcario's
Home Since 1958

Former Grain
Threshing Field

revised from National Park Service, Historic American Building Survey Map   (Borchers, P. E. : 1973)

Scale — Feet

*Fig. 2-36 Map of the older section of Santa Clara Pueblo
in 1982.*

Her teacher was a spinster named Clara D. True who lived with her housekeeper mother (figure 2-35). Miss True would go on to become a leading officer in the nearby Española school system and a self appointed local historian. Later, she would also teach some of Margaret's children. In particular, Virginia Ebelacker has fond memories of Clara True and the special attention which the teacher gave her and the assistance she gave the Tafoya family when they were unfairly treated at the pueblo. Miss True purchased a ranch near the southwest corner of Santa Clara land and named it the Pajarito Ranch (Harrington 1916: 262). In spite of the fact that she had been a leading citizen of the community and had established many friendships in the Española Valley, she eventually chose to retire to her childhood home in Tulsa, Oklahoma.

Outside of school, the life of a child growing up in the pueblo was not an easy one. Everyone was required to contribute work necessary for family survival. One of the first chores for a young girl was carrying water in a large water jar from the Santa Clara Creek to her home, a distance of about a quarter of a mile. The load was about twenty pounds. Other work included helping with the digging and kneading of clay, doing the necessary household chores and—most difficult—working in the fields.

The very survival of the family depended on the successful planting, tending, harvesting, and preserving of the crops (figure 2-37). Family and friends from within and outside the pueblo, came to help with the harvest. These times were always marked by feasts, not only at the Tafoya home, but also at most homes in the pueblo. It was then that the very large pieces of pottery, up to two feet in diameter, were brought out and filled with freshly prepared food for all to share. With the chili con carne, green chili and corn, posole with meat and green chili, pumpkin dishes, squash dishes, beans prepared in various manners (mostly with chili), came the bread. The latter had been prepared days in advance in the *hornos* outside. Hornos (beehive shaped bread baking ovens) would hold thirty to forty round loaves of bread in one baking, and there were several bakings for one feast. Meals were

Fig. 2-37 Museum of New Mexico, Photo Archives, Santa Fe, NM. Neg. No.4137. Harmon Parkhurst photographer. "Harvest, Santa Clara Pueblo, ca. 1925." One of the last of the bountiful Santa Clara harvests. The Los Alamos Scientific Laboratories would be established in a few years offering paying jobs outside of the pueblo so that farming was no longer necessary, and the de-emphasis of farming was a major factor in the demise of large utilitarian vessels.

accompanied by the most common food of all, the corn tortilla. Beverages included prepared fruit juices, coffee, and more recently commercially available Kool Aid®, jokingly called "Tewa beer." Indian pudding, dried fruit and the Indian fruit pies were offered for dessert.

There were also poor harvests and following these, survival became difficult. Margaret recalls one of these disasters. "My dad had fresh corn, and we had started to eat that fresh corn. Then came a cloudburst. All those fields were full of water, just cover them, the whole place. .....Our winter food— we lost it. We lost our oats, our wheat, our corn, and our garden. All the fields just full of water. [Later] from the heat of the sun and all that water, there was just no way that we could drain. It just kill all that, and all that rot. All that work just gone, all that work." Food for the coming winter was almost nonexistent. A small amount, preserved from past years crops, had been saved, but it was not enough to sustain the family. Work outside of the pueblo, which was hard to find, was sought to obtain food money; and some possessions with which they would not normally part had to be sold or bartered. Times such as this emphasize how valuable pottery production was in procuring necessary income.

Margaret remembers the date of that flood, late summer of 1916, because it occurred just prior to her brother Juan Isidro's wedding. Margaret spent time with her brother and his wife at their San Juan home.[5] Although she was in her teens at that time, she was able to learn the characteristic pottery-making techniques of the classic San Juan potters, and this would influence some of her later work and have a profound influence on the work of one of her daughters. (Discussed in Chapter 4)

After receiving the meager education provided by the pueblo school which supposedly took her to the seventh grade level, Margaret and all other Santa Clara children her age were required to attend one of the several Indian high schools. She and her family selected Santa Fe Indian School, probably because of its proximity to home. From 1915 until 1918, she spent most of her time attending this boarding school away from her home, her ceremonial life, her family, and her friends. The fall semester began the first week in September and the schooling continued without a break through the middle of June. Although parents were permitted to visit their children at any time, they were limited by the difficulties of travel and weather restrictions, therefore they seldom exceeded three visits a year.

The infrequent journeys to Santa Fe included one to deliver Margaret in September, at least one visit in April or May—depending on weather—and one necessary to return her home in June. Each of these trips required four or more days to complete with a horse and wagon. The first day ended at Tesuque Pueblo where the Tafoyas spent the

evening with friends. The remaining ten miles to Santa Fe were completed the morning of the second day. In addition to spending time with Margaret at the school, Sara Fina and Geronimo would devote a least one extra day selling their pottery at various outlets in the city which had been established previously and in purchasing necessary supplies for the family at home. The fourth day was spent entirely on the return journey.

During Margaret's first summer break from school in Santa Fe, Sara Fina decided that the time had come to teach her the secrets of producing fine pottery. Mother and daughter spent much of the time that summer working together with Mother Clay. Some of the lessons were harsh, but well remembered. Margaret remembers a piece of greenware she had made which she felt would result in a fine fired piece. She was rather proud of her work, but Sara Fina was not impressed. In the student's words, "It looked good to me. It should be baked, but Mother she get a little yucca brush. Then she put it in water and tell me, 'Look, I'm going to drop this water right on that polishing, and that going to bubble, and that will chip [when fired] .... you didn't polish it good.' It kind of make me feel angry—all that work, but [I learned] it's true. It will chip if we bake it like that." At this point, the vessel had to have the polish removed and reapplied. Although she only smiles when asked if she taught the same lesson to her children, they remember her instructing them in the same manner.

Late in the year of 1918, Margaret was forced to leave school before her education was completed. Disaster had struck the pueblo, as it had the entire country, in the form of a flu epidemic. Many friends and relatives were affected by the disease, but the worst blow was the death of her sister Tomacita. In Margaret's words, "At that time I came [home] my Dad and Mom were sick with it. A lot of people around here were very sick. So many deaths every day, old people and small children. There was no doctor that I know of. When my mother recovered from that flu, she went around carrying water for the people and help them make food. She was the only one first to recover from that flu. I lost my sister Tomacita, Nicollassa's mother, at that time. That far back 1918, she pass away in November, but I don't remember the day. She left a little boy, just about a month and a half [José Alcario], and her sister-in-law raise that little one. He didn't live very long. That coming summer that baby pass away with diarrhea. My sister Tomacita left about six children, I think. [Six exactly ranging in age from one and a half months to fourteen years]. Since then, I never went back to school. We work with pottery by my mother."

Since the church restoration was about complete at that time (1918) it would have been expected that the priests from Santa Cruz would visit at least once a month to say Mass and administer the sacraments. Margaret and others remember that few, if any, medical people or priests visited, and the almost nonexistent church records for that time period bear her out. There must have been a tremendous shortage of doctors because of the severity of this widespread epidemic. Certainly, priests were not immune to flu, and it is probable that it was physically impossible to minister to the large territory assigned to them. The practice of ringing the church bell had started many years before at Santa Clara. A rapid ringing announced a joyous event such as birth, and slow tolling—death. The frequent slow tolling of the bell during that time must have been very depressing to the Tewa people.

Among the many other victims was Andreita Tafoya (at that time no relation to Margaret), the mother of Alcario, who later became Margaret's husband.

The flu epidemic dictated that Margaret leave school. Also, the death of Tomacita, the marriage of siblings Dolorita, Christina and Manuel all resulted in a shifting and increasing of responsibilities, and the support of the family rested on fewer shoulders. Margaret was needed at home, especially for help with the pottery production.

In addition to the work at home, Margaret earned additional income outside of her pueblo. Her first paying job was that of a waitress at the Ganado Hotel in Española. The hotel was formerly located where the present Ford automobile agency now stands. It was owned and managed by the Holmquist and Khonol families who were exacting and meticulous people and provided training which young Margaret would always appreciate and remember. It never occurred to her to resent the fact that she had to walk to and from work.

Margaret had developed into a dainty and beautiful young woman who naturally attracted suitors. Those who knew her then, say she was unusually pretty and early photos attest to this fact. At age seventeen, she considered marrying a young Jicarilla Apache. "I thought I was going to marry that Apache boy. His mother and sister made me a dress (figure 2-38). The Apache buckskin is different, made with no sleeves to it, just a shoulder part, and it was beaded. But afterwards, I don't like that Apache life, so I just kind of get away from him and went to work in Santa Fe."

The job she undertook in Santa Fe was that of a live-in housekeeper. She stayed only a short time. The threat of marrying the Apache had passed, she could not work on her pottery in the city, and she missed her family and ceremonial life. Margaret moved back to Santa Clara.

The hotel work, cooking for the Santa Fe family, and preparing meals for her own family, provided

Fig. 2-38 Margaret Tafoya collection. Cross of Santa Fe photographer, ca. 1921. About seventeen years old, Margaret poses in a beaded Jicarilla Apache dress.

her with a background which allowed her to secure a job as an assistant cook at the school in Dulce, New Mexico, on the Jicarilla Apache Indian Reservation. When the head cook departed, Margaret was promoted to this position. She worked in this beautiful mountainous section of the country from 1921 until 1924.

Her family and friends both within and outside of the pueblo, all agree that this must have been the best of training because Margaret is an outstanding cook. In 1931, Margaret's friend Blanche Fulton wrote, "We have spent several days at Margaret's. She is a very good cook, and sets a very nice table. The best chicken dinner I've had in a long time was at her house—a platter full of delicious fried chicken, and more was brought in as needed." Kenneth Canfield (1975: 2C) was so impressed with her cooking that he wrote an article about it which was published in the Kansas City Star newspaper.

The journey to Dulce was made on the Denver and Rio Grande Western (narrow gauge) Railroad. The first part of the trip was on the "Chili Line" from Española to its branch terminal at Antonito, Colorado. This portion was one hundred twenty five miles long. lasted for six and one half hours, and ended at Antonito sometime after 5:35 P.M., the scheduled arrival time (Chappell 1969: 28). Since the next connecting train for Dulce would not arrvie from Denver until approximately 8:00 A.M. the following morning, it was necessary to spend the night in Antonito. Another seven hours were required to complete the ride the following day, but to Margaret this never seemed long because she spent her time enjoying the beautiful mountain scenery. (This portion of the railroad is still in operation and is run as an historical landmark by the states of Colorado and New Mexico. It runs only in the summer months for tourists using the original rolling stock and engines. Occasionally, a diesel of later vintage is substituted for the old Bladwin steam engines.)

Alcario Tafoya, "Swallow in the Mist", had grown up with Margaret at their home pueblo of Santa Clara and, possibly not wanting to wait for the arrival of another Apache on the scene, asked Margaret to marry him early in the year if 1924. She had made a commitment not to leave her job at the Dulce school, so Alcario moved there after having obtained government work in a nearby area. On June 23, 1924, they were married by Father Barnabas Meyer in the small Roman Catholic Church at Lumberton, New Mexico.

Alcario was born on November 11, 1900. For the purposes of the church records at Santa Cruz, his mother is listed as Andreita Baca Tafoya and his father as Leandro Tafoya. This confuses the genealogist because in fact Leandro was actually his grandfather. He was raised by his mother, the grandfather and an uncle, Casimiro, whom he refers to as his father.

It is said that Andreita was a good friend of Maria Martinez, the famous potter from San Ildefonso, and was very near her age. The church records verify this. Maria was born on April 5, 1887, and Andreita was born close to that time the same year. The two families were close and used to exchange visits during feast days and harvesting time, each assisting the other with the chores.

Through his family, Alcario is related to other famous potters. He is a distant relation to, the now deceased Santa Clara-Santo Domingo potter, Monica Silva. Her mother, Benina Tafoya, and his grandfather, Leandro, were sister and brother. Monica Silva contributed to pottery development at both the Santa Clara and Santo Domingo Pueblos, especially in finding and developing clay slips which are responsible for the high luster finishes of today's fine work. Monica had an influence on Margaret. When asked if she remembered Monica Silva, the reply was, "Yes, she was born here [Santa Clara]. She often come here when she was living. She always call us 'my children'. We always liked her." Is she the one who found the slip at Santo Domingo? "Yes, that could be true." Did her son, Martin Lovato, provide the Santa Clara potter with slip? "Yes, he comes here to do that, but we have our own secret slip. She got married and moved to Santo Domingo. I've seen her pottery, the red, the black, and the Santo Domingo kind, but when I knew her she was only making the red and black Santa Clara pottery."

Shortly after their marriage, the young Tafoyas made two important decisions. The first of these was to pool their resources to buy two horses, and the second was to return to Santa Clara and settle down. To accomplish this in the most economical manner, their belongings (except the horses) were shipped to Española by rail where they could be recovered at a later time and the two set off for their old pueblo home on their newly acquired horses.

The route they followed from Dulce to Santa Clara was shorter than that of the railroad, but it naturally took a longer time. The scenery of the first leg of their journey was and is spectacular. Their path took them from Dulce to Chama, New Mexico, some twenty five miles roughly paralleling the narrow gauge tracks. They crossed the Continental Divide between the towns of Monero and Chama. They continued in a southeasterly direction, ever losing altitude, through the town of Tierra Amaria and on to Santa Clara. Margaret, an expert equestrian, remembers that she was not at all uncomfortable during the long ride, and it was enjoyable making camp each evening. It is interesting to note that the route they followed was roughly the same as that said to have been taken by their migrating ancestors hundreds of years earlier.

Should one, for some reason wish to divide Margaret's ceramic art career into phases, it would be logical to term this time the end of the first or developmental phase. A period of unusual productivity and creativity was about to begin.

The Tewa people like many native American groups, seem to be endowed with a profusion of highly artistic individuals. Their art is an expression of their feelings from the dim past and their religious beliefs associated with both the past and the present. At the same time it is meant to show their close bond with nature and their relationship to the present-day world which surrounds them.[6] The combination of Margaret's artistic heritage, the close association with other gifted people, and her talent which was nurtured by this environment, could result in nothing but the production of outstanding ceramic art. Fortunately, Margaret has been productive for many years. She and other Indian artists give little thought to being artists, they simply do what their people before them and their people around them do. It is not their way of life to set themselves above the next person. Margaret is reluctant to be involved in gallery shows and will not give public demonstrations. "No, I never did [give demonstrations]. My mother told me that it is not right for me to show myself at different places... I still kind of feel that way because I always obeyed my mother whatever she tells me, and I take it seriously whatever she tells me." Her later attendance at "Indian Market" and the Inter-Tribal Ceremonial are considered by her more as social gatherings than shows.

The rare example of Margaret "showing herself", is found in a National Geographic Society publication (Ortiz 1974: 122, 173) which shows in five colored photographs Margaret working on various stages of her pottery production. The disturbing element in these pictures or others of Margaret working is that she is dressed in her best Indian clothes and jewelry, articles of attire which she would not normally wear while engaged in the dirty tasks of clay mixing and firing. Margaret remains a partial holdout in this respect, largely restricting herself to quality publications and museum exhibitions. Although Margaret does not wish to do demonstrations, she does not object to her children and grandchildren doing so.

When the newly married Margaret and Alcario returned to their Santa Clara home, they lived with Sara Fina and Geronimo and began in earnest to make pottery. A latent talent in Alcario bloomed when he first applied painted, and later carved decoration to Margaret's pottery. Although he never cosigned their work, Margaret is quick to give him his due and is proud of this talent. Together, they are now credited with bringing carving to a high state of development. It was at this time, that the Tafoya family became a well coordinated team. All

shared in the work of their lands, all assisted in providing the group with the necessities of life, all worked on the making and selling of crafts and pottery, and all shared in their ceremonial life.

The men usually provided the leather articles of clothing and ceremonial dress, while the women sewed or traded for clothing or materials which could be converted into clothing. Geronimo either sold or traded family pottery to obtain a treadle sewing machine which he packed home on his burro. This machine was used to make many articles of family clothing as well as other items such as gathered skirts which were popular with the Santa Clara ladies of that time. The products of this machine would be traded to others for items necessary for family maintenance.

In later years, Margaret and Sara Fina would trade their pottery for clothing for the family. From 1931 to 1935, and again after 1943, they exchanged some of their work with Blanche and Clarence Fulton of Albuquerque, New Mexico, for clothes for the Tafoya children. "She used to come around selling young kids' dresses and pants. She said that she had finished a school for seamstresses, so she is making things like that—children's clothes, baby bonnets, crocheted items. So I traded pottery." It is fortunate that Mrs. Fulton (figure 2-39) kept a diary of sorts and also maintained a fine collection of Margaret's and Sara Fina's pottery much of which is still intact. Not only does it contain examples of a wide variety of their work, but it has proved a basis for dating many of Margaret's pieces in other collections.

The Fulton's came west from Indiana, settling in Albuquerque in 1929. They were attracted to the Southwest and its people, especially the pueblo Indians. Of her first meeting with Margaret, Mrs. Fulton wrote, "We met Margaret Tafoya and her father and mother and her family [in 1931]. I don't know the exact number of children she has, but family does not bother her any and only delays her pottery making about once each year. [to have another baby]. Margaret is very well educated and very pretty. She speaks English well and is a grand pottery maker."

"---Our trips were to trade old clothes for pottery, not worn out clothes, but things that were clean and could be worn. It was so exciting and so much fun. Sometimes we got the best of the bargain and sometimes they did. ---I've made lots of dresses for Margaret's girls in exchange for pottery and we do have some lovely pieces."

"---We were thrilled with the pottery we obtained on our first trip. ---We are still more thrilled with it since we learned to appreciate the tremendous amount of work concerned with it."

This friendship lasted for a number of years as evidenced by the number of letters Margaret wrote and the fact that Mrs. Fulton carefully preserved them.

Fig. 2-39 Donald Fulton collection. Unknown photographer. Blanche and Clarence Fulton, friends of the Tafoya family and pottery collectors from 1931 until Blanche's death in 1970. They moved from Indiana to Albuquerque, NM in 1929. They resided in Albuquerque until 1935 before moving to El Paso. In 1943 they returned to Albuquerque. Blanche's scrapbook and unpublished notes have been helpful in validating facts and dates concerning the lifestyle and pottery of the Tafoya family.

Within a year of their return to Santa Clara, Margaret bore Alcario their first child, Virginia. From that time through the year of 1947, they would have twelve children, two of whom, Priscilla May (1933) and Martha Nora (1940) would not survive the first year. The other children led normal pueblo lives and, as they grew and became able, they assumed family chores. After Virginia came Lee (1927), then Jennie (1929), Mela (1931), Toni (1935), Leo (1936), Lu Ann (1938), Mary Esther (1942), Roger (1944), and Shirley Anne (1947). Margaret took each arrival in her stride and spent only what time was absolutely necessary for the birth process away from the routine of her normal life.

Mrs. Fulton described the early Tafoya household. "Margaret's living house consists of only two rooms, a kitchen and a bedroom, and I never could figure out where they all slept. One other house has two bedrooms and a display room. Their furniture is quite modern, and recently they had electric light put into their home." This was in the early 1930's.

The Tafoyas have always been a busy and productive family. Beginning with the dealer relationships already established by Sara Fina and Geronimo, Margaret began marketing arrangements which were to last for years. The pottery was carefully wrapped and loaded into a horsedrawn wagon during these early years for delivery to the dealers who were located either in Taos or Santa Fe.

The journey to Taos used to follow a road located near the east bank of the Rio Grande River but west of the present Highway 64. The first rest stop was at the Pueblo of San Juan where the Tafoyas might elect to visit friends and relatives or, time permitting, spend the evening. From San Juan, the road continued northward, flanked by huge cottonwood trees, and passed through the old settlements of Alcalde and La Villita to the farming community of Velarde located at the head of the Española Valley. (It is at Velarde that the Rio Grande completely changes its character. South of here it is silt laden and winds its way slowly through and around the many sandbars which have been deposited in previous years along the length of the Española Valley. North of this point it is a clear, swift-flowing stream that passes over an almost continuous run of cascades and rapids as it drops in elevation through the rugged canyon.) Leaving Velarde, the road entered the Rio Grande Canyon following the path of the present highway on the east bank of the river through the towns of Embudo to Pilar. The gray, basaltic cliffs, pockmarked with remnants of bubbles left by volcanic gases, increased in height and steepness as their wagon proceeded northeard. At Pilar, the old road followed the river to the northeast. The present highway takes off on its own, leaving the river, to make its climb to the plains of Taos. A short way up the river on the old road at a location where the present state Highway 96 crosses the river and meets the old road, camp was made for the evening. In Margaret's words, "We stayed for the night near the going up place." These few words vividly describe the location because the dirt road from here climbs abruptly up the steep wall of a side canyon and suddenly emerges on the plains south of Taos (figure 2-40). Once out of the canyon, Taos can be seen in the distance with its backdrop of the snow-capped Sangre de Cristo Mountains and the Blue Mountain, so sacred to the Taos Indian people.

Fig. 2-40 Museum of New Mexico, Photo Archives, Santa Fe, NM. Neg. No. 49234. Ellen S. Quillen photographer. Portion of the old road from the Española Valley to Taos, NM, which Margaret calls "the going up place." It was over this precipitous track that the Tafoyas drove their horse drawn wagons loaded with pottery to sell to Taos dealers.

Upon arriving in Taos, the first business trans-action took place at a trading post owned by Ralph Meyers (figure 2-41) which is still operated by his window, Rowena Meyers Martinez. Ralph was a well-known citizen of the community and had the respect of the English, Spanish and Indian residents of Taos.

Most of the Taos shops and businesses were located on or near the central plaza (figure 2-42) and rounds could be made without too much travel. In addition to Ralph Meyers, there were Francis Fausta, Mrs. Gustoff, and a Mr. Travis. This group was later joined by Tony Reyna (figure 2-43), Mr. and Mrs. Carl Schlosser, and Mr. and Mrs. Harold Street. In retrospect, these traders strongly influ-enced Margaret's pottery development, not so much from an artistic or utilitarian standpoint, but from the view of what was marketable at that time. For example, the Streets purchased many of her large pieces, converted them into lamps and sold them either to businesses or private collectors (figure 2-44). In addition to the beautiful lamps still in Mrs. Street's collection, a fine display of lamps were sold to the owner of the La Fonda Inn at Taos, and may still be seen in the upstairs lobby of that historic old hotel where they are surrounded by an extensive collection of writings and art (including much by D. H. Lawrence).

Upon completion of their downtown business, the remainder of the day was sent with friends and relatives at the Taos Pueblo. Again, Margaret traded or sold pottery, some of which was probably resold to passing tourists. Here they stayed the night. Early in the morning of the third day, the horses were hitched to the wagon for the return trip to Santa Clara. The wagon was lighter, the trip was mostly downhill (a drop of 1375 feet in approximately 52

Fig. 2-41 Rowena Meyers Martinez collection. Photo-grapher unknown. 1912 studio picture postcard of Ralph Meyers, Taos, NM, which he sent to his sister in Denver. One of the first Indian traders with whom Margaret Tafoya dealt. The fictional character Rodolfo Byers in the book The Man who Killed the Deer (Waters, F. 1965) is said to be based on Ralph Meyers. His widow, Rowena Meyers Martinez, still operates the El Rincon Trading Post in Taos.

Fig. 2-42 Courtesy of the Santa Fe Southern Pacific Corp., Chicago,, IL. Photographer unknown. Pre-1929 picture of the Don Fernando Hotel where Margaret Tafoya traded early in her career. This building, on the plaza in Taos, burned in 1929 and was never rebuilt. Writing in upper left corner is that of Blanche Fulton.

Fig. 2-43 and Fig. 2-44, see color page 63.

Don Fernando hotel, Taos, New Mexico

Fig. 2-45 Museum of New Mexico, Photo Archives, Santa Fe, NM. Neg. No. 10685. Photographer unknown. Seligman Store in Santa Fe, ca. 1855. This mercantile could be considered the original southwest Indian art gallery. Descendants of the owner of this store were good customers for Tafoya pottery when they operated a trading post in a nearby location.

miles), so usually only a little over one day was required for the journey home.

Sales trips were also made to Santa Fe to sell to dealers in that area. Although the jaunt was not as beautiful or spectacular as that to Taos, it was enjoyable. The first stop was made at either Tesuque or Nambe Pueblo, where they spent the evening at the home of friends. Continuing the next day, it was only about ten miles to Santa Fe, so there was time in the late morning and the afternoon to sell, trade and buy needed household goods.

Although a fair percentage of Margaret's and Sara Fina's pottery was sold in Taos, much more went into the Santa Fe market. Some was sold directly to businesses, some through dealers, and during the summer season at fiestas, fairs and later at the popular Indian Market.

A memorable dealer in Santa Fe was James Seligman (figure 2-45) who, in Margaret's youth purchased the first piece of pottery she ever marketed.[7] "I sold that piece to Mr. James Seligman who used to have a jewelry store right by the cathedral, but one time I went there and that building was just torn down. I sure don't remember

how much I got. It was a small piece, you know. It made me feel good. I felt I should make some more."

Another associate of her mother's was J. S. Candelario, who owned The Original Old Curio Store located on San Francisco Street from 1905 until 1915 (figures 2-46 and 2-47). When the store changed hands, she continued to do business with the new owners for many years. During a recent inspection of pottery at the School of American Research, Margaret immediately spotted some old, large, beautiful pieces which she identified as having been made by either Sara Fina or herself, or the two together, which had been originally sold to Mr. Candelario. Commenting on a repaired large piece of her work, she said, "I sold that to Mr. Candelario, but it wasn't broken when I sold it to him." (figure 2-48).

At one time, twenty-four of these large pieces were sold for use in the El Fidel Hotel in Santa Fe. These included a double-banded water jar which is extremely difficult to form. In the 1940's and early 1950's, these works were not yet appreciated by the collector or the galleries. The large, beautiful black

Fig. 2-46 Museum of New Mexico, Photo Archives, Santa Fe, NM. Neg. No. 11334. Photographer unknown. Candelario's Original Trading Post, Santa Fe, ca. 1925. Margaret has vivid memories of going with her mother to Mr. Candelario's at about the time that this photo was taken. Museum archives sometimes contain records of pottery obtained from Mr. Candelario. (Figure 2-29)

Fig. 2-47 Museum of New Mexico, Photo Archives. Neg. No. 14039. Photographer unknown. "Interior, Candelario's Original Curio Store, San Francisco St., Santa Fe, NM, ca. 1915" From an old cracked glass slide, this pictures a collector's dream. Margaret identified the man on the right as Mr. Candelario.

Fig. 2-48 School of American Research, Santa Fe, NM. #880. Large black polished storage jar with bear paw decoration by Margaret Tafoya. 23" height, 21" diameter. Though unsigned it was identified by Margaret as one of her earlier works because the sides are quite vertical—easier to form than her later, more slanted ones.

Fig. 2-49 The Heard Museum, Phoenix, AZ. Fred Harvey collection. Neg. No. 28-546. Harvey Detour party in Santa Clara. Photographer unknown. Christina Naranjo. Margaret Tafoya's sister, standing third from right, is selling pottery to Harvey clients. On her left is another potter, Domingita Naranjo. Identifications by Margaret and Christina's daughter, Mary Cain. License plate on limosine dated 1929.

jars brought from twenty-five to fifty dollars each at wholesale and were difficult to resell at that time. With the passing years, these pieces have become recognized as true works of art and their value has increased much more than most art purchased for speculation.

Pottery marketing required that Santa Clara potters become increasingly aware of the ways of the American tourist and even tourists who came from across the oceans. Early visitors to the pueblo came by train and automobile, but only sporadically and in limited numbers. This changed in 1926 when Margaret was twenty-two years old and the famous Fred Harvey Detours were inaugurated.

Luxuriously appointed motor coaches and cars transported tourists from their comfortable quarters at the La Fonda Hotel in Santa Fe to the pueblo; forty five minutes ride which included a brief stop at the Tesuque Pueblo on the way. From the beginning, the Santa Clara stop was included in the itinerary, while the sister pueblo of San Ildefonso was not. As the system expanded, San Ildefonso and other points of interest were gradually included. At first, only twenty minutes were allowed between the time the tour stopped at Santa Clara until it reached Española some two miles away. Later, the schedule was revised, Santa Clara substituted for Española as a lunch stop, and the layover time at the pueblo was extended to an hour and a half—ample time to shop for the beautiful black and red wares produced at the village (figure 2-49). Margaret remembers that there was always someone in the pueblo who give them notice as to the time of arrival of the tourists (referred to as "dudes" by the Harvey employees) so that the pottery would be on display when the buses arrived. The Indian children also proclaimed the buses arrival by shouting, "Here come the Harley buses!" In 1928, the lunch stop was moved to Puyé in Santa Clara Canyon where permanent stone buildings were erected by the Harvey Company which are still standing. The stop at the pueblo was again limited to twenty minutes.

The Detours business did not appear to be affected by the 1929 stock market crash, but continued to thrive until February of 1931. Probably sensing that recovery was further away than many realized, Byron S. Harvey sold the Detours on March 16, 1931, to Major Hunter Clarkson, manager of the company. By 1933, the American tourist had discovered the fun and economy of touring in the family car and only the very wealthly continued to travel by train. In addition, Clarkson was a lavish spender and drained the company of its resources at a time when they were badly needed. Business fell off, and the advent of World War II, made things even worse. Amazingly, the company held on until it was sold to the Grey Line Company in 1968. (Thomas 1978: 56, 182, 305-307, 324).

Both trains and the Detours transformed Santa Clara from a remote, seldom visited pueblo to one where the sighting of outsiders became a common occurence. Again, the Tewa people showed their remarkable ability to accommodate without changing. Sara Fina's life spanned this period of sudden change and, though she accepted it, she probably did not approve of the many new customs which were introduced to her people by aggressive visitors.

The most enjoyable places for Margaret's early pottery sales were the fiestas at Santa Fe and other fairs and ceremonials. These were looked upon as mini-vacations or social gatherings as well as outlets for arts and crafts. This attitude continues to the present time.

For a period of years, the Tafoya family travelled by horse and wagon to the fiesta held each September in Santa Fe. A corral for the horses and housing for the family was provided at Indian House, located on the grounds of the Santa Fe Indian School. Margaret recalls that in the early days of this event there were no buildings north of the former location of St. Vincent's Hospital so that space was allotted for the participating Indians to "play cowboys and Indians. It was really nice. We all enjoy it."

These fiestas lasted for three days. The first day was devoted to "Indian Scenes, Ceremonial, and Episodes." The second day was a Spanish event entitled "Santa Fe Antigua" and the third day was a patriotic celebration featuring ceremonies honoring the U.S. war dead which was followed by a grand parade. The Santa Fe Fiesta is probably the oldest fair of its kind in this country. It was started sixty-four years before the signing of the Declaration of Independence, to commemorate the reconquest of the colony of New Mexico by the Spaniards in 1692, led by De Vargas (Walter 1920: 3). It was at this fair in the early 1920's that Margaret won her first award for the making of excellent pottery. This award was a fringed, blue Pendelton shawl with gray and red designs which she highly values and still has among her possessions (figure 2-50). Pottery was exhibited and sold then, as it is today in front of the Governor's Palace (referred to as "under the portal"). *See color page 63*

The fiesta grew in scope and popularity to such an extent that it became necessary to separate the native American exhibits and activities and to hold them as an event apart at a different time of year. This began under the direction of E. L. Hewett, and with judges appointed by him, an Indian Fair which emphasized pottery was held in the State Armory (Toulouse 1977: 33-38). This event has grown in stature and developed into the present "Indian Market", today the largest happening of its kind in the country. Sponsored by the Southwestern Association of Indian Affairs, the Market demands the undivided attention of merchants, inn keepers, municipal authorities, musem officials, and many citizens of the city part time throughout the year and full time for much of the month of August. The market is held the weekend two weeks prior to Labor Day.

In spite of the fact that Indian Market is considered by many to be the most prestigious show in which to compete for awards and sales, its real attraction is that of a social event where much is learned from the art of others. "It's really nice to go and see your friends," Margaret states, "and see what kind of things they have—the art they know. They will be different the next year. If you keep coming every year, you see many different things."

With each market, ceremonial or fair, Margaret's reputation and that of her offspring continue to grow. In 1977, they collectively won 69 awards at judged shows. For two years running, Margaret won the "Best of Division, Best of Class, and Best of Show" at Indian Market—first in 1978 for her large, red storage jar with impressed bear paw design and in 1979 for her large, black storage jar with the same decoration. In 1980, due to the death of her sister Christina and other family problems, she did not participate at Market, but in 1981 she and her family returned in style, winning 21 awards. It was this year beginning at six o'clock in the morning before the fair officially opened, that twenty-six prospective buyers left their names at her booth hoping to have preference in selecting a piece of pottery. At the appointed time Margaret appeared with only eight pieces.

During the late 1930's and until the time of his tragic death in 1943 of Julian Martinez and his son John are remembered as having purchased unfired pottery at Santa Clara. This fact has been verified by some of that pueblo's people who either recall selling directly to the Martinezes or being present when their relatives were involved in these transactions. Margaret states, "That's true. I am one of her [Maria's] pottery makers—also my mother, my sister Christina, and also Mrs. Candelario Swazo." Commonly referred to as "greenware" it is said to have been pottery that was polished, decorated, and fired at San Ildefonso. Probably because of the great demand for Maria's work, production could not satisfy demand and outside assistance was necessary.

When asked if the pottery that Julian Martinez bought was fired or unfired, Margaret replied, "Unfired, except for one piece. It was finished when I gave it to Mr. Julian Marinez when he was still alive. That was around 1936 or 1937. He always admired that pot so I told him I give it to him. I washed it—I was using it. He was very happy to get it." ... "Did you make mostly large pieces to sell to Julian and John?" "No, all kinds, the kind they order—wedding jars, small pieces, thunderbirds,

bowls, and little baskets, bowls with little handles in the center and sometime they order bigger wedding jars, large pieces and medium size and water jars." Some of Margaret's and Christina's children remember these visits of Julian and John to their homes. Virginia Ebelacker said, "I remember Julian and Juan Diego [John] because he always gave me a nickel or a dime. He always used to tease me. They came down to pick up my grandmother's pottery, and they also bought a lot of it from my mother. I remember one with a rainbow band. I remember that so well because my dad and I took that same type of lamp base to Santa Fe. I was probably about ten or twelve."

Although Margaret does resent the fact that much of their work has not been recognized, she remains philosophical on the subject. "Those days were hard and we were sure glad to get the money. We didn't know that they would be marked up so high." Money was scare then, especially for the native American. They raised and preserved most of their food as well as sewing most of their clothes. Work outside of the pueblo was difficult to obtain, and prices paid for their pottery yielded no more than five cents for each hour of work that went into the making.[8]

The 1940's brought a profound change in the pueblo way of life and in the Tafoya family's lifestyle as well. They were able to buy their first car, a Ford stake truck. More children were born. The outlet for greenware pottery was almost cut off with the death of Julian Martinez. Alcario obtained a job at Los Alamos, New Mexico, where the U.S. Government had taken over land and began building scientific laboratories for the development of the atomic bomb. In 1945, he was elected governor of Santa Clara Pueblo, and so was unable to continue working in Los Alamos (figure 2-51).

A governor's position is much more demanding than simply holding an honorary rank which allows one to display the canes of office prominently in his home or carrying them during celebrations (Faris 1954). A newly elected governor and his family must host a feast for the entire pueblo, opening his home to all. The affairs of the pueblo are complicated and change daily. "Every day there is people, people with problems, people with complaints, Indian people, Spanish people, even white people. They want to have disputes settled or want to rent land or lease land. Always seem to come when we are eating. He would have to stand up and leave his meals all the time," Margaret remembers. The duties of his office demanded that Alcario spend full time at governing, even though, governors received no salary or expense money. With the main source of income removed, the Tafoyas had to maintain the family by raising as much food as possible and selling as much pottery as possible. As the wife of the governor, much of Margaret's time

Fig. 2-52 New Mexico State Economic Development and Tourism Dept., Santa Fe, NM. Neg. No. 14,226. Photographer unknown. Inter-Tribal Ceremonial, Gallup, NM. 1956. This photo illustrates the size and diversity of Margaret Tafoya's production. The large jar is still in a private collection. Alcario well remembers moving it from the exhibition hall for the purchaser.

was required assisting Alcario, and her pottery production was restricted. When asked to serve for a second term, Alcario, finding the family resources severly depleted, was forced to refuse the honor. Today, there is a complex of pueblo offices at Santa Clara as well as salary and expense money for the governor and other tribal officials.

With a family car, Margaret's pottery marketing covered greater geographic areas. She was now able to attend the famous Inter-Tribal Ceremonial to exhibit and sell her work (figure 2-52). The Ceremonial was started in 1922 by a group of Gallup, New Mexico civic leaders. It did not become financially stable until it was recognized by the New Mexico legislature as the outstanding tourist attraction for the state and was given the status of an official agency entitled to an annual appropriation from state funds (Anon. 1972). The character and flavor of the event has changed through the years and it has become more com-

mercially oriented. In times gone by, Indians from all tribes would come in their horse-drawn wagons or pickup trucks and camp on the small hills which encircled the old fair grounds in Gallup. Their campfires at night were spectacular and added something of beauty which is now gone. These grounds were condemned in 1972 because they stood in the right of way of the approaching U.S. Highway 40. The new site, located some ten miles east of Gallup surrounded by natural red rock splendor, was opened in 1973 as a state park.

Margaret does not remember in what year she first exhibited at Inter-Tribal, but she attended for many years. "My children always stay with my mother. She was still living at that time. It's too far away to leave the children. But we did good. We sold our pottery and our beads, so the next year I make it again. Even our feast day was going to be during that time, but I put it back—the feast day—and I went to Gallup. I enjoyed it more over there.

All those four days—the things you can see. I haven't been there for years. Just some of the rest of the family go."

The years from 1946 through 1948 were turbulent and sad for Margaret. Trouble developed with the Roman Catholic Church over the right of the Tafoyas to enroll their children in a non-Catholic private school.

As a settlement of a legal dispute, some Catholic schools were closed and they could not accommodate daughter Mela. The Tafoyas were pleased with Mela's progress at McCurdy School just outside Española and so the decision was made to enroll Toni. Later, when room became available in the Catholic school, the children were not sent there. This began a disagreement with church officials, a disagreement which has left scars to this day.

In 1949, the inevitable happened. Sara Fina passed away after living a full and worthwhile life of approximately ninety years. (Figure 2-36 shows approximate grave location.) Partially because of her strict adherence to her Tewa ways, her reluctance to "show herself", and the times in which she lived, she has never received the artistic recognition she so well deserved. Her burial was marred by the family's disagreement with the church at that time.

Although the school and burial arguments are in no way connected to the history of Margaret's life as it relates to her pottery, her comments on the subject do give deep insight into the character of this strong, impressive person. "[In the past] when somebody died no one is there to pray for them, only the old Indians say their prayers. That poor body is laid there, but up there the Great Spirit bless it. Why is the same not true today? If she have the Great Spirit, if she have the love—she is going up there. If you are living the wrong way, the Almighty Father won't help. Some day when I die, ask the older people to pray for me. Until then I say my own Indian prayer. I have my own way, I pray my own way. The Spirit I pray to is the same as the one that they [the Christians] worship. In the other language [Tewa] we pray. We come from the same Father, we all did. This is our understanding from our first people. We must pray. We can't live in this world without Him. We can't be on our feet without Him."

For a time, Margaret changed to another Christian faith. This may be the reason that her son Lee studied to be a Protestant minister. However, when she attended a different church, she was told that whoever believed in the Indian religion or worshipped idols was evil and would never go to heaven. With her background and strong inherited beliefs in the ways of her ancestors, this was more than Margaret could stand. "So I went out of there and never went back to church. I say my own Indian prayers." Although Margaret has strong feelings about her personal religion, she has no objections

when her children select Christian religions for themselves. She knows that they have all been raised the Tewa way and that they all, in one way or another, maintain their connections with it and the past.

Today, there is no trace of Sara Fina's grave. "It has been so long. We put crosses there, but that was before the yard was fenced or adobe around. Before that, the cows and horses walk around and during then all the crosses were destoryed." Sara Fina's grave and much of her pottery have gone unmarked.

In the mid 1940's, the composition of the Tafoya family began to undergo many changes. In the nine years between 1945 and 1954, five of the children had either married or left the pueblo to pursue careers of their own. Following the death of Sara Fina, Geronimo had only three years of life remaining, most of which he was bedridden and required constant attention—a chore that none of the family resented. He, like his wife, lies in an unmarked grave and the many contributions he made to his people go largely unrecognized. (figure 2-36)

During the second half of the 1950's, Margaret and Alcario decided they needed new and larger quarters and so built a home on the southeast side of the pueblo near one of the plazas. Brother Manuel who was very close to the family assisted in the construction. The beams, the carefully plastered walls, and the beautiful adobe fire place were all the result of his fine touch and were nearing completion when Manuel was murdered in October of 1958. His body way found face down in the Santa Clara irrigation ditch, all of his money from a cashed pay check missing. His violent death left the family in a state of shock. They worked closely with Manuel, especially on pottery production, and felt a deep attachment for him. The old house continually reminded them of him, so a decision was made to move as quickly as possible into the new home. This was done just before Christmas in spite of the fact that all the work was not completed.

The Tafoya's contact with the tourist was not limited to those who came to the pueblo, but they also left their homes for the summer to perform Indian dances and sell to the tourists who were visiting the natural wonders of the front range of the Rocky Mountains in Colorado. Pioneers in Indian tourist entertainment were Margaret's uncles Tomas ("Lightning") and Jose Maria ("Red Bird").[9] They established contacts at Manitou Springs, Seven Falls, Garden of the Gods, and other resorts and brought their families for the summer season to sell their wares and entertain the tourists with Indian dances. They enjoyed this summer occupation—to some it was more like a vacation.

Realizing the popularity of the Indian groups at the resorts, a Mr. Wann, began to search for a family

Fig. 2-53 M.E. Archuleta collection. Clarence and Donald Fulton photographers. The Tafoya family at Royal Gorge, Co. in dance dress, ca. 1955. **Left to right: back row-***Alcario and Leo,* **middle row-***Margaret and Mary Esther Archuleta,* **front row-***Shirley Tafoya, Gordon Trammel, Richard Ebelacker, and Roger Tafoya.*

to work for him in the summer at Royal Gorge. He learned of the Alcario Tafoyas through their daughter Mela who was working in Colorado Springs at the time. He went to Santa Clara in the spring of 1952 to contact them and explained that Royal Gorge was near Cañon City, urging them to go and look before making a decision. He was sure they would enjoy staying there. Margaret was reluctant to go because the family had never left home for such a long period of time, but she finally agreed.

Mr. Wann must have been a man of persistence and courage. "So we went. He drove us with pottery, moccasins, drums, costumes for the children—Toni, Leo, Esther, LuLu [Lu Ann], Berde [Shirley], Roger, Gordon, and grandson Richard Lee. Toni and LuLu worked at the store. For a few weeks they didn't like it—kind of homesick. They got used to it, and the next summer they are glad to go back" (figure 2-53).

For ten ensuing summers, the younger members of the family returned to Royal Gorge with Margaret and Alcario. They invested in a small, two-wheeled trailer to attach to their truck for these summer moves, and many of their belongings were loaded in this for the 265 mile trip. The income from this venture consisted of tips from the tourists who witnessed their dances, and a house was provided for the family. Almost all of the cash they received was put aside to purchase clothes for the children for the coming school year.

Each day, just before the dance performance, Alcario would set up an advertising sign that read "Chief Foggy Bird". This was an odd translation of his Tewa name. The Tewa name for mist had been translated to fog and the Tewa for swallow or diving bird was simply called bird. Thus, "Swallow in the Mist" became "Foggy Bird", a name by which many still remember him.

At Royal Gorge, Margaret was able to sell pottery which she had made at Santa Clara. During the summer, she simply did not have the materials, the place or the time to make pottery in Colorado. "Up there the children keep me busy. Moccasins that they wore lasted only three or four days and need repair. At night I put new soles on, sewed beads on, and fixed everything that the dance costumes need. I make my own moccasins." People at Royal Gorge remember that she supplied the family with a change of costume every week.

In the following years, other younger members of the family joined the group, while some of the older children would drop out to pursue other endeavors. One of the children remembers thinking, "Oh, boy! School just closed, and we are going back to our Colorado." Margaret was happy that the children had a change of scene and were kept busy during school vacations.

Although these summers were pleasant and busy times, the exposure which they gave Margaret did very little to promote her in the right areas as a potter. Her attendance at summer events where Indian art was featured was consequently very limited for eleven of the most productive years of her life.

Following the years at Royal Gorge, a change began in the marketing of Indian art. The public was becoming increasingly aware and appreciative of the value of the work of many Indian artisans and was beginning to look on these as a different art form. The complexion of the stores handling Indian work changed from cheap souvenir outlets to craft shops, and then to galleries specializing in native Americn art which became increasingly popular. As demand increased, the number of stores carrying Indian art multiplied, and competition grew to obtain the work of the better artists. The dealers now began to pursue the artists, rather than the artists having to bring their work to the dealers. At first, a dealer would go to the work place, where he would select a limited number of completed works. Gradually, due to increased demand, selection was elimated and dealers took what was available, with little opportunity to choose. Today, buyers place a blind order for a number of pieces in advance, and often these orders cannot be filled. Should dealers not appear on agreed dates to collect work, it is sold to the next buyer and sometimes the next order from that dealer is not honored. In many instances, a mistrust between the buyer and seller has occurred. This, in turn, has led some non-Indians to unjustly criticize the trade practices of Indians in general.

Margaret and her family have remained remarkably free from dealer conflict. Over the years, she has developed a group of dealer associates with whom she has an excellent rapport. She gives them discounts which allows them to sell to the collector at a profit—a profit Margaret could have kept for herself.

Even after the need to leave the pueblo to sell her work no longer existed, Margaret attended the Gallup Inter-Tribal Ceremonial, the New Mexico State Fair, and Indian Market on an almost regular annual basis. Transportation was available, and the pleasure of meeting friends and exchanging ideas with other potters had always been irresistible. It was during one of her early visits to Gallup that she first met the famous potter Nampeyo and her daughter Rachel.

"So I met Nampeyo in 1935 or 1937—along there, you know. I even talked to her in 1937 when we were up there, but she must have died soon after, around 1940. [Nampeyo died in 1942]. I met her over there. she was with a young fellow. Didn't even ask her if that was her son. She had some pottery on a shelf and on a counter she had a big storage jar. It was all decorated pretty. I asked her where she took her pottery for exhibit and she told me Phoenix, Arizona. I didn't think she ever signed her pieces. Way back we never do, but just by looking at it, we know our work. I told her that we both belonged to the Corn Clan. I told her I make these kind of big pieces, Sister, really big ones. They look almost like yours, only yours is painted and mine are either all black or all red. She said, 'Yes, you know why. We're Corn Clan you and me. We are smart and can make these big things'."

The Tafoya potters have, more than many, shown an interest in the work of other potters. When visiting museum collections, they are inquisitive and spend much time studying and noting the finish, shapes, and decorations of Santa Clara and other pueblo pottery. Margaret enjoys these observation visits almost as much as she does any other form of recreation.

It was not until the 1960's and 1970's that Margaret began to receive the recognition which she had merited for such a long time, but it was still slow in coming. The literature finally and almost grudgingly began to recognize her accomplishments. Harlow (1977: 28) wrote as follows: "As at all the other pottery making pueblos, the general trend during this commercially oriented period has been toward making smaller vessels and ceramic sculpture, and to develop new forms such as ashtrays and candlesticks. At Santa Clara, however, there are still a few potters capable and willing to make very large vessels. Margaret Tafoya usually makes one huge black jar every year, a real *tour de force* requiring months of careful drying of the clay body, many tedious hours of polishing to achieve the incredibly beautiful surface, and a most careful firing to achieve uniform deep black color and avoid cracking the vessel. At present, no other potter from any village will attempt such a feat, although some at Santa Clara and elsewhere still occasionally produce vessels up to two-thirds the size of Mrs. Tafoya's."

On October 8 and 9, 1977, Rick Dillingham arranged a pottery exhibition for the Dewey-Kofron Gallery in Santa Fe.[10] Not only was this exhibit outstanding, it was an event whose quality and potter participation may never be duplicated. Fifty-one potters representing eleven different tribes attended and Margaret spent her time talking to and studying the work of others. It was noted that she darted from one vessel to another throughout the reception period, carefully examining each piece.

Two important things happened to Margaret because of this show. First, she and her estranged sister Christina became and were to remain very close until Christina's death in 1980. Second, she met Grace Chapella, an outstanding Hopi-Tewa potter (Collins 1977: 9, 10). Grace and her daughter Alma Tahbo accepted Margaret's invitation to visit her home at Santa Clara after the reception.

The meeting at Margaret's home was an event which many anthropologists would gladly have paid a good admission price to attend. Grace, who was then possibly 103 years old, and Margaret carried on a conversation in the old Tewa language about their ancestors and their art. Some of Margaret's daughters remember this distinctly because they, in spite of the fact that they speak Tewa, could not understand many of the old words used during this dialog. Old Tewa is to today's Tewa as Elizabethan English is to the present English language. The Tafoya daughters were told that it was rude to interrupt with questions, so they missed much of conversation. Unfortunately, a reunion of these two impressive ladies would never occur. Grace passed away on June 19, 1980. She may well have been over 106 years of age.

Christina's death cut Margaret deeply. She remembers the last time that she saw her sister. "This was when she was in the hospital. She just turned her face the other way. I asked, 'Christina, are you very sick?' 'No,' she said, 'but when I am lying on this bed some things come to my mind. Someday when I'm going, I want to go back to the old religion.' [Christina had left the Catholic Church years before and now wanted to return]. So I guess she told the same thing to the her daughters, and the girls ask the Catholic priest just the day before she pass away. He [Father Conran] was there." In addition to returning to the old religion, she also returned to the old, old religion and was given a beautiful "send-off" in the Tewa tradition.

A Tewa burial is very ecological. The deceased is simply wrapped in a blanket and interred the next day. Four days after the death, the relatives go to the home of the departed, bringing all kinds of food. Some of this is put aside for the deceased, and the rest is divided among those present. Thus, a loved one is "sent off" to the next world. A year later a similar ceremony is observed, and this is considered the final "send off".

With the exception of the inconvenience brought on by notoriety, Margaret lives much as she always has. In the late morning through the remainder of the day, she is often besieged by dealers phoning or knocking at the door, requests for interviews, or tourists or collectors who wish to talk or buy pottery which she almost never has available. She concentrates very hard when polishing or firing and can tolerate no disturbing influences. At these times, she rejects all outside contacts.

Throughout the years, Margaret's way of life and remarkable work habits have changed little. A normal day would see the Tafoyas rising about 5:30 A.M. to tend the livestock. In the words of a grandson, "She has a milk cow I have been trying to get her to get rid of. It's too much work. Early many mornings it's cold down there. Grandpa takes her down. She milks the cow." Wayne helps with some of the chores, but his time is limited because he maintains a full time job outside the pueblo. There are just a few Tewa left who raise chickens and Margaret is among them. "I love just to be walking with chickens and doing something with them. I always like chickens. I like to milk cows, and we have a milk cow. Her name is Nancy. We had Charmin too. [Called Charmin® because she was so squeezable]. We used to have an old milk cow called Judy. We didn't want to sell her or kill her. We just turned her loose out in the pasture. She was a second mother of ours, we don't want to hurt her. Somehow she got stuck in a ditch where there was water and she died." Margaret still prefers to churn her own butter by hand from the milk they obtain that day.

Following the farm chores comes breakfast. Even then, Margaret is not quite relaxed and is thinking of other animals. "I always think when I'm finishing my breakfast that the dog wants to eat. Sometimes I see them outside, and even if I've fed them I think maybe she's hungry and I feed that dog again." Breakfast time and shortly thereafter, is one of the favorite visiting times for children and grandchildren. Richard Ebelacker says, "I like to talk to them in the morning. If you catch them about seven o'clock when they are having their breakfast, they like to talk. In the afternoon, they have too much to do, too many things on their mind. If you start talking about a certain pot or design or some procedure or something about the pueblo, they will go way back. Tell about people you don't remember. They have many flashbacks, but as old as they are they will come back to where they left off and start in again." Some of the Tafoya daughters enjoy lunch with their parents for the same reasons.

The remainder of the day is spent on many different kinds of jobs, depending on what needs doing. One day might be devoted to any of the various aspects of pottery making. During certain seasons, there are crops to be harvested or food that needs to be preserved. Days of preparation are still required for some ceremonial or feast day functions. Before each of these occasions, the house is cleaned from top to bottom, including polishing the vigas, (exposed rafters). Son Leo tries unsuccessfully to get his mother to reduce her work load and accept more help from others. "I enjoy it, I tell him. At night, I sew my apron or maybe a dress that has ripped up. I rip a lot of old dresses to make aprons for work. I'm always doing something. repairing moccasins like this. I never like to watch TV. When I see it, I go to sleep." The day for the senior Tafoyas often ends near midnight.

Christmas Eve is a special and private time for the family. Again, Margaret requires days of preparation for this annual event. All of the family, spouses and children dress for the occasion and make their way back to the house in the pueblo for feasting and the exchange of presents. Many times, they give each other pottery which they have made, or sometimes give older heirlooms that they feel should be in the hands of the younger generation. Gifts are stacked in the living room in a pile so high that it is impossible to imagine. Grandma Margaret usually selects one person each year to receive a special present from her. A grandson describes one of these occasions: "She saw me. I guess it was my turn that year. She went running to the corner and took off the top of a lamp which I thought she was going to take into another room. 'This is yours,' she told me."

Margaret Tafoya's pottery has, from the time she was a young woman until today, been outstanding, if not the best, in its field. One wonders why it has taken so long for her to receive this overdue recognition. There are several possible reasons for this oversight, the main one being Margaret's heritage and personality. There are many things in her life which she rates above artists' reception, gallery shows, honorary degrees, and world fairs which seem to be necessary to successfully promote an artist. (figure 2-54) She is reluctant to take part in any publicity about herself and she has never had a prestigious sponsor. She has rejected several attempts to write her biography and has refused an offer to participate in a public television program about her life and work because she simply had too much to do and could not spare the time. Above all else she puts the welfare of her family.

In the summer of 1983, the first major showing of Margaret's work was held at the Wheelwright Museum in Santa Fe with Margaret in attenance. This was followed by more comprehensive exhibitions in the fall of 1983 at the Denver Museum of Natural History and later at the Colorado Springs Fine Art Center and Taylor Museum. Unfortunately, Margaret was seriously ill during the

fall and winter of 1983-84 and missed seeing these exhibitions as well as not being able to attend a one person show given for her at a private gallery in Scottsdale, Arizona.

Margaret Tafoya's work speaks for itself, and her reputation has grown almost solely by word of mouth by far-sighted collectors and a few dealers who saw the unique beauty she has produced.

By Spring 1984, Margaret had almost completely recovererd from the previous winter's illness, and in June of that year she was elected Folk Artist of the Year by the National Endowment for the Arts in recognition of her accomplishments. In addition to a generous cash award, she was given a trip to Washington, D.C. to attend a ceremony to receive this honor.

"The Folk Arts Program of the National Endowment for the Arts recognizes Margaret Tafoya as a Master Traditional Artist who has contributed to the shaping of our artistic traditions and to preserving the cultural diversity of the United States."

Upon receiving the governor of New Mexico's award for outstanding achievement in the arts in 1985, Margaret responded with reticence and simplicity, "I never thought I'd be here. Thank you very much." ·

Margaret Tafoya with Larry and Mary Ellen Blair. New Mexico Governor's award. Santa Fe, NM.

Chapter 3
The Making of Traditional Santa Clara Pottery

"Just by Watching my Grandma."

Margaret Tafoya

What is meant by traditional Tewa pottery, and what are considered traditional pottery-making techniques? Is a work decorated with carved designs traditional? Is the famous Black-on-black traditional? These methods of decoration were not the norm in the 1920's when they were being developed, but are now certainly considered traditional among contemporary Tewa potters. Commercial kiln firing is not conventional today, but the metal cans, sheets, and grates used in the firing process are devices of white civilization, and their use by the Indian artist is quite acceptable by traditionalists. Presently, some Tewa potters may consider a piece of pottery traditional, while their contemporaries with the same background do not.

After many discussions on the subject with various Tewa potters, one comes up with the following general requirements which traditional Tewa ware must satisfy:

1. The article must be formed from raw materials available from tribal lands. These materials should be beneficiated and purified manually, preferably by the potter or close members of the potter's family.

2. The ware must be formed and finished by hand methods such as coiling or pinching which have their roots in the prehistoric or historic Tewa past. The use of the potter's wheel, jiggers, or plaster molds is frowned upon by the classic Tewa potter.[1]

3. The work must be fired in temporary kilns built on the spot at the time of each individual firing, using only wood or manure as fuel. Firing in commerically available kilns, heated with secondary fuels such as gas, oil, or electricity, is considered an especially poor practice.

Traditional forming and firing is a matter of great concern and discussion among Tewa potters. Due to the very nature of the pueblos, with competing potters living in close proximity, the topic is often and heatedly debated. All Santa Clara potters, however, agree that Margaret Tafoya is as close as one can be to a true traditional Tewa potter today. She is conservative by contemporary standards, both in her approach to her work and the methods used in production. To the traditional potter,

designs should have a meaning rooted in the Tewa past and not simply be forms used without any purpose except artistic effect. In this vein, Margaret feels that "jewelry does not belong on pottery," referring to the heshi and semi-precious gem stones which are added to some of the ware after firing.

Margaret's pottery-making techniques, though mostly inherited, are not exactly like those of her ancestors, nor are they exactly like those of her nearby contempraries. It logically follows that the methods of her descendants differ slightly from hers and from one another. Even with traditional potters there must be some innovation or the art will become stagnant.

In some respects, Margaret is an enigma. She was one of the first at Santa Clara to work with the Black-on-black decoration, she produced outstanding polychrome painting and orange-outlined decorations at the same time as similar work was created by Lela and Van Gutierrez, and she adpoted Greek and Roman forms to Santa Clara shapes. She and Alcario were among the earliest carvers at the pueblo. While using these innovative techniques, much of her output remained traditional and each would be abandoned while she returned to making the traditional Tewa shapes. Today, with the exception of some forms of decoration, much of which was done by Alcario, she has limited herself to beautiful and graceful adaptations of the old forms. Fortunately a few artists, such as Margaret and her mother, clung strongly to the ways of the past, thereby allowing all to share in this beauty before it is lost and its techniques are forgotten.

Changes in Santa Clara pottery shape and design have come slowly, but, like other art and technology since World War II, are increasing at a rapidly accelerating rate. This, combined with impatience at mastering the old techniques, is resulting in a decrease in the production of traditional pottery at the pueblo.

Beginning with Adolph Bandelier's work in 1890, archeologists, anthropologists, and other technical reseachers have contributed to the knowledge of how present-day Tewa pottery

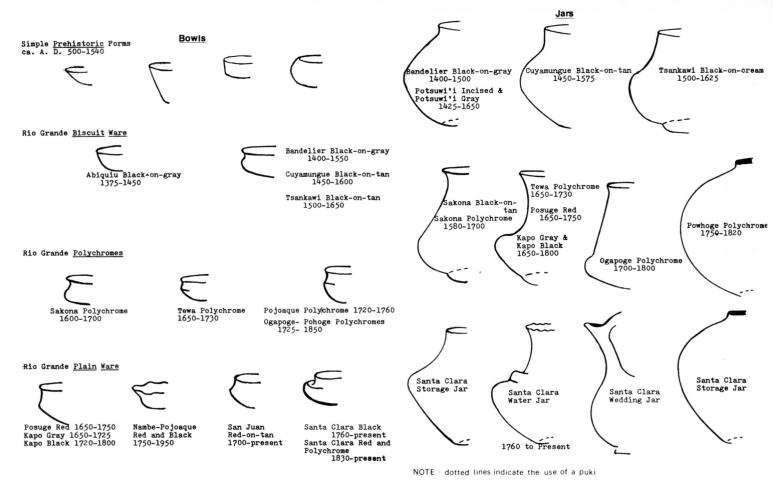

Bowls

Simple Prehistoric Forms
ca. A.D. 500-1540

Rio Grande Biscuit Ware

Abiquiu Black-on-gray
1375-1450

Bandelier Black-on-gray
1400-1550

Cuyamungue Black-on-tan
1450-1600

Tsankawi Black-on-tan
1500-1650

Rio Grande Polychromes

Sakona Polychrome
1600-1700

Tewa Polychrome
1650-1730

Pojoaque Polychrome 1720-1760
Ogapoge-Pohoge Polychromes
1725-1850

Rio Grande Plain Ware

Posuge Red 1650-1750
Kapo Gray 1650-1725
Kapo Black 1720-1800

Nambe-Pojoaque
Red and Black
1750-1950

San Juan
Red-on-tan
1700-present

Santa Clara Black
1760-present
Santa Clara Red and
Polychrome
1830-present

Jars

Bandelier Black-on-gray
1400-1500

Potsuwi'i Incised &
Potsuwi'i Gray
1425-1650

Cuyamungue Black-on-tan
1450-1575

Tsankawi Black-on-cream
1500-1625

Sakona Black-on-tan
Sakona Polychrome
1580-1700

Tewa Polychrome
1650-1730

Posuge Red
1650-1750

Kapo Gray &
Kapo Black
1650-1800

Ogapoge Polychrome
1700-1800

Powhoge Polychrome
1750-1820

Santa Clara
Storage Jar

Santa Clara
Water Jar

Santa Clara
Wedding Jar

Santa Clara
Storage Jar

1760 to Present

NOTE · dotted lines indicate the use of a puki

Fig. 3-1 Ceramic shapes that were produced in the Rio Grande region that have influenced the development of Santa Clara pottery. Dates are averaged.

emerged from its prehistoric past, and newly developed research tools continue to add to this knowledge. In spite of what appears to be a tremendous amount of work, there is much more remaining to be done. Information is so highly fragmented and contradictory that a clear picture of Tewa pottery evolution is simply not available in spite of many firm expert opinions.

It was not until the arrival of the Spanish that any written records on the subject of southwest American Indian pottery were kept, and searching these old records reveals much about historic pottery development, but very little about the ceramic work of the Tewa in particular.

There are conflicting scholarly evaluations on the importance of Spanish contact to Tewa pottery. Adams (1982: 596) states that some elements of Santa Clara pottery design, such as rim fluting, were influenced by the Spanish. Some pueblos increased their use of the color red at this time, and this too has been suggested as reflecting Spanish tastes (Dittert and Plog 1980: 131). In view of their reluctance to assimilate anything that was Spanish in nature, however, it it seems doubtful that the Santa Clarans made an exception for pottery. Harlow (1973: 60) states that the pottery of other pueblos was affected neither positively nor negatively by Spanish occupation. Tewa potters, particularly those at the Santa Clara and San Juan

Pueblos, remained true to their inheritance, producing hard-fired, utilitarian pottery that improved in quality with each generation.

Excavations of Tewa-occupied pueblos such as Sacona and Cuyamungue (fig. 1-2), which were abandoned after the Pueblo Indian revolt, have yielded pottery pieces which clearly demonstrate that pottery not only survived Spanish occupation, but thrived. Undoubtedly, some potters who abandoned these sites moved to neighboring villages and continued their work. The pueblos of Nambe, Pojoaque, Tesuque, San Ildefonso, and Santa Clara may have benefitted from these migrations. The beautiful Ka'po Grey, one of the forerunners of present-day Santa Clara ware, appeared at the end of this period (Harlow 1973: 200). Beautiful examples of pottery shapes and decoration made during this time continue to be found.

In the late eighteen hundreds, Tewa pottery was recognized as a separate art form. The making of Santa Clara pottery was first described by Jeançon in 1931, and publication on the subject proliferated. A complete work concerning Santa Clara pottery was published by LeFree in 1975. Figure 3-1 shows pottery forms that influenced the development of pottery shapes at Santa Clara. Other influences on the evolution of Santa Clara pottery are summarized in Appendix 1.

The Clay

The word "clay" according to the Winston Dictonary is earth or mud; and in a practical or Scriptural use—the human body. In this context then, the Tewa term of "Mother Earth" or "Mother Clay" in reference to the basic material for pottery is easily understood. Margaret speaks of "respect for Mother Earth" and considers it a commodity that is loaned for human use, but never owned. Potters are grateful that they may use it for their maintenance and well being. As true Tewa gathering clay, Margaret and her family still practice the age-old inherited rituals, with sacred cornmeal, of saying prayers and thanking Mother Earth for leanding of herself. Continuing with this philosophy, the traditional potter does not waste the clay, and even meager scraps of unfired material are saved and recycled. This applies to the tempered clay and slip as well.

Fortunately, clay deposits are plentiful in the southwestern United States, and Tewa potters have been digging the red, tan, or gray sedimentary material in the Rio Grande Valley since they moved from their ancestral homes in the Chama Valley in the 11th century and later from the Pajarito Plateau in the 14th century, when they brought their knowledge of pottery with them. With only sticks and stones as tools, clay mining must have been unbelievably hard work for these early people. It was not until the Spanish brought draft animals and metal working tools, that the chore was made easier.

In the horse and wagon days of Margaret Tafoya's youth, clay digging was an all day expedition, though the deposits were not far from the pueblo. To alleviate the drudgery, the Tafoyas, as was the pueblo custom, made it a day for a picnic. Later in 1941, it was written, "We drove up to the sand hills, a few miles from here, where each of the pottery makers have their own clay pit. These pits are shallow, and one must be on one's knee to get into one to dig out the clay which is placed in a large square of material and carried down to the truck or wagon. Many trips were made on foot by the Indians when no other means of making the trip was available".[2] (figure 3-2)

Fig. 3-2 Clarence and Donald Fulton, 1951, 1952. Alcario Tafoya digging clay illustrates the potential danger from collapsing over-burden. One of a series of postcards sold at Royal Gorge, Co. where the Tafoyas spent eleven summers.

Margaret tells us that the "old clay" that was used to make the very large vessels of the late 19th and early 20th centuries was quite different from that used now, both in location and consistency. She describes it as "more slick" so that it could be worked into much thinner walled pieces. Both Hill (1982: 83) and LeFree (1975: 7) mention this older deposit which was used to produce utilitarian ware at Santa Clara. The steep earth walls which bordered this location, eventually eroded and collapsed and the clay is now covered by many feet of rubble so "you can't get there", according to Margaret.

Santa Clara potters including the Tafoyas remember a deposit of micaceous clay which was used in the past, but this too has been eradicated by flood waters. Micaceous ware was produced at Santa Clara until the 1940's with clay that required no tempering (Hill 1982: 86). Pottery made from this deposit by Margaret's mother has been located in private collections (figure 2-15).

Though Santa Clara men have always helped with pottery chores, the actual forming and decorating was previously considered women's work. Starting in the early 1920's, men began to admit to decorating and later to actually forming pottery (Chapman 1970: 26). The men's earth working reponsibilities formerly were limited to clay digging and mixing, adobe work on the houses and fireplaces, and the construction of hornos (outdoor beehive shaped bread baking ovens).

After their marriage, Margaret's husband Alcario joined her brothers Manuel and Camilio in helping dig clay for the entire family. With Margaret and Alcario clay digging is still a family affair, with the younger males (sons, sons-in-law, and grandsons) taking the responsibility for the heavy work while Margaret, acting as mine superintendent and pit geologist, points out the clay veins worth mining.

Because pottery making is economically important to the Santa Clara Tribe, the Council now employs bulldozers to clear the overburden from the deposits presently being quarried. Thus, the collection of clay is a much lighter burden than it was in the past. It is available near the surface, and the danger of overhanging dirt and rock collapsing to kill or maim the clay digger is almost eliminated. There are several known instances of this happening to pueblo potters including the mother of the Hopi potter Garnet Pavatea who died when the earth collapsed on her.

Most important to the traditional Santa Clara potter is that the clay used be dug from what is considered Santa Clara land. To the discerning collector, there is something warm about the colors of ware made from reservation clay as compared to any commercial clay which is readily available from hobby art dealers. Commercially available clay products seem cold and sterile by comparison, though certainly the "store bought" product is easier to work, contains no impurities such as roots, and can be used to form a thinner walled and lighter weight product.

The Temper

Temper is commonly referred to as "sand" by the Tewa potters and as "grog" to the professional ceramic engineer. The temper used at Santa Clara is in reality a volcanic tuff—the traditional additive to Tewa clay. Undoubtedly, fine silica sand temper has found occasional use, but never to Margaret's knowledge have ground shards been put to use, as the Keres people of Acoma Pueblo do today. However, Jeançon claimed that shard temper was used at Santa Clara between 1904 and 1930 (Hill 1982: 84, 85).

The tempering agent performs important functions in a ceramic body. It modifies the stickiness of the raw wet clay, making it easier to handle and more pliable. Importantly, it controls drying shrinkage of the ware, thereby elimating cracking and distortion of the unfired work. Finally, it reduces firing shrinkage and warping.

Margaret has two sources of temper. The first occurs on Santa Clara land, and the second is purchased from the neighboring Pueblo of Pojoaque. Santa Clara tuff or sand is located about nine feet beneath the surface, thus requiring the removal of overburden and much digging. What is referred to as "Pojoaque sand" is preferred by most Santa Clara potters and is sold as a dig-it-yourself mineral by the Pojoaque people. The going price in 1983 was ten dollars for a 33 gallon container. The material is bluish in color and, according to Margaret, cannot be distinguished from Santa Clara sand in a fired pot. Unlike clay, washing is not necessary, but some potters sift the temper to remove any particles or impurities.

Formerly, temper was obtained as close to home as possible to avoid hauling, but now it is permissible to purchase it, as long as it comes from Indian land. Micaceous clay, such as that formerly used at Santa Clara for utilitarian vessels and that presently used at Picuris and Taos Pueblos, does not need to have temper added since the mica present in the clay, as a major impurity, performs all of the functions of a grog.

Recently, microscopic techniques have been so refined as to provide a valuable tool to the archeologist when studying the life habits of prehistoric and early historic pueblos. Using these techniques, a specific temper can be identified and thus traced to its source. With this information it is now possible to tell if a piece of pottery was a local product or if it was brought to the site as trade material from distant peoples.

Sifting

In the development of prehistoric native American arts, basketry preceded pottery, consequently potters have always had some kind of woven sifters at their

Fig. 3-3 Clarence and Donald Fulton photographers, 1951 or 1952. Clay and pottery drying outside the old Tafoya house.

disposal for removing large particles of foreign marterial from their clay or temper. As the women of countless generations of Tewa potters before her, Margaret breaks the dry lumps of clay and treats them in a basket by a method paralleling that of winnowing grain. By throwing the dry lumps of material up in the air, the wind removed contaminants such as sticks and roots, while the clay returns to the basket. small pieces of impurities which are not removed by air classification must then be separated by hand. In earlier times, old maños and metates that were no longer adequate for corn grinding were used to crumble the winnowed clay lumps for further sifting. Some sieves used at Santa Clara during the early twentieth century were made of woven horse hair supported on circular oak frames (Hill 1982: 85).

Presently, one sees a change in the process by which the impurities are removed. although Margaret has not adopted the change, her children prefer to clean their clay wet. The raw clay cannot be dispersed in water unless it is thoroughly dried first, and all potters agree that the initial drying step is necessary. This is accomplished by breaking the clay into small pieces, spreading them on a table to dry thoroughly, which usually takes about three continuous days of dry weather (figure 3-3).

After the clay is well dispersed in water, most potters remove impurities by a series of treatments. some of the debris is floated off, some is removed by a screening process, and the soluble impurities are removed by allowing the clay to settle and decanting the water in which the contaminating salts are dissolved. One observer mentioned the use of warm water for this purpose.[2]

Unfortunately, the clays used presently by some of the Acoma and Zuni potters contain a high amount of water-soluble salts. Unless these are removed by thorough washing, the salts are carried over into the finished ware in the form of dehydrated compounds. With time, under higher humidity conditions, these salts will rehydrate and swell, thus generating very high pressures on the masses surrounding them. The pressure will eventually increase until small pieces of the surface break off, a condition which is termed "spalling". Santa Clara potters are fortunate in that the clays which they use seem to be relatively salt-free.

Mixing

Mixing clay is a strenuous and dirty job. In her younger days, Margaret performed this task by laboriously kneading each batch by hand for up to two hours. Now she is helped by the younger men in her family.

91

Briefly, the standard procedure is to add dry temper to a plastic mass of clay and thoroughly blend the mixture with either hands or bare feet. (The Tafoya family remembers Geronimo tieing back his two hair braids, removing his shoes and stockings, and attacking the sticky clay mass with his feet). Should the addition of temper make the mass too dry or not plastic enough to work, small amounts of water or clay are added to restore the desired pliability to the batch. Because Margaret works with dry clay, the clay and temper are mixed first in about equal portions and then the water is added with small adjustments being made as required.

There is no way a potter can give specific information on the proportations of a proper clay mix. It is tested by feel and is deemed to be correct when a slight crack appears when a coil is bent. If it feels too sticky, more temper is added. If it crumbles, the mixture probably has too large a proportion of temper and requires additions of clay and water. The consistancy of the mix also depends on the size of the piece being made, the drier masses being used for larger pots. The potter continues to add to and work the raw materials until the mixture feels "right".

Noticeable defects or broken ware will result if the mixing is not thorough. Non-uniform distribution of the components will produce drying, polishing and firing defects which will either ruin or severely mar the final work. Hours must be spent on this seemingly insignificant step in the process.

Forming

It is an accepted fact that no one person can claim complete responsibility for the production of a piece of pottery from the digging of the clay through the firing process, but in forming a vessel it is a "hands off" one person procedure. In the past when pieces were signed at Santa Clara, there was generally only one signature which was that of the one who formed the vessel. The work of others, even that of a decorator, was not acknowledged. Traditionally, decorators such as Alcario preferred to remain anonymous, in spite of the fact that they were accomplished artists who were proud of their work. This is as it should be since the skill, the creativity, and the artistry of the potter are the prime contributors to the beauty of the final work. Recently, there is a trend toward multiple signatures which may include not only that of the person who formed the piece, but can also include the decorator and/or polisher as well.

The traditionally large family contributed to a pueblo child's early pottery training. Children help with all pottery chores in the home, so naturally acquire a feel for the clay. Margaret quotes her mother on how Sara Fina learned to make pottery: "I learned it myself just be watching my grandma. I was left when I was quite young, twelve years old when my mother died." The story of most potters is similar; they gained the knowledge from observation of their environment. This is their way of life. A child's first ceramic endeavors usually take the form of toys, crude animals, or small bowls (figure 3-4) and impatient to get into the business, they have been known to have sold items to tourists in an unfired form. Imagine the feeling of the buyers when these souvenirs gradually disintegrate into a pile of dust!

The habit of geophagy (eating raw clay mixtures) is acquired by some potters at the pueblo during childhood, and this often carries on to later life. Many adult potters admit to the habit and state that the taste is "real good." It has been likened by some to the taste of unsweetened chocolate (Hill 1982: 84).

Having an inquisitive mind, Margaret learned pottery making from Sara Fina not only by observation, but also by a form of instruction through answers to her questions. When asked, Margaret also provides the same teaching methods to her descendants. Without exception, her children and grandchildren are all appreciative for what she has taught them.

Necessary to a Tewa potter is a working surface and several forms of primitive tools. Before railroads and other modern means of freight haulage brought kitchen tables to the pueblos, a board or slab resting on the lap of the potter was her working area. The Tafoya family has vivid memories of Sara Fina, her back supported by a mattress leaning against a wall, feet extended straight out, sitting with a board on her lap forming pottery (figure 3-5). In 1931 Blanche Fulton, Margaret's friend, wrote, "The women usually sit on the floor to make pottery. Margaret at Santa Clara always works with her pottery on a chair and she sits on a chair to polish pottery." In other words she sits on a chair to both form and polish pottery (figure 3-6, 3-10 and 3-11).

Many times, a potter has no idea at the start what the final appearance of a vessel will be. The Tafoyas claim that the clay has a mind of its own, and they say this is often particularly noticeable when trying to make a specified shape for a special order. We are told that the clay will not always be molded to the potter's wish, and the final shape of the piece under construction may result in something quite different from that visualized.

In forming the clay, the potter must remove any of the debris which had been missed in previous cleaning processes. Air bubbles, which will destroy the pot during firing, should also be eliminated. The more the clay is worked to remove these unwanted inclusions, the better chance the ware has of surviving the firing process. Some Tafoya potters prefer to work their clay drier than others since it is claimed that the wetter the clay, the

Fig. 3-5 Museum of the American Indian, Heye Foundation, New York, N.Y. Neg. No. 31755, Fred Harvey collection, ca. 1910. Unidentified woman at

Santa Clara forming pottery on a stone slab. Modern potters have trouble believing that so many wedding jars could be under construction at the same time.

harder it is to locate entrapped air.

In hand-coiling a vessel, particularly a large one, a "puki" is usually used to assist in forming a base and supporting the lower sections of a piece. The word "puki" in Tewa is said to mean simply "form." Just where the word originated is not well defined and it is interesting to note that Harrington, (1909 and 1916) in his excellent Tewa language translations, does not even mention the word.

Baskets were probably the first form of puki, as they predated American Indian pottery; examples of mud-lined baskets have been found on this continent which date back to the first century A.D. Some examples of early prehistoric pottery show the imprint of baskets on their bases. It is suggested that this imprinting may have been imitated in clay and led to the development of corrugated decoration which continued in many varieties through the

centuries.

As pottery pieces became available, they replaced baskets for use as pukis. Pukis of this type which date to the fourteenth century, have been found on the homesites of Margaret's ancestors (figure 3-7).

Early prehistoric ware produced in the southwest had bases that were either flat or convex, indicating the shape of the pukis in use at that time. Early in the 15th century, the first jars made on a concave puki appeared. This was identified as the pottery of the Tewa people then living in the lower Chama Valley and on the Pajarito Plateau in New Mexico. This first type of concave based pottery, known as Potsuwi'i Incised and Potsuwi'i Grey, was followed by the concave-based Tsankawi Black-on-tan which was produced in the Rio Grande Valley as well as on the Pajarito Platea (Harlow 1973: 37, and figure 3-1 and Appendix 1).

Fig. 3-6 Clarence and Donald Fulton photographers, 1951 or 1952. Margaret Tafoya demonstrates hand coiling pottery. Note the bucket of mixed clay and her large puki at her feet.

Fig. 3-7 Museum of New Mexico, Anthropology Laboratory, Santa Fe, N.M. #21745/11. Mary Fredenburgh, photographer. Black-on-gray Pueblo IV period puki. 7⅛" diameter, 1⅞" height. Excavated at Puyé Ruin by Edgar L. Hewett, it has a concave bottom and contains a clay base as though the potter had started a vessel and then abandoned the work.

Margaret is the proud possessor of what is probably the finest collection of older style pukis now in existence, and claims she could not produce the large vessels which have made her so famous without them. Especially treasured are two pukis given her by her mother and her aunt Santana, the first used for making large storage jars and the second for large water jars (figure 3-8). Each has a comparatively narrow base with ascending walls which are steeper on the water jar puki.

These concave-based types, as well as the later Ka'po Grey and Ka'po Black types, have all been found at Puyé Ruins, the previous home of the Santa Clara people on the Pajarito Plateau. The last type, Ka'po Black, is considered the forerunner of the present Santa Clara Black ware. Thus, it is seen that the use of the puki at Santa Clara has roots that extend several centuries into the past, with the concave type arriving on the scene during late prehistoric times.

In addition to baskets, bases of old pottery, and deliberately manufactured ceramic pukis, it has been recorded that pieces of dried gourd have been used as forms for pottery bases.[2] Finally, it is the modern practice of most Tewa potters to use either wooden boards or factory-glazed bowls, plates, or other dinnerware pieces which can be readily purchased from merchants in nearby towns. Finely pulverized sand or temper is sometimes spread over the glazed surface to prevent the pliable coils from adhering to the form.

The purpose of a concave base on a jar is generally thought to be to facilitate carrying it on the head, a logical conclusion especially for a water jar. The fact that many of the very large storage jars also show a concave base form leads one to specuate that the use of the concave puki may result in the vessel having increased strength and stability.

The older pukis now in use at the pueblo to form larger pieces, are hard-fired, hand-made shapes. some have holes drilled around the periphery, perhaps to allow for the escape of water vapor and hasten drying. It is interesting to note that these usually older pukis require no treatment to keep them from adhering to the new clay. A newly formed properly dried vessel can always be cleanly removed from them, probably due to their some what porous nature.

Fig. 3-8 Private collection, Mary Fredenburgh photographer. Margaret's pukis. **Top:** *for water jars—14¾" diameter at widest, 6" diameter convex base which rises to a height of 1½" in the center, 5" height and ½" average wall thickness.* **Bottom:** *for storage jars—20¾" diameter at widest, 15⅛" diameter convex vase which rises 1½" at the center, 7" height, and ⅝" average wall thickness.*

The storage jar puki is of particular interest. Due to age and hard use, it has cracked and been mended in Indian fashion by drilling holes on either side of the crack and then lashing together for stabilization. Margaret remembers her father Geronimo mending it with leather strips for her mother. The leather deteriorated over a period of time, and Alcario replaced it with wire at a later date. Because of the breaks and the mending, this puki has been flat on one side for as long as Margaret can remember.

Vessels can be identified by the characteristics of the puki which have been imparted to it during formation. Taking into consideration shrinkage from drying, materials removed by the sanding and smoothing processes, and firing shrinkage, these characteristics still influence the outside form and may be transmitted through the plastic form to the interior of the pot where they may leave their distinctive signatures. Maria Martinez of San Ildefonso claimed that she could identify her old unsigned polychrome water jars by the shape imparted to their bases by her puki. She said the base had a certain feel when placed on her head.[3]

Margaret identified a very large storage jar in the Laboratory of Anthropology, Museum of New Mexico in Santa Fe as her mother's work in spite of the fact that it bore Maria's signature[4]. This happened during her first visit to the Laboratory, and the jar obviously had been decorated with beautiful Black-on-black San Ildefonso designs. Without close inspection or touching it, she described how far down the inside of the lip would be smooth and the characteristics of the interior base. She accurately predicted how high the center of the base would rise above its support, and also portrayed a flat area near the bottom which was caused by the previously mentioned mend in her puki. Thus, she offered convincing evidence that members of the Tafoya family, as claimed, had sold greenware (undecorated and unfaired) pottery to Julian Martinez, and that these were finished as the beautiful pieces often photographed with Maria (Spivey 1979: 1, 46 and Peterson 1977: 258).[5]

Once the puki has been placed on the working surface, the potter begins the task of forming. The first step is to select a lump of plastic clay whose volume depends on the size of the vessel to be formed and pound it by hand into a pancake shape of the correct thickness. This is placed on the center of the puki or board. When a puki is being used, the clay is forced down until it conforms to the shape of the mold.

When the base of the piece is in place, the sides are formed by adding coils of clay, one at a time, beginning around the bottom (figure 3-9). By experience, the potter knows how much of the remaining clay to select to form each coil. These lumps are either rolled between the palms of the hands or on a flat board until coils are the proper length and diameter. The first coil is mounted on the formed base and is pinched until it forms a secure bond. Further pinching around the circumference builds up the vessel wall by reducing the diameter of the coil. Each coil in succession is treated in the same manner until the wall of the vessel is of the desired shape and height. "The potter has in her mind the shape, the design, and

Fig. 3-9 Clarence and Donald Fulton photographers, 1951 or 1952. Margaret Tafoya demonstrates the adding of the first coil to the pancake of clay in place in her storage jar puki.

Fig. 3-10 Courtesy of and photo by Rick Dillingham, 1983. Margaret Tafoya smoothing the vessel wall with a wet piece of gourd as she works the damp clay, making sure all air and impurities are removed.

the way the finished product must look before she starts".[2]

Bottom coils are smoothed and allowed to harden only to the point where they will support each new coil being placed on top. Much know-how is required to insure that the clay dries at just the right rate. If for some reason the work must be abandoned temporarily, the vessel must be covered with damp cloths or plastic to prevent evaporation.

During the final shaping and forming of the wet coils, the skill and dexterity of the master potter becomes apparent. One hand must support the vessel from the inside, another hand holds the forming tool against the outer surface at precisely the right pressure, while the piece must be turned simultaneously to insure symmetry. In reality, a puki is converted to a very primitive form of the potter's wheel, but requires much more skill for manipulation than does the wheel.

As the work progresses, many different aids or

tools are used in the completion of the forming. Today, these may include pieces of gourd, cocoanut shells, tongue depressors, wooden spoons, spatulas, and other sundry items which the potter wishes to utilize.

Some use tools called "kajapes", which originated in Europe and probably came to the pueblos via Meso-America. In its simplest form, a kajape consists of a piece of wire bent into a triangular shape having its apex fastened to a slender wood handle. The purpose of this tool is to remove thin slices of clay from the damp work to assist in shaping. Margaret has never used this tool.

Because she is traditional, Margaret's tools consist only of pieces of gourds having a wide variety of shapes (figure 3-10). In order to finish the surface properly, the tools including the gourd pieces are kept wet. Under these conditions, they soften to the extent that it becomes impossible to handle them and therefore frequent replacement is necessary.

It was during the plastic stage of forming one particular pot that an event occurred which had an outstanding influence on Margaret's development as a potter and gave her encouragement to perfect the techniques of large pottery artistry. This event left such a deep impression on her that she remembers not only the exact date, October 4, 1926, but almost the exact time of day of its occurence. Mother Sara Fina let few things interfere with her pottery making, but one of these was her duty as a midwife. On that day, she was called about ten o'clock in the morning to go to the home of a cousin who had gone into labor, and she was forced to leave a vessel before she had finished forming it. Labor proved longer than anticipated, and as the day wore on, Margaret became concerned about the fate of the unfinished pot. Because this was before plastic was available, the pot had been covered with damp cloths which had to be kept moist, but were beginning to dry.

Time passed and finally, in the middle of the afternoon, Margaret asked her father Geronimo if she could add the additional coils (about four) and finish the vessel before the clay became too dry to be worked properly. Being a little hesitant about interfering in any way with the pottery work of his wife, Geronimo gave Margaret a strange sort of permission to proceed. He told her to go ahead, but not to tell her mother that he had agreed in any way.

With the baby safely delivered, Sara Fina returned home about 9:00 P.M. Margaret continues the story: "She [Sara Fina] said, 'Oh, who finish it?' 'My dad finish it for you,' I said. And then my dad said, 'I didn't want her to finish it. Don't blame me.' I was kind of afraid. I don't know what I am going to get from her. But she turned it [the pot] around and said, 'You did exactly what I would do. That's like my work.' So my mom come and kiss me and she said, 'Thank the Lord that you can do it.' Before that time, I had been making different shapes, even storage jars, but not that big." Thus, Margaret had begun a career of producing large, beautiful jars which no other contemporary Indian ceramic artist has been able to approach (figure 3-11).

This is a classic example of a master potter with a very observant student daughter. Between that time and the time that Margaret started to sign her pieces, it is almost impossible to identify whether the mother, daughter, or both were the artists responsible for the work. Until Sara Fina's death in 1949, mother and daughter often collaborated.

Margaret stated that it is an old belief that a pot in the process of completion should be covered until it is ready to be fired. This is said to be necessary because any bad character traits of those looking at the pot will infect the work and eventually cause its destruction. "Sometimes you can't believe, but it does come true—Mother Clay knows."

Some potters toil long and hard over their work,—others work at a quick pace. Margaret is among the latter. In her younger years she was especially fast, working deftly with Mother Clay, at times able to shape many pieces a day from the already prepared clay.

Following the final shaping of the ware, the piece is allowed to dry to the point where it can be sanded or smoothed. María Martinez took credit as the first to use sandpaper to smooth pottery, although no date is specified. As told to Richard Spivey, "And I was the one that start the sandpaper. And before that time we just scraped it and rubbed it...I start the sandpaper. I learned it from the museum. I watch them. They make those chairs and tables, and then they smooth them with sandpaper. There is where I got that sandpaper business." (Spivey 1979: 25). Jeançon (1931) mentions that the potters of Santa Clara were using sandpaper prior to 1931, which may have been after the time of María's start.

Smoothing by past generations, was accomplished by the use of corn cobs or shaped pieces of pumice. After an ear of corn was dekernelled, the cob was brushed with a flat surfaced stone to smooth it. After smoothing, the cob was dampened with water and rubbed over the surface of the vessel. Some of Margaret's early work was treated in this manner before she too began to use sandpaper. Sara Fina never did adopt the use of sandpaper when it came into vogue at the pueblos, though some family members sanded her pottery for her in her later years.

The practice of smoothing with porous lava rock (sometimes mistakenly referred to as sandstone) probably preceded corn cobs. The Tewa people who fled to the First Mesa of Hopi from the Santa Clara area taught their pottery-making descendants how to use the porous rocks to smooth, and this tool is still in use by some Tewa-Hopis.[6]

Shapes

It is generally accepted that the first fired ceramics, in the form of utilitarian ware, appeared in the southwest United States in the areas inhabited by the Hohokam or Mogollon people, between 300-200 B.C. Margaret's ancestors, the Anasazi, did not form pottery until after 400 A.D., some six hundred years later (Tanner 1968:85). Both were preceded for well over one thousand years by the pottery making of the Olmecas, an Indian tribe which had settled on the Gulf Coast of Mexico (Chan 1965: 20-25). Why did pottery making make its appearance so late among the peoples of our Southwest? The answer lies in the time of development,—of agriculture which, because of climatic and soil conditions, took place much earlier on the east coast of Mexico.

In prehistoric times, the native peoples of the American continents banded together in small

Fig. 3-11 Courtesy of and photo by M.E. Archuleta, ca. 1960. This snapshot illustrates the enormity of Margaret Tafoya's pottery and how prolific and varied has been her production.

units, probably limited to immediate family groups. These units had no need for heavy, fragile containers until they organized into larger, more sedentary agricultural groups. Pottery containers were then needed for the storage, preparation and serving of food.

Bowls and jars were the earliest utilitarian forms since they lent themselves to agricultural needs (Dittert and Plog 1908: 73 and Woodbury and Zubrow 1979: 43-45). As cultures developed their living habits and religion, pottery shapes became more complicated, and the formation of more sophisticated non-utilitarian ceramic shapes gradually became common practice.

In the history of Santa Clara pottery, the shapes of vessels emerge as important identifying characteristics. Although the potters of the pueblo have and do produce some painted ware, Tewa plainware has been the people's prime inheritance. Their jars and bowls have followed the shapes that were developed by the Rio Grande Tewas in the Tewa Polychrome type (1650-1730) (figures 3-1 and Appendix 1). Most of the credit for the preservation of this tradition is given to Santa Clara potters, although San Juan Pueblo also contributed to the continuance of Tewa Polychrome shapes, particularly in bowl forms (Harlow 1973: 31).

Other Tewa pueblos either let the pottery art die altogether or became distracted with painted designs, allowing shape to be sacrificed. Such was the case at San Ildefonso. By 1750 A.D., pottery production was almost extinct there and, when reinstated, it was in the form referred to as Pojoge Polychrome (1760-1850). The jars were globular with little grace of line and the focus was on the painting of these vessels. After the demise of Pojoge Polychrome, a pottery revival occurred at San Ildefonso toward the end of the 19th century in a type named Tunyo Polychrome. In this type, the jar forms resemble the classic Tewa Polychrome shapes. Were it not for Santa Clara potters steadfastly producing shapes of the type known as Tewa Polychrome all through this time period, the classic shapes would not have been available to the San Ildefonso potters (Harlow 1973: 31, 40, 41). The revival of plain black and red wares of later date produced at San Ildefonso also owes its inheritance to Santa Clara traditional potters.

In restoring pueblo pottery, both prehistoric and historic, from shards, archeologists have been greatly aided by the painted designs in piecing vessels together. Plain shards do not necessarily give any indication as to their location on the master form, and so restoring plainware is rather like putting together a one-color, three dimensional jigsaw puzzle. The knowledge of plainware shapes therefore is derived mostly from a few complete or almost complete vessels which have survived. Because of this difficulty of restoration, there has been little work done on plainware. (Figure 3-1 and Appendix 1 are condensations of the available information.)

Bowls and jars developed more or less simultaneously at different pueblo sites. There was trading between villages of both ideas and the vessels themselves.

Bowls. A bowl is a "a vessel with the smallest diameter (point of constriction) more than the overall height, and more than half the maximum diameter (point of greatest expansion)." (Dutton 1966: 8).

One of the most graceful bowl forms is termed "Tewa" which originated as Tewa Polychrome, continued as the Ka'po and Santa Clara Black types at Santa Clara, and as Posuge Red at San Juan Pueblo (Harlow 1973: 81). Modifications of this form are still produced occasionally by contemporary potters and it is hoped this beautiful shape will be perpetuated.

Bowls have served many purposes, from mixing large batches of bread dough to containers for washing clothes. They have even been used to pop corn when first filled with heated sand (Hill 1982: 89). Margaret has produced bowls of infinite sizes and shapes including utilitarian, decorative and ceremonial pieces, both shallow and deep with either incurving or outcurving sides, and plain and fluted rims (figures 3-12 through 3-20 and 2-14).

In April 1981, at the home of one of her daughters, Margaret had an unexpected and pleasant reunion with two older bowls, both in the tradition of the period 1760-1950 A.D. A black one was Sara Fina's and the other was a red piece of her own making—almost a duplicate of that shown in figure 3-13. Both were well polished, slipped on the outside with gently fluted, outflaring rims. Margaret explained that the fluting not only made the utensils more attractive for festive occassions, but also served the practical purpose of making the ware easier to handle.

Bowls with irregular walls carved in the shape of "kiva steps" are sometimes referred to as *ceremonial bowls.* Four holes, one located in each apex of a set of converging stairs, are used to hold four different colored feathers, each denoting a different cardinal direction (figure 3-17).[7] There seems to be some disgreement in the literature as to which color represents which direction.

Although not built to any particular shape or size, the "*naming bowl*" deserves mention as a Santa Clara or Tewa type which is made in the traditional manner (figure 3-18). It is used to hold water during the naming ceremony for a child in a manner similar to the utensil used during a Christian baptism. Customarily, a grandmother gives a child a Tewa name, traditionally on the fouth day after birth. (Ortiz 1969: 30-35) With today's complications of inter-marriages outside of the pueblo and Santa Clarans sometimes living great distances away, a naming ceremony occurs when the child first comes to the pueblo which could be some years after birth. If an outsider marries a Santa Claran, he or she may also be given a Tewa name, and a naming bowl given to him or her as a permanent possession. As of April 1984, Margaret had roughly 42 grandchildren and great grandchildren. Since the senior woman in the immediate family is the one most called on to perform this ceremony, Margaret has made many naming bowls.

A "*melon bowl*" and a "*gourd pot*" are sometimes confused, but these represent two distinct types. The former is so named for the vegetable it represents, and the gourd pot for the tool used in its construction, although it also was gourd-shaped in its original form (Tanner 1976: 109). The exterior of the melon bowl is grooved around its entire circumference, from top to bottom, sometimes vertically, sometimes at an angle, or sometimes swirled (figures 2-44, 4-14, 4-18). The most difficult and rare type of melon bowl to form shows grooves inside as well as outside, indicating that the design was impressed rather than carved. Such a bowl can only be formed when the clay is rather plastic, but not too wet.

On the origin of the gourd pot, Margaret says, "Mother Clay said, 'Put my design on a pot. Gourds come from earth too'." Figure 3-12 shows the concave impressions which are formed by pressing a gourd into the pliable clay in desired depth running horizontally around the upper body of the vessel, while the inside wall is supported with the other hand. This requires much skill, as the range of plasticity of the clay when this operation can be successfully performed is limited. If the clay is too

soft, the shape will sag, if too hard or dry, it will crack.

These and other impressed shapes including various forms representing different fruits, have been found in prehistoric burials of Meso-American cultures which predate any of our southwest ceramics.[8]

A two-lipped bowl has one lip opposite the other with a ceramic strap handle at right angles to the lips (figure 3-19). Margaret notes that this type was originally used for serving or pouring food in either direction. Later, smaller versions of this type were made for tourist consumption. These are often referred to as "baskets" because of the location of the handle.

Also found in Margaret's vast repertoire of bowls are those decorated with carved designs, bowls decorated with Black-on-Black or Red-on-Red designs, and bowls with different types of graceful handles (figures 3-15 and 3-20).

Plates. A dish is "a vessel with depth less than 1/5 of the maximum diameter." (Dutton 1966: 11).

Apparently, flat plates were not made in the Southwest until historic times after the arrival of the Spaniards. Prehistoric Anasazi and Tewa had no use for such a utensil and their cultures had no contact with this item. Plates, especially the carved ones made today, are difficult shapes to form and fire, and many well known potters lack the necessary skill to produce them. Margaret has been producing plates since the latter part of the 1920's in a great variety of decorated types (figures 3-21 through 3-27).

Jars. A jar is "a vessel with a restricted orifice and the smallest diameter less than the overall height and less than the maximum diameter." (Dutton 1966: 9). (figure 3-28 and 3-29)

One pottery shape often associated with Santa Clara and particularly the Tafoyas, is the water jar or olla (figures 2-8, 2-13, 2-24, 3-30, and 3-31). With its usually concave base, wide, squat body, rainbow band shoulder (discussed in the design section), and often fluted rim topping a gently curved long neck, it is almost a Santa Clara trademark. By referring to figure 3-1, one can see its Tewa inheritance. Thanks to Margaret Tafoya and a few Santa Clara potters, its unique form has been preserved. Santa Clarans lay claim to this shape as exclusively theirs, and certainly they are to be credited for the preservation of this graceful and beautiful container.

Pueblo pottery is not waterproof. Modern and contemporary water jars are formed of relatively porous clay, fired at quite low temperatures, and are considered pieces of art. Older historic utilitarian water containers were only sightly porous and more vitreous, having been made of higher quality clay and fired for longer periods of time. A little porosity was a distinct advantage in these vessels

Fig. 3-34 Enchanted Mesa, Indian Arts, Albuquerque, N.M. collection. Black carved and polished wedding vase, signed Margaret Tafoya, ca. 1960. 19¼" height, 13⅜" diameter. Too big to be used for a ceremony, this was made for collector consumption.

because the water they contained was kept cool by slow leakage and evaporation. While the Apaches and Navajos have used pine gum and the Papagos grease for waterproofing, there is little evidence that this was done extensively at Santa Clara. There is mention made, however, of rubbing grease on micaceous ware immediately after firing, but it is stated that this practice existed before 1880 (Hill 1982: 86).

Margaret and Sara Fina have been responsible for the production of many outstanding *"wedding vases"*, formerly called *"love jars"*.[9] Margaret's jars vary in height from eight inches to over two feet (figures 3-32 through 3-34). She has made these distinct vessels for many close members of the family on the occasion of their marriages. The wedding jar has an easily recognized shaped bowl

with two spouts connected by a strap handle. The necks have two opposed open spouts. The wider of the two spouts is reserved for drinking by the groom, we are told. Generally, Margaret's wedding jars can be distinguished from her mother's because the necks are more vertical, while Sara Fina's are more flaring (compare figures 3-35 and 3-36).

Two-necked vessels have appeared in various forms in many parts of the world throughout history. The Olmeca culture which existed on the eastern Gulf Coast in the pre-classic period of Mexican ceramics (1500-800 B.C) made a two-necked vessel without a connecting strap or stirrup. Later, the Tlatilco people who existed until about 600 A.D. near present day Mexico City, produced the first verified two-necked piece with a strap handle on this continent. Interestingly, the Mexican examples were always oxidized fired, so were red in color. Although how these were used by the prehistoric Indians of Mexico has not been determined; it is thought that they had ceremonial significance because they have been found in burial sites.[10]

Many forms of double-necked vessels were made by the Anasazi ancestors of the Santa Clara people (Lister and Lister 1969: 14, Breternitz and Rohn 1974: 3, and Dockstader 1972: 42). The present day version of the wedding jar or vase at Santa Clara appears to have arrived at the pueblo during the latter half of the 19th century. Wedding jars have been produced by other non-Tewa tribes in the United States, and though Santa Clarans may be the only Indians using them ceremonially today, references are found that claim previous matrimonial use of them. The Catawba Indians of South Carolina occasionally made them and used them in marriage ceremonies (Pennypacker 1937: 147).

One of the most important Tewa pottery forms is the sometimes lidded *"storage jar"*, the "largest vessel ever made by pueblo Indians." (Frank and Harlow 1974: 30). Its history follows almost the same progression as the water jar. Margaret states that storage jars with flat, wide bases and vertical walls indicate that the potter was a novice because damp clay is more easily supported in a vertical position than at an angle. A vertically sided piece which she identified as hers, she claimed was one of her first (figure 2-48). Her later, better shaped storage jars always show that she used her concave puki which, as previously discussed, perhaps gave more stability not only to the damp clay, but also to the finished ware. The sides of her storage jars ascend from the base at an astonishing outward angle to broad shoulders where there is an abrupt, but smooth, insloping to a comparatively small unflared neck opening. Beautiful in their simplicity, with possibly impressed "bear paws" as their only decoration, Margaret has won much recognition for these masterpieces. She has made them in both black and red, and considers them to be her outstanding accompishments (figures 3-37 and 3-38).

While researching this book, approximately forty of Margaret's large storage jars were located. These were in both museums and private collections, with the museum' having a slight majority. It is estimated that at least that many more, privately owned have been overlooked. The amount of work that must have been expended to produce this estimated number of pieces is staggering to comprehend, and yet Margaret minimizes her efforts.

Alcario remembers Margaret taking an order for two of these large jars from "a man from the East, either St. Louis or Texas." This was sometime before 1942 because the prospective buyer had a son enrolled in the Los Alamos Boys' School so had occasion to visit the area and learned of Margaret's skills as a potter. Before the order was completed, she had made twelve tries which failed before two acceptable pots were finished. Some of these had cracked during drying, while others broke in the fire. When asked about this order and the time and work that it took to complete, Margaret simply shrugged and commented that it didn't seem like such a chore at the time.

This provides an excellent example of the Tafoya philosophy and of the love of her work. Alcario also remembers packing these large jars (long before plastic) into soft but dry field straw, not only to ensure safe transporation, but also to guard against scratching the highly polished surfaces.

1750 through 1800 (Harlow 1973: 31), marks the end of an era when the beautifully sculptured jars were made at the Tewa villages with the exception of Santa Clara. A few exceptions may be found at the other pueblos, but the Santa Clara potters, especially the Tafoya family, must be given credit for the perpetuation of these large jars. At present, there are very few potters at Santa Clara who possess the skill or the time to produce these outstanding pieces, so the output is limited compared to that of Margaret's earlier production and that of Sara Fina's (figures 3-39 and 4-2).

Margaret's storage jar forms have been limited to the older classic forms. In addition to small imaginative replicas of the large forms, she has made smaller, lidded utilitarian jars sometimes to hold cookies (figure 3-40). A few of her large pieces have been converted into art forms by adding carved decorations, handles, or a combination of both (figure 3-41). Many of the intermediate-sized jars with and without carved decorations have been converted into lamps (fig. 2-44). Judging from the specimens studied, one is led to speculate that Margaret has made more jars with carved decorations than any other shape.

Fig. 3-41 Enchanted Mesa, Indian Arts, Albuquerque, N.M. collection. Black carved and polished handled vase signed Margaret Tafoya, ca. 1950. 20½" height, 14¼" diameter. Not only is this a large vessel, but is probably one of the most ornate carved pieces made by the senior Tafoyas.

Vases

These are vessels whose heights clearly exceed their widths and may be cylindrical or of varying diameters (Dutton 1966: 11). Latecomers to southwest pottery forms, vases were probably adaptations and outgrowths of jars. In fact, a vase could be a jar with an elongated neck.

Margaret has produced beautifully formed vases for over sixty years. Many of her earlier works came complete with interestingly formed handles similar to those produced by her sister Tomacita (figure 3-42 and figure 2-25) and with handles which terminate in hands or claws similar to those of her mother (figures 3-15 and 2-22). Vases with these handle types date back to the early part of the 20th century, Margaret's to the early 1920's, and it is doubtful that many were made after 1935.

Overlapping and following the handled vessels, Margaret produced many slender and graceful vases, often decorated with carved designs (figure 3-43). These were usually larger than those being made by her contemporaries (figure 3-44 and 3-45).

Miscellaneous Shapes

An interesting utility piece made formerly at Santa Clara was a type of griddle used to make a kind of tortillas or piki bread. Using a dark stone, which was probably volcanic in origin and which had been scraped flat, a layer of pottery clay was smoothed on, dried, slipped, stone-polished, and the combination fired until the polished clay became fairly vitreous. This low porosity was the result of firing with manure for an extended period of time—up to 24 hours (Hill 1982: 93).

Blanche Fulton, while visiting Santa Clara, witnessed the making of one of these griddles: "They put the clay on the hot rock to fill [it] in, to make it smooth, [then] polished it with a polishing stone. Next day they repeated the procedure, and after polishing they rubbed in fat to make the polish smooth. After a week or five days they take the fat off. They then wipe it off with corn husks, and it is now ready to make paper bread for wedding and feast ceremonies."[2] It is doubtful that any of these cooking utensils remain in existence at Santa Clara, but many Hopi people still use flat stones for making piki bread.

For centuries, Margaret's ancestors have made open, rectangular ceramic pieces for use as receptacles for their holy cornmeal (figure 3-46). This form was duplicated through time, with later potters adding lids, some topped with a figure or animal (figure 2-28). These lidded ceremonial box replicas were sold to tourists and collectors who used them as candy or cigarette containers. Margaret has made such boxes since the early 1930's, usually with handled lids.

A figurine is defined as "a small molded, or carved figure" which probably had its origin in the effigy vessel—"a primary vessel form modified to imitate a life form (animal, bird, human, etc)." (Dutton 1966: 9). Many effigies have been found in prehistoric Tewa ruins, and these continue as figurines today, particularly at Santa Clara. They are attactive to the tourist, reasonable in price, and are easily transported reaching a high degree of popularity beginning in the 1930's. Figurines range in size from one to approximately eight inches in length and are mostly black, although red forms are not uncommon. They may be carved or decorated with a dull or polished slip. The Gutierrez family is identified with humorous polychrome figurines.

To the potters of the Southwest, animal figurines are know as *"animalitos",* and the figures in a creche scene are termed *"nacimientos"* (Monthan and Monthan 1979: xi and xii), a carryover from the days when Spanish was the second language of the Tewa. Compared to most Indian-formed figurines, nacimientos are late arrivals in pottery, with early examples being made about 1940 (Anon. 1979: 1).

The Tafoyas often make figurines as a way of relaxing, and these are distinguished by their brilliant polish. Margaret has made many artistically formed, beautifully polished, and fairly large pieces, some of which were presented as gifts which accompanied jar forms to bring good fortune to the recipient. These are now prized collector's items (figure 3-47a).

Judging from older photographs of Margaret surrounded by her pottery of many shapes, one form—that of the candlestick—is often seen (figure 2-52). In general, they are characterized by twisted holders formed from two equally proportioned coils of clay mounted on various simple bases (figure 3-47 b). These are not often found among her later works.

Of a curious nature, whenever she saw a different shaped ceramic piece in an exhibition, shop, or photographed in a magazine which not only appealed to her, but which she felt might have commercial appeal, Margaret would try adopting it to her work. She has even produced a tea service consisting of a lidded teapot, cream pitcher, sugar bowl, and cups with saucers.[11] However, in spite of these side excursions and experimentation, she has never lost sight of her Tewa inheritance, and she concentrates on making her major productions adhere to traditional forms.

Although not always able to pinpoint the date when pieces were made, Margaret is expert at identifying the maker of a vessel by its shape, the type of decoration, and how it was polished. Not long ago, an unsigned wedding jar was shown to her for maker identification because it had been suggested to the owners that the shape was very much like that of others made by Margaret (Figure 3-32). It had been assumed to be of San Ildefonso origin because of its Black-on-black decoration. With no prompting, Margaret not only identified the work as hers, but also remembered selling it to the Original Trading Post in Santa Fe just before Bob Ward assumed ownership. In fact, the piece had been purchased from Bob Ward almost immediately after he began to operate the store. This identification ability also applies to her recognizing the older work of other Tafoyas—her mother's—her aunt's, etc. which has been a great aid in identifying the makers of older unsigned pieces.

Impressing

Impressed designs are simply dents, lines, or knobs (usually on the necks or shoulders of vessels) made in the damp clay during the forming process. They began to appear at Santa Clara on

Fig. 3-4 Private collection. Small polychrome bowl with Avanyu design by Margaret Tafoya, ca. 1914 to 1916. Unsigned, identified by Margaret. 1⅞" height, 1⅞" diameter. One of her first pieces, this was made when she was about ten or twelve years old. It was saved by Margaret's mother and passed on to her on Sara Fina's death in 1947. Red slipped top and bottom with natural polished clay around the middle. Not shown in the picture are two small black designs painted with guaco. The serpent is outlined with lead pencil.

Fig. 3-13 Private collection. Red slipped and unslipped polished bowl with scallopped rim by Margaret Tafoya, 1983, signed. 9½" diameter, 4" height. This type of bowl is used at celebrations. The only slipped section is around the inside rim because it is the only part that shows when holding food.

Fig. 3-12 Grant Wilkins collection. Black polished bowl with impressed gourd design by Margaret Tafoya, ca. 1975, signed. This is a difficult shape to form without the walls either collapsing or cracking.

Fig. 3-14 Colorado Springs Fine Arts Center and Taylor Museum, Colorado Springs, Co. #351. Black polished dough bowl with four impressed bear paws by Margaret Tafoya, ca. 1935, signed. 23" diameter, 15½" height. Formed in her large storage jar puki, this bowl could hold enormous amounts of dough—a necessity for feast days.

Fig. 3-15 Walton Youngblood collection. Black-on-black bowl outlined in orange designs with two claw handles by Margaret Tafoya, ca. 1928, signed. 10½" diameter, 6½" height. This paint was in vogue for only a short period of time, a fact not regretted by the potters because of difficulty of application.

Fig. 3-16 Private collection. Black-on-black with orange outlined designs on a bowl (or deep dish) by Margaret Tafoya, ca. 1932, signed. 11¾" diameter, 3" height. Her husband Alcario painted the matte black design while Margaret accomplished the difficult task of outlining the decoration with orange.

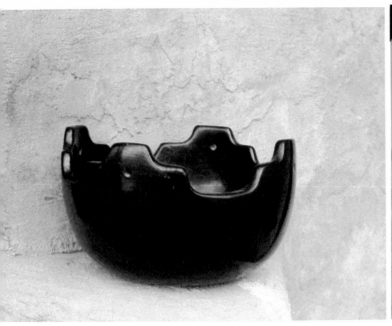

Fig. 3-17 Private collection. L. Blair photographer. Black polished fruit bowl with kiva step walls by Margaret Tafoya, ca. 1950, signed. 11½" diameter, 7" height. A kiva bowl is required to have a hole in each of its four sides to hold feathers.

Fig. 3-18 Naming bowls, C. Lewis and S. Whittington collections. **Left:** Kiva step bowl with bear paw design by Jennie Trammel for Charlie Lewis on the occasion of his being named "Goldfinch." 10" height, 8" diameter. **Right:** Made by Margaret Tafoya in 1955 for Susan Roller, "Rose by the Water," for her naming ceremony. 7½" diameter, 5" height. There are no set conditions governing the size, shape or decoration of a Santa Clara naming bowl.

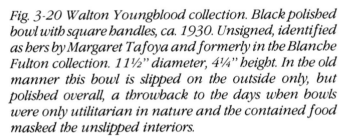

Fig. 3-20 Walton Youngblood collection. Black polished bowl with square handles, ca. 1930. Unsigned, identified as hers by Margaret Tafoya and formerly in the Blanche Fulton collection. 11½" diameter, 4¼" height. In the old manner this bowl is slipped on the outside only, but polished overall, a throwback to the days when bowls were only utilitarian in nature and the contained food masked the unslipped interiors.

Fig. 3-22 Walton Youngblood collection. Four colored polychrome plate signed Margaret Tafoya, 1930's. 12¼" diameter, 1¼" height. The Avanyu and buffalo designs indicate two life-giving elements in Tewa existance— water and meat. Compared to the volume of Margaret's other shapes and designs, very few polychrome plates were produced. The rim and back of this plate are slipped and polished.

Fig. 3-21 Lowie Museum of Anthropology, University of California, Berkeley, Ca. #2-17072. Unknown photographer. Polychrome plate signed Margaret Tafoya, ca. 1935. 12¼" diameter, 1½" height. A unique and beautiful five colored piece decorated with a detailed, black outlined, segmented Avanyu design.

Fig. 3-23 University of New Mexico, Maxwell Museum of Anthropology, Albuquerque, N.M. #82-56-1. Black carved and polished plate with twisted "friendship handles" signed Margaret Tafoya, ca. 1960. 11½" diameter, 2" height. Carved plates crack easily both in forming and firing due to expansion. Large, perfect plates are the hallmark of an accomplished potter.

Fig. 3-24 Millicent Rogers Museum, Taos, N.M. #81-56-5. Red carved and polished plate signed Margaret Tafoya, cà. 1950's. 14" diameter, 1½" height. A large handsome example of a Tafoya plate with simple graceful carving.

Fig. 3-25 **Left:** *Black-on-black plate signed Margaret Tafoya, ca. 1935. 9⅝" diameter, 1½" height. Margaret formed this plate, but the Avanyu painting was done by her husband, Alcario. Margaret jokes that his serpents have thin necks so they can't be well fed.* **Right:** *Walton Youngblood collection. Black-on-black plate signed Margaret Tafoya, ca. 1935. 12½" diameter, 2" height. This plate was both formed and the Avanyu painted by Margaret, whose serpents can be differentiated from her husband's (Alcario) by their thicker necks.*

Fig. 3-26 Private collection. Red-on-red plate with Avanyu design signed Margaret Tafoya, ca. 1940. 14" diameter, 2⅜" height. White outlines enhance many of the Tafoya pieces of this period, and some of Margaret's daughters remember the long and tedious hours they spent on this procedure. Since this photo was taken this piece has been broken beyond repair.

Fig. 3-27 Denver Museum of Natural History, Denver, Co. #11,738. Black carved and polished plate signed Margaret Tafoya, ca. 1925-1930. 11" diameter, 1¾" height. An early example of the Tafoya work has shallow carving. The horn motif was used as a symbol which would bring meat for the plate.

Fig. 3-28 Heard Museum, Phoenix, Az. #A-10-28. A black carved Avanyu encircles this classic polished vessel by Margaret Tafoya, 1973, signed. 6" height, 6" diameter. This jar is an excellent example of Margaret's carving.

Fig. 3-29 Private collection. Black polished jar with three carved bear paws, signed Margaret Tafoya, 1983. 7⅞" height, 8" diameter. Simplistically beautiful modern adaption of the storage jar design.

Fig. 3-30 Tony Reyna collection. Black polished water jar with rainbow band and four bear paws, signed Margaret Tafoya, 1973. 12" height, 12" diameter. This is one of the classic and unique Santa Clara shapes that Margaret has perpetuated and one of her most often reproduced.

Fig. 3-31 Tony Reyna collection. Red polished water jar with rainbow band and four bear paws, signed Margaret Tafoya, 1970. 16" height, 14" diameter. One of the larger examples of Margaret's water jars.

Fig. 3-32 Private collection. Black-on-black wedding jar, signed Margaret Tafoya, ca. 1960. 8" height, 6¼" diameter. Margaret and Alcario painted many similar Avanyu designs on different shapes. This is a late example for its type.

Fig. 3-33 Museum of Northern Arizona, Flagstaff, Az. #E7708. Red carved and polished wedding jar with two Avanyus, signed Margaret Tafoya, ca. 1960. 12½" height, 7⅜" diameter. The proportions on this piece are particularly pleasing. A tan slip in the recessed areas accentuate the detail of this complicated carving.

Fig. 3-35 Tony Reyna collection. Black carved and polished wedding vase, signed Margaret Tafoya, 1950's. 21½" height, 13" diameter. One characteristic by which one can distinguish a Margaret wedding vase is the necks, which often rise almost vertically or with a gentle outward slope. Compare with Figures 3-36, 4-16, and 4-25.

Fig. 3-36 Denver Art Museum, Denver, Co. #XSC57G. Black polished wedding vase with four impressed bear paws. Unsigned, identified by Margaret as Sara Fina's work from a photo. 14½" height, 12⅛" diameter. Acquired by F. H. Douglas in 1940. Typical Sara Fina flattened base shape which is squat compared to Margaret's. See Figures 3-32 through 3-34.

Fig. 3-37 Tony Reyna collection. Black polished storage jar with three impressed bear paws, signed Margaret Tafoya, ca. 1958. 21¾" height, 21¾" diameter. A classic design for a large storage jar, and typical of Margaret's storage jars.

Fig. 3-38 Denver Art Museum, Denver, Co. #XSC32P. Red polished storage jar with paw decoration, signed Margaret Tafoya, 1932. 21" height, 20" diameter. The high lip and the shape of the paw are very like Sara Fina's. As in most red storage jars, there are slight firing marks due to the difficulty in firing such a large vessel, and though the potter tries to avoid them, such marks add beauty and authenticity for some collectors.

Fig. 3-39 Private collection. Mary Fredenburgh photographer. Three generations of Tafoya storage jars. Left to right: Mela Youngblood (ca. 1975), Margaret Tafoya (1936), and Sara Fina Tafoya (1936). The Margaret and Sara Fina jars took first prizes at the Inter-Tribal Ceremonial in Gallup in 1936. All were signed, but the two on the right lost their signatures by water damage when left standing on an open porch. When asked who made which pot, Margaret replied, "That's easy. The one with the smaller bear paw (center) is mine. My mother would never let me make the bear paw as big as hers." (Quote from Webb Young, Phoenix, Az., the original owner.) These jars all measure over 21 inches.

Fig. 3-40 Mrs. J. B. Jobe collection. Black carved cookie jar with lid, signed Margaret Tafoya, 1978. 9" height, 8½" diameter. Both jar and lid are completely polished inside and out. Margaret explained that a polished interior is easier to keep clean.

Fig. 3-42 Maurine Grammer collection. Black polished handled vase by Margaret Tafoya, ca. 1930. 11⅛" height, 8⅞" diameter. Adding handles, especially the more complicated ones, to any vessel is difficult. Margaret refers to these as her "Egyptian handles." Handled vessels were sometimes converted to lamps.

Fig. 3-43 Tony Reyna collection. Red carved and polished Avanyu vase signed Margaret Tafoya, 1965. 16" height, 12½" diameter. Typical of the large carved vases that the Tafoyas made from about 1955 through 1980. This type that was often converted into lamps.

Fig. 3-44 Private collection. Black carved and polished vase signed Margaret Tafoya, 1974. 8" height, 5¾" diameter. The low shoulder gives this piece interesting proportions. The design suggests kiva steps.

Fig. 3-45 Tony Reyna collection. Black polished and carved vase signed Margaret Tafoya, 1968. 16" height, 12¼" diameter. It is amazing that this piece and Figure 3-43 are almost exactly the same size, yet were hand coiled years apart.

Fig. 3-46 Museum of New Mexico, Anthropology Laboratory, Santa Fe, N.M. #20991/11. Mary Fredenburgh photographer. Glaze D corn meal box, ca. A.D. 1500, excavated by Edgar Hewett from Puyé Ruin. 2¼" x 3" x 1½" height. Prehistoric forerunner of later Tafoya corn meal and candy containers. Compare to Figure 2-28.

Fig. 3-47a Streets of Taos, Santa Fe, N.M. Black polished frog by Margaret Tafoya, identified by Hilda Street. ca. 1955. 6" long, 3¾" height. Unusually large animalito form with flawless polish.

Fig. 3-47b Black polished twisted candlesticks by Margaret Tafoya. ca. 1950's. 6⅜" height, 3¼" diameter base. Forms such as this are found in old photos of Margaret and her work. See Figure 2-52.

Fig. 3-48 Private collection. Close-up section of a red carved and polished jar signed Margaret Tafoya. ca. 1975-1980. 5" height, 6" diameter. Tan slip painted in the recessed carved out areas help to bring out and enhance the design. The horizontal grooves pictured here are ¼" wide and ⅛" deep.

Fig. 3-49 Clark Field collection, Philbrook Art Center, Tulsa, Ok. #PO-179. Red slipped and polished bowl by María Nestora Naranjo, ca. 1865. Unsigned, identified by Christina Naranjo. 14½" diameter. 9¾" height. A very early Santa Clara red piece. Thought to have been used for ceremonial purposes.

plain, slipped polished ware during the first half of the nineteenth century. During the fifty years between 1880 and 1930, this type of design was widely produced at Santa Clara (LeFree 1975: 51), but it gradually died out. Today only a few potters, including some members of the Tafoya family, are still able to do this difficult work. The clay must be exactly the right consistency (too damp collapses, too dry cracks) to allow the design to be pushed into the clay with one hand while the interior wall is supported with the other hand. The potters ability to judge the state of the clay is crucial to success.

Specific impressed designs are discussed in the section on decoration.

Carving

The Indians of Meso-America carved stone before Christ and did relief carving on pottery in pre-Hispanic times, but in North America, outside of a few simple scratches (primitive incising), no real carving (clay removal) occurred until the 1920's.

Following a certain degree of drying of a formed piece, the potter decides if the ware is to be decorated by carving. "Leather hard" is the term generally used to describe the state of the vessel before its final drying, at which time it is ready to be carved. It must be dry enough to withstand handling, but not so hard that the clay is brittle. If the ware overdries, most carvers will moisten it enough so that it becomes easily tooled. Alcario must be given

Fig. 3-54 Clark Field collection, Philbrook Art Center, Tulsa, Ok. #PO-178. Black polished water jar with two impressed bear paw designs by Filomena Cajete Gutierrez. ca. 1865. Unsigned, identified by Christina Naranjo. 12¼" height, 12" diameter. This jar is said to have been used for ceremonial purposes.

was polished, and then reduced fired. Several of these unique pieces have been located in various museum archives (Figure 2-16 and 2-17).

Margaret relates how she and Alcario first started to carve designs into their pottery. In the middle 1920's, when they were doing painted designs on their work, she suggested that he carve between the proposed design outlines. "So he did, he carved it, then I polish it, and it looks nice." When questioned on the possibility of increased difficulty in firing carved pieces because of differences in wall thickness, Margaret said it didn't seem to make any difference.

Carving styles differ from shallow to deep, straight to slanted, and from sharp to rounded edges. Each variety is beautiful in its own way, with uniformity of depth being the important factor. Margaret's carving is straight-sided, fairly deep and very uniform, while Alcario's is deeper, more bold in design and is also uniform. The edges of Margaret's work tend to be more rounded.

Tools used by the carver vary from person to person and may range from screwdrivers to dentists' picks, each being altered to fit personal needs. Margaret and Alcario prefer wood chisels. They spurn the use of any electrically-powered tool for either carving or etching.

In order to make carved designs more uniform in appearance, the carved-out portion is usually given a coat of slip of the same or a complementary color. Occasionally, to further enhance the design, this is done with a slip whose color is different from that of the main body of the work (Figure 3-48).

credit for his skill in carving because he is one of the few who is capable of artistically carving a very dry surface. (This skill presently is a blessing because arthritis pains him when working with damp pottery.)

Several potters at Santa Clara claim to be the originators of the modern carving process. The earliest known work which appears to be the forerunner of today's carving, is that of Sara Fina. It is documented that she produced twelve jars with zoomorphic designs in 1922 or 1923.[12] These designs were apparently formed in two stages. When the clay body was still sufficiently plastic, a rough form of the design was impressed into the piece. It was then allowed to dry to the desired state when the impression could be sharpened with a gouging instrument. Examination of these pieces reveals that the initial impression was carried over to the interior of these vessels. It appears that the depressed design was slipped, the entire exterior

Fig. 3-60 Courtesy of Nathan Youngblood. 1984. Black firing smudges on red bowl caused by flying coals when oxidized firing is done in a high wind.

Slips

A slip may be defined as a low viscosity fluid which is formed by suspending particles of finely divided clay and possibly other materials, such as fine grog, in water. Usually the grog is in the from of silica sand flower rather than the volcanic ash used by the Tewa potter. A modern Indian potter may use a slip in two ways: one, as an application to an unfired piece for decorative purposes; and second, it can be poured into a hydrated gypsum or plaster of Paris mold to produce cheap, untraditional greenware bodies suitable for firing.

Decorative Slips. Decorative slips are thinly applied suspensions of iron-colored, reservation-produced clays over the green form. These are applied by either wiping or brushing after the ware is dry, smooth and dust-free.

The Anasazi people of the Four Corners area first practiced slipping pottery with the development of black-on-white wares about 725 A.D. (Dittert and Plog 1980: 77). As small bands of these people began to migrate from this area to the south and east in the thirteenth century, slipped and polished black-on-white pottery began to appear in the lower Chama drainage and upper Rio Grande Valley regions. With the establishment of villages on the Pajarito Plateau shortly before and during the fourteenth century, the Tewas began producing slipped and polished ware.

Red slipped pottery first appeared in the Colorado Plateau region about 1000 A.D. The first examples were decorated with black line designs in the manner of their white slipped predecessors; later, white lines were added to replace the black. Red grew in popularity, so that by 1200 A.D. equal amounts of red and the earlier black-on-white styles were being made. By 1300 A.D., the black-on whites had almost disappeared in favor of red slipped vessels (Harlow 1977: 11, 12). However, black-on-whites lingered on in areas such as the Santa Cruz Valley until the time of the Second Pueblo Revolt in 1694.

The Tewas of the Rio Grande region started using red slip between 1600 and 1650 A.D. Tewa Polychrome, circa 1650 to 1725, with its heavy red slip on top and bottom sections, may have been the result of Spanish influence, though it seems more likely that the use of red was an idea imported from the glaze-paint pottery made in the lower Rio Grande Valley area intermittently from 1370 to 1730 A.D. (Harlow 1973: 28). Perhaps some Acoma people who, disrupted by the Spanish, came to the area in the early 17th century, contributed their knowledge in the use of slips (Dittert and Plog 1980: 133).

The Pueblo Revolt and subsequent reconquest by the Spanish seems to have had little effect on the increased use of red slips, although it was a time of great upheaval, migration, and incorporation of other outside influences. A small portion of the Tewa people who fled from the Spanish to the land of the Hopi, returned with new ideas and techniques. However, with time conditions became more settled, work from individual villages could be distinguished, and the identification and location of pottery types became easier.

As previously discussed, at Santa Clara Pueblo plain well polished pottery without slip was produced from 1650 to 1725 A.D. in the classic Tewa Polychrome and Ogapoge shapes, and was designated Ka'po Grey. Santa Clara was the center for this fine, well made utilitarian type of pottery. It was thin-walled and hard, the color varying from tan to grey, and was the forerunner of all plain ware, either slipped or unslipped, along the Rio Grande. The potters of the San Juan and Nambe Pueblos added a slip to plain ware and fired in an oxidizing atmosphere, thus producing a type called Posuge Red (1650-1750 A.D.). LeFree (1975: 79) states that "there are no documented specimens prior to 1880, "referring to red polished ware at Santa Clara. However, a documented piece was located at the Philbrook Art Center in Tulsa, Oklahoma, dated 1865 (Figure 3-49). By 1920, an all-over red polished slip ware was popular and therefore considered traditional at most of the pueblos (Frank and Harlow 1974: 29).

Of prime importance is the development of slipped polished black pottery which claims Santa Clara as its traditional home. María Martinez in discussing Tewa black ware stated, "Those Santa Clara Indians always know how to fire black, long before we discovered how to do it...When I was a little girl, I was a baby sitter at Santa Clara Pueblo sometimes. I liked to watch them make pots over there. They make ollas for water and kitchen, which they fire black." (Peterson 1977: 93). Margaret confirmed this. "Marie used to be here. My husband's mother [Andreita Baca Tafoya, born 1887, the same year as María] was a friend of hers. They used to work together when they were young."[13]

In the chronology of Tewa slipped plain polished ware, red takes precedence over black. Later, when a slip was added to Ka'po Grey and reduced fired, Ka'po Black was the result. In finishing this type of pottery, the slip was applied from just inside the lip of a vessel to about one half to two thirds of the way down the outside (Figure 3-50). The line created by this practice (that which separated the upper two thirds of the black slipped surface from the lower one third grey unslipped portion), corresponds to that of the line between the lower slipped red portion and the decorated top two thirds of polychrome ware being produced at that time at other pueblos.

Researchers have stated that Ka'po Black was made for only a short time, 1720-1780. It was during

Fig. 3-50 Private collection. Black Santa Clara slipped and polished wedding jar, ca. 1890. Maker unknown. A very definite line can be seen where the slip has been applied from the top about two thirds of the way down on the outside of the vessel. The difference between the slipped and unslipped polished portions is very obvious. Note the interesting base. Though Sara Fina did not make this piece, she did produce some pottery with this type base.

this Ka'po Black period that some of the finest pottery ever fashioned by the American Indian was produced. It was both beautiful and utilitarian. These hard, thin-walled vessels also occurred at both Nambe and Pojoaque Pueblos, with those from Nambe being distinguished by their mica-bearing clays (Harlow 1973: 40, 41).

The main feature which distinguishes Ka'po Black from pre and post 1930 Santa Clara Black is that of wall thickness. Ka'po Black ware has an average wall thickness about 1/16 of an inch thinner than later Santa Clara pottery. Measurement of the Tafoya Santa Clara vessels made before 1930 shows them to have an average wall thickness of 0.2125 inch. Pottery produced by the same family after 1930 had an average wall thickness of 0.4018 inch. This is probably due to the change in clay deposits as well as the need to make thicker-walled pieces for carving.

In 1908, Stroup indicated that the demise of plain polished ware was at hand. He stated, "The last of the plain polished [slipped and polished] ware comes from the northeastern village of Santa Clara...it is still beautiful for itself and of intense ethnological interest. In the history of American ceramic art, the chapter which shall tell of the earthenware of the pueblo women will be one of the most interesting." (Stroup 1908: 112). Interesting—yes, but the last of beautiful plain polished ware—no.

A traditional Santa Clara potter of the 1980's feels strongly that the material used for slipping must originate on Indian land, although not necessarily Santa Clara land. Many purchase their slip from a Santo Domingan. This material, also known as red ochre, presently sells for five dollars a volume, which will fill a number three-sized fruit can.[14] Materials suitable for slips also have been located on Santa Clara land. Margaret states, "We can use two slips to bring it up, a real dark kind, dark red. Nobody knows, just in the family, but we get it here." Also, contrary to what has been previously published, some of the Tafoyas use different slips depending on whether a red or a black color is the desired end result.

This information is given further credibility by Margaret's friend, Blanche Fulton, who wrote, "This is a slick dark red clay that has been brought from Santo Domingo to be used on pottery that is intended to be black. For red, a clay is found close to Santa Clara which has sand in it of a darker red color. [For a] dull design on a polished surface, [they] use polish clay [or slip] to paint design and leave a dull finish on [the] polished surface."[2]

The slip used for black ware contains more iron oxide as an impurity, and more readily produces a black color in a reducing fire. When the black type is fired under oxidizing conditions which would normally produce red ware, a dark brownish red color is the result.

Care must be taken to ensure that slip is applied in the proper thickness. If too thin, it will result in a streaky surface, and if too thick, it will either peel off during drying or crack during firing. It is said that some slips accidentally spilled on a polished surface will destroy the finish, necessitating complete repolishing.

Slips may be applied either with a rag or a brush (Figure 3-51). Margaret's daughters generally paint the slip on with a brush, while other Tafoyas prefer rag application (Young 1975: 11). Today's brushes are purchased from commercial outlets, but in the past they were made of yucca leaves.

Fig. 3-51 Rick Dillingham collection and photo. 1983. A close up of Margaret Tafoya applying slip to a bowl with a paint brush. This tool has replaced hand made yucca brushes with all but a very few potters.

The high degree of slip technology and processing which has been developed by the pueblo Indian is truly amazing, unfortunately the contribution of the many pueblo potters over the centuries who have helped bring the art to a state of perfection will never be fully appreciated.

Polishing and Polishing Stones

No glaze is ever used on pueblo pottery; the high gloss is achieved by polishing the surface with a smooth stone. Polishing is a tedious process that must not be hurried if a good finish is desired. Two or three layers of slip are thinly applied on the smooth dried work, allowing a little time between coats for partial drying. Next, a fatty or lubricating substance is added over the slip and the ware is ready for polishing. Formerly, marrow was used as a lubricant (Hill 1982: 85), and at present a wide range of materials are utilized depending on the individual preference of the potter. Some contemporary Hopi-Tewa potters use Vaseline but prefer chicken fat when it is available. Margaret has used bacon fat, but says that almost any kind of grease will do.

The lubricant has two purposes: it prevents the polishing stone from sticking to the surface of the ware and it also holds in the moisture, keeping the slip damp so that the polisher can work for longer periods of time.

More lubricant is required with the red slipped pot than with a black one. Excessive applications of lubricant applied to black ware is said to produce surface bubbles and other defects that develop during firing.[15] In Guthe's (1925: 61) study, he observed that some potters did not apply any fat until the polishing was finished, a practice that would make polishing more difficult as the lubricant helps the stone glide. Grease may be applied after firing to further enhance the sheen.

Polishing stones are prized possessions among Tewa potters; often being passed from one generation to the next. These may be presented during holidays and feast days as presents, and sometimes make valued wedding gifts. Along with pukis, polishing stones have been found at many perhistoric sites including Santa Clara's Puyé Ruin (Figure 3-52a).

Margaret has a fine collection of polishing stones, many of which she inherited and considers her family treasures. Some were given to her by her paternal grandmother, Nestora Naranjo Tafoya, and two others once belonged to her aunt Santana Tafoya Gutierrez. Sara Fina gave her some that had been her great grandmother's (Figure 3-52 b). Margaret's sisters, Christina and Dolorita, were also given stones by their mother, but Margaret states that because she was more deeply involved in the production of large pottery at the time, she received the greater share of the stones. This was given

credence by Christina who said, "I used to make big pots, but not as big as Margaret's, but big."[16]

It does not necessarily follow that larger stones are used for polishing larger pieces. More important is that the stone feels right to the hand of the polisher. A potter who produces large vessels may prefer small stones and one who makes miniatures may feel more comfortable polishing with a larger one. Thus, the size and shape of the stone is governed by personal preference.[17]

The origin of Margaret's stones has been long forgotten, but according to tradition, they will someday be passed on to her pottery producing descendants. In this respect, it is interesting to note that Daisy Nampeyo Hooee, now a resident of Zuni, has a stone which is remarkably similar to one of Margaret's (Bottom, third from left. Figure 3-52b). This was given to Daisy by her Hopi-Tewa grandmother, the original Nampeyo of Hano. One is led to speculate that both stones came from the same parent rock somewhere in the Rio Grande or Santa Cruz Valleys. During the Second Pueblo Revolt, it is conceivable that when the Tewa moved to Hopi, they brought their prized stones with them. Therefore, it is possible that the stone migrated from the Santa Cruz Valley to First Mesa and from there to Zuni.

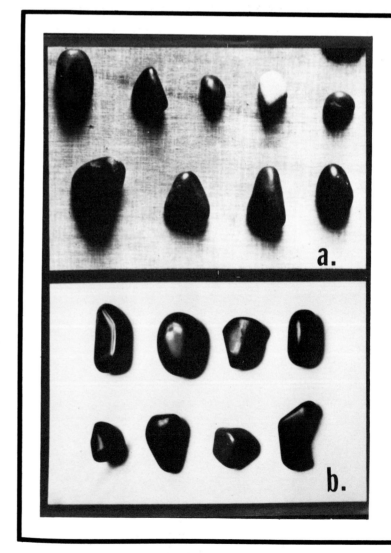

An old polishing stone is unbelievably smooth and often strangely shaped from centuries of use. Each stone in a potter's collection has a particular use depending on the size and shape of the vessel to be polished and the complexity of the design on it. Stones with thin edges such as those used in crevasses of miniature pieces wear down faster and become unusable for this purpose.[18]

During polishing, clay has a tendency to accumulate on the polishing stone to the point where it will gouge the surface. To alleviate this and to aid the lubricant, the potter will moisten the stone by either dipping it in water or licking it.

Once polishing is started, any unbroken or continuous design surface must be complete. Stopping and restarting polishing leaves noticeable lines on plain surfaces and detracts from the appearance and value of the work. Often, carved designs on a pot will result in producing a number of separate continuous surfaces. In this instance, each surface can be considered a distinct entity and polishing can be postponed once a continuous unit is complete. For example, an Avanyu carved design often results in three continuous surfaces which include the top section of the piece, the serpent itself, and the bottom section. Such a work may be polished in three different sessions.

Fig. 3-53 Rick Dillingham collection and photo. 1983. Margaret Tafoya demonstrates her polishing technique. A very smooth stone is rubbed over a slipped area to achieve a luster. Due to a muscular disability, Margaret is now an ambidextrous polisher, but is naturally right handed.

Fig. 3-52a Museum of New Mexico, Photo Archives, Santa Fe, N.M. A section of Neg. No. 90127. Wesley Bradford photographer, 1917. "Material Found at Puye" shows a fine selection of polishing stones used by Santa Clara forebears. Some modern potters use stones such as this which have been recovered from prehistoric pueblo ruins.

b.Private collection. Mary Fredenburgh photographer. 1981. Margaret's inherited polishing stones.

Reading from left to right the stones formerly belonged to:
Top: Sara Fina's great grandmother, name unknown. Candelaria Tafoya Gutierrez's (Sara Fina's grandmother) Pottery shown in Figure 1-7. Maria Nestora Naranjo's. Candelaria Tafoya Gutierrez's.

Bottom: Maria Nestora Naranjo's (Geronimo's mother). Pottery shown Figure 1-8. Gift from Santana Tafoya Gutierrez (Margaret's aunt) to Margaret when she married Alcario Tafoya. Pottery shown in Figure 2-23 and 2-24. Gift from Maria Nestora Naranjo. Filomena Cajete Gutierrez's (Sara Fina's mother). Pottery shown in Figure 3-54.

Margaret has the following to say on polishing interruptions, "Sometimes you leave it for some reason. That's what cracks it. That is why we don't want anyone to bother us when we are polishing. We even give up our eating. Like maybe around noontime we haven't finished that piece of pot, we don't eat until it's done...You have to dry by polishing it. If I'm making pottery, that's not too bad, just have to wash my hands. But when I'm polishing, I can't stand up. I am going to ruin that pot. That's the only way." (Figure 3-53).

Presently, polishing is one of the most difficult operations in pottery making for Margaret. In winter, the stones are cold to the touch and must be warmed by her fireplace. The joints and muscles of the hands can become stiff after a long session. Margaret is naturally right-handed, and so polished with her right hand until 1974 when a muscle in her right thumb collapsed and she was no longer able to polish in her usual manner. With typical pluck, she also taught herself to polish left-handed. Presently she uses either hand.

When a large plain jar is to be polished, the potter usually requires assistance from other family members because it is impossible for one person to adequately cover such a large unbroken surface before the slip begins to dry and lump on the polishing stone. According to Guthe, "The secret of good polishing seems to lie in the ability of the potter to go over her work as many times as possible after the slip has been applied and before it becomes too dry." (Guthe 1925: 62).

In addition to the very large pieces, swirled designs such as those on some melon bowls are difficult to polish. This is probably due to the fact that it is hard to maintain constant hard pressure on curved and slanted surfaces, plus the fact that the surface area on a melon bowl is increased so there is more area to polish.

In the Tafoya family, polishing of a piece is not necessarily done by the potter who formed the piece, but may be the work of anyone in the family who has the skill. In a few instances, the polisher is given recognition by being allowed to sign also, but usually they go unrecognized (Figure 4-8). Some of Margaret's daughters enjoy polishing more than the other processes of pottery production and are willing to polish pieces made by other members of the family. So familiar are these potters with each other's polishing that they can often tell, from the slant of the stroke or marks around handles, who in the family has polished a particular vessel, regardless of the signature on the work. One member may prefer polishing horizontally, while others may work at an angle or vertically.

Polishing can be achieved by smoothing a pottery piece with a stone without the use of a slip, a process called "floating". A vessel is wet with water, and by stroking with a smooth stone, smaller clay particles float to the surface to produce a glossy surface. Obtaining a high gloss by this method is difficult because of the coarse temper that is mixed with the clay. This type of work must be oxidized fired to achieve the natural tan color of fired clay. (Figure 3-13 and 4-17) The practice can be traced back to the Anasazi of the Basket Maker III—Pueblo I period (Tanner 1976: 108), and is best illustrated by the Ka'po Grey type. Today, there are relatively few pieces produced with unslipped polished surfaces, but occasionally a Tafoya vessel appears that has a section thus finished, and it is very striking.

Decoration and Designs

The first crude Anasazi pottery was strictly utilitarian, however it was not long before design elements appeared which logically imitated the intricate designs woven into the baskets made by their predecessors (Tierney 1976: 51). The early Tewa were master pottery decorators, but it was not until the second half of the nineteenth century that designs on polished plainware appeared at Santa Clara.

In designing a pot, the artist must decide what area is to be decorated. A banding arrangement is quite traditional, but in search for originality, the potter is becoming more innovative. Margaret notes that she and Alcario condsider the shape and size of a piece before a design for it is chosen. The success of this approach is confirmed by Clara Lee Tanner who states, "Several beautiful pieces by Margaret Tafoya observed in 1962 are gracefully formed and their simple designs were effectively placed in relation to shape. Three of these were large, with two wedding vases over 18 inches high and a long necked jar over 15 inches tall. The carving was deep, the lines of the pattern even and sure." (Tanner 1968: 100).

A modern Tewa potter has a choice of four different ways to decorate pottery. This can be done by impression, carving, painting or incising. Impressing and carving (carving has been described above) are both done prior to polishing, while painting and incising are done after the polishing procedure is complete.

Incising

The prehistoric decorative process of incising (not to be confused with carving) was revived in the 1930's at the pueblo of San Juan where geometric designs were scratched in the damp clay. Currently it is practiced at most of the pueblos, including Santa Clara, where some exquisite and delicate designs are sometimes incised after polishing.

Neither Margaret or her mother ever felt that incising was a true form of Tewa decoration. Margaret quotes her mother as saying, "My people never did put design by scratching on their pots." She was undoubtedly referring to contemporary incised decoration now produced at the pueblo by some potters and not the carving, since it is not uncommon to find later carved pieces which bear her signature.

When decorating by either painting or incising, the polished, unfired pot must be handled with care. Unfired polished surfaces are very vulnerable to damage and may be marred even by the oil from human skin. For this reason, they are usually handled with a soft rag.

According to LeFree (1975: 74), the first impressed "bear paw" design appeared at Santa Clara about 1903, although Frank and Harlow state that this motif dates to about 1850 (Frank and Harlow 1974: 41). A well documented piece in the Philbrook Art Center in Tulsa, Oklahoma, is dated circa 1865 (Figure 3-54) and would give credence to the Frank and Harlow dates.

Margaret tells us that the bear paw is a good luck symbol which must be placed in the upright position in an attitude of prayer, asking for rain and everlasting life for the Santa Clara people. Athough the bear is often associated with healing at the pueblo, there is a prevalent story that long ago during a period of severe drought, the bear led the people to a water source, thus accounting for the recognition of the bear on pieces of pottery, especially those which were made to contain water or food.

Modern decorators sometimes tend to neglect tradition, especially that of bear paw design size. By old custom, the matriarch of her family has the right to place the largest paw on her work. Often these designs are as distinctive as a signature, and the work of one potter can be distinguished from that of the others.[19]

"Rainbow Bands" impressed in a water jar are structurally part of the vessel but are also considered to be part of the design, as are gourd and melon bowls. Rainbow bands are raised portions on the shoulders, at the joining of the neck and bowl, that encircle the entire water jar. There may be one, two, or even three bands, and each is considered a prayer to keep the water from evaporating. In spite of their simplicity, they require a great deal of skill to form (Figures 2-8, 2-13, 2-24, and 3-30, 3-31).

Often associated with older water jars and rainbow bands were "rain drop" rims. Rain drops are rather small, crimped indentations around the rim that may also be fluted. The purpose of this addition was the request that water in the container stay sweet and drinkable (Figure 3-55).

Margaret is adamant that the bear paw and rainbow band symbols originated with the ancestors of the Santa Clara people and that their symbolism is rooted in Santa Clara tradition. She considers their use by potters of other pueblos as plagiarism. It is apparent that bear paws are historically unique to Santa Clara and nothing can be found at the other pueblos which resembles them. Shouldered jars are prevalent among many prehistoric cultures and have been found in as many as three distinct

Fig. 3-55 Detail of Figure 2-24 shows the rim of a water jar decorated with an impressed raindrop design—a prayer to preserve the water.

separations in early Meso-American jars, but the rainbow band shoulder on the classic water jar form is a unique Santa Clara trademark.[8]

Presently, many Santa Clara potters decorate their work with a type of shallow carving which closely resembles impressed decoration. In addition to being shallow, the carving is wider at the surface than at the depth of the cut, and is made very smooth by cleaning the cut with a wet sponge or rag. The bear paw designs on Margaret's later work are made in this manner, and without examining the inside wall of the design, one would not be able to tell the difference (Figure 3-29). Impressed pottery is now a collector's item, as most of the makers of impressed shapes are gone.

Perhaps the decline of impressed decoration came with the introduction of carving, perhaps good clay deposits were lost or depleted which resulted in thicker walled vessels that were more difficult to work, or it is possible that many modern potters have simply lost the skills of their ancestors.

Painted Decoration

The earliest forms of painted decoration used by Margaret's Anasazi ancestors were the many types of black-on-white pottery. First appearing ca. 600 A.D. (Dittert and Plog 1980: 75), designs were applied by painting with a so-called carbon paint (vegetable material) or a mineral paint (iron bearing clay), or a mixture of the two, on a white slipped surface. Particularly interesting in Margaret's background are those who settled above the Rio Grande Valley on the Pajarito Plateau. About 1350 A.D. a distinction can be made in the work of the northern Tewa potters of the upper Rio Grande from their neighbors to the south. The dividing line was located near La Bajada Hill, south of the present day Santa Fe (Dittert and Plog 1980: 129). The northern Tewa continued to produce ware of carbon painted black-on-white (Figure 3-56). This pottery was probably traded for the southern Tewa's glaze-paint and polychrome vessels and may explain why glaze-paint shards are seen at Puyé Ruins even though Santa Clara people claim no knowledge of their ancestors producing any of this type. To follow the Tewa migrations and the development of their pottery see figure 1-1 and Appendix 1.

The black pigment for carbon painted wares is usually derived from a water extract of the leaves and stems of the guaco plant. *Guaco* is the Spanish name of a plant also known as Rocky Mountain beeweed, wild spinach or Cleome (Taylor 1936: 152). The plant not only grows wild in the west, but is at times deliberately cultivated in areas where bees are kept, and so the common name beeweed. The Tewa people have used it as an herb, medicine, and writing vehicle (Hill 1982: 86). According to Guthe (1925: 66), the bitter taste of the wild spinach plant disappears after boiling and it can be

Fig. 3-56 Private collection. Abiquiu Black-on-gray (1375-1450 A.D.) 13½" diameter, 5½" height. Some think this Tewa design, excavated from the Pajarito Plateau, is an early form of the Avanyu.

eaten, but of more interest here is its use as a binder for pottery pigments and as a pigment itself.

To convert the guaco plant into a paint medium, Margaret described the procedure she used, which was passed on to her from her forebears. "We boil it [the young plant leaves and stems] to syrup. Then we put it into a little dish. When it's dry we cut it, but we have to try to keep it away from flies or bees. Sometimes it looks like it is getting mold. Then we take it outside, but we cover it so the flies won't get in. If they get in they ruin that color. Before it gets too hard we cut it in little layers so we know just how much [water] to put in. The guaco syrup is what turns different colors of clay into different colors after it is baked." The longer the material is stored, the darker color it will produce, and the fact that it should be kept over a period of several years is well documented (Tierney 1976: 50, Spivey 1979: 25, 26, and Peterson 1977: 96). If it is applied before it has matured, a weakly colored, streaky finish will result.

The term used to describe the black decoration, "carbon black" or "carbon glaze", are not truly descriptive of the chemical makeup of the final form of the decoration, nor what is responsible for the final black color. The sap of the guaco plant contains organic compounds which contain high amounts of iron. The sap is removed from the plant by boiling and the iron compounds are further concentrated by further boiling. When painted on, dried and fired to a high temperature the concentrated sap decomposes and the iron containing organic compounds break down to form a black reduced oxide of iron and elemental carbon. It is this reduced iron compound which is the prime contributor to the black color. The carbon, if it has not entirely burned off, only contributes in a minor way.

Following the discovery that guaco could be used as a pigment, the pueblo potters of the Rio Grande area began to learn that this material could be used with other natural mineral pigments in the region, and by applying various combinations of materials, they could produce different colors. Polychrome pottery has more than two colors used for decoration. Historically, polychromes succeeded bichromes (two colors) and made their appearance as Tewa potters experimented with various pigments. Thus, by 1650 A.D., a center for polychrome ware had developed around the now extinct pueblos of Cuyamungue, Sacona, and the old areas of San Ildefonso (Harlow 1973: 30, 31). Although polychrome decoration reached its zenith in the early 1900's at San Ildefonso, the Santa Clara people, for the most part, preferred to remain with their tradition of plain unpainted pottery.

Jeançon claimed that some polychromes with a cream slip were produced at Santa Clara prior to 1900. T.S. Dozier reported that some potters were using aniline dyes in the early 1900's, although this was a fad that didn't last long (Hill 1982: 83). An undocumented piece of this type was found at the Smithsonian Institution in Washington, D.C., and another at the New York Museum of Natural History which is a bowl with interior decoration of this type collected by George Pepper in 1903. These are most unusual specimens because the colors are bright and gaudy, and almost transparent in appearance.[21]

The use of polychrome decoration has diminished but is still produced at San Ildefonso by potters such as Blue Corn, and at Santa Clara by Margaret and Luther Gutierrez and Belen Tapia. Today, potters who paint use purchased brushes almost exclusively, though there may be still a few conservatives who make their own brushes from the yucca leaf. There is an excellent description of the making of yucca brushes by Chapman (1938: 12, 13).

Tewa pigments today are usually some form of clay which is highly contaminated with inorganic compounds of iron. Margaret speaks fondly of the days of her youth which were spent in collecting these colored clays near Puyé Cliffs. These collection trips took the form of family picnics or outings similar to the clay digging expeditions, and the locations of the sources of many of these coloring materials are still fresh in her memory.

Most potters agree that painting polychrome decoration is more difficult than carving. From the collection and preparation of pigments to the actual application, and perhaps including black or white outlining of the designs, producing polychromes is a time-consuming operation, and removing mistakes is difficult. For these reasons and economic factors, Margaret's polychrome decoration is limited to times past. In the 1930's and 1940's, Margaret and Alcario produced beautiful polychrome ware (Figures 3-21, and 3-22), but this ended abruptly when Alcario became governor of the pueblo in 1945. In more recent years, their work has concentrated on larger well shaped pieces which were more lucrative to produce and not as time-consuming to decorate.

One well-published form of painted design was developed at San Ildefonso Pueblo by María and Julian Martinez beginning in 1918 (Peterson 1977: 91 and Chapman 1970: 9, 10). This is the famous black matte design on a polished black background, now referred to as "Black-on-black." This was gradually adopted by other potters at both San Ildefonso and Santa Clara, accelerating in popularity until about 1927 and maintaining its popularity as an art form through the present (Figures 3-16 and 3-32). During the early development at Santa Clara, an effort was made to produce the matte black effect by simply painting the design in guaco over the polished surface before the piece was reduced fired. It was soon found that a fine clay mixed with the guaco produced a thicker, more uniform matte, and finally the guaco was abandoned altogether. Today, a thin, finely screened clay slip is painted over the polish. A similar pattern of development occurred for the red-on-red designs except the red pieces are oxidized fired.

A final form of Margaret's painted decoration which deserves mention is the type referred to by LeFree (1975: 85) as Duco painted ware. This is a rare example of modern Santa Clara pottery where painted decoration was added after firing. Although LeFree is correct in stating that some potters used hardware or Duco paint to achieve the orange line designs, Margaret claims that she made an orange vehicle from a mixture of old and new pine gums with as light a colored clay as possible. A similar decorating process is described by Tierney (1976:50) and witnessed by Blanche Fulton who wrote, "The Santa Clara Indians for a while used hot pine gum for decorating. It is an orange color and put on pottery while boiling hot."[2]

Margaret found that pine gum was a difficult medium with which to work. The dispersion had to be carefully and constantly stirred to keep the clay in suspension. The resultant color was orange. Should the temperature of the mixture be low, the viscosity increased to the point that it could not be applied to the vessel, and too high a temperature caused the gum to carbonize and turn brown. An example of her work in this medium is shown in Figures 3-15 and 3-16.

Like the polychrome, this type of ware occupied only a short period of time (probably the early 1930's) in Margaret's career. It was a short-lived fad

with the collectors and demand for it passed quickly.

Presently, traditional ceramic pigments of the Tewa potters are usually colored clays highly contaminated with inorganic compounds of iron. Individual families have their favorite locations for obtaining these materials and often keep these locations secret. Fortunately or unfortunately, other color producing transition elements if available to the Tewa at all, are found in only trace amounts. With this limitation, they have become masters in the utilization of iron as a coloring element and have been able to produce a remarkably wide range of colors from that element.

In addition to iron, manganese, which is often found in trace amounts with iron in the region, probably also influences the Tewa color palette. This element is capable of producing subtle color variations when mixed with iron in minor quantities.

A final coloring transition element which may make a small contribution to the iron colors is vanadium. Like manganese it is often associated with iron in very small amounts, and traces have been found incorporated in the Tewa clays. Again, when present, it may make subtle changes in the iron colors.

Copper is another transition element which is found in some minerals available to the Tewa artist, but it is doubtful that it has ever been used as a ceramic pigment. Copper colors (greens, blues and reds) are brought out when the element is incorporated in low melting glazes and under specially controlled firing conditions. Today, all traditional Tewa pottery is glaze-free and the primitive firing controls which are now used are such that satisfactory and reproducible colors from the element are practically impossible to produce. Copper is responsible for the colors turquoise (bright blue), malachite (bright green), and azurite (deep blue).

Polychrome ware must be fired under oxidizing conditions. The coloring agents, especially those containing iron, when subjected to reduced firing conditions, will always either turn black by themselves or be unattractively masked by the black carbon soot which penetrates the pores of the piece and adheres to the surface.

For this reason, the background color of Santa Clara polychrome pieces is the characteristic oxidized brownish red of the polished slip, the tan color of the polished unslipped clay body, or a few matte slipped white or tan vessels. The subtle ochres, bluish greys, yellows, white, and subdued red colors of the design itself are obtained from the carefully selected, finely ground minerals. White is obtained by using iron-free clay. Bright blues, greens, and reds are claimed by some potters to be produced by mining undisclosed desposits or by using the extracts from secret undiscovered plants, but to the eyes of anyone trained in ceramic color technology, these colors are obviously from oxides of cobalt, chromium, vanadium, or chrome tin mixtures obtained commercially and, by no stretch of the imagination available naturally to the Tewa potter.[22] Some pueblo ceramic artists are using commercial products,and are producing fine pieces of art. However, they are unfairly placed in competition with traditional Indian pottery which requires more time, knowledge and skill. Margaret disdains commercial aids and considers work which incorporates them as not being representative of the art of her people.

The years between 1920 and 1935 were a time of rapid and radical pottery design changes by the Tewas, especially those of Santa Clara. The railroad had recently opened the pueblo to tourists, and so the number of visitors increased rapidly in the period following World War I. Roads in the Southwest were improved, which not only increased the tourist flow, but also improved access to pottery markets in nearby towns. Finally, people with vision and an appreciation of Indian art began to supply attractive outlets for the art that provided incentive for the potters who were capable of creating these fine works.

In 1917, Mme. Vera van Blumenthal and Miss Rose Dougan built a summer home west of San Ildefonso Pueblo which was to be used as a base where a few selected potters could work with the purpose of improving the quality of their output (Figure 1-2). Mme. van Blumenthal had previously developed a profitable business in reviving and improving the quality of lace produced in various Russian villages and possibly thought she could do the same with pueblo pottery. Because they could devote only limited time to the endeavor, in 1919 the ladies turned over their project and two hundred dollars to the School of American Research in Santa Fe, then directed by Dr. Edgar L. Hewett. For a period of several years before this, Dr. Hewett had been encouraging potters at San Ildefonso to improve the quality of their work (Toulouse 1977: 33, 34).

To further the project established at the school, Dr. Hewett enlisted the efforts of two very capable men, Kenneth Chapman and Wesley Bradford. They proposed a formula which they hoped the pueblo potters would follow.

"1. Inviting the potters to submit their wares to us at the Museum before offering them for sale elsewhere.

2. Asking each potter to set her price, piece by piece.

3. Selecting a few outstanding pieces, if any, and explaining why they were chosen (for form, finish, decoration, etc.).

4. Adding at least twenty-five percent to the price named by the potter for those selected, and promising still higher prices for further improvements.

5. Explaining that selected pieces would be sold at the Museum at a markup sufficient only to repay the school for the time devoted to the project by Bradford and me." (Chapman 1970: 28)

Finally, during the Santa Fe Fiesta starting in 1922, the pueblo potters were, for the first time, encouraged to exhibit and sell their wares to a waiting market, and this market seemed to hunger for decorated rather than plain pottery.

Realizing that the market for decorated ware was growing and that making pottery of this type would be more financially rewarding, the Tafoya family was quick to produce pieces which would satisfy the new demands. In short order, they began to create the Black-on-black type, at the same time making multi-colored or polychrome decoration at the pueblo. In the 1920's, Margaret and Alcario pioneered in the development of carved decoration. Impressed pottery, while not entirely disappearing, became only a minor part of the total output.

Design Symbolism

Blanche Fulton, an observer of Tewa design application, particularly that of the Tafoyas in the 1930's wrote, "After a piece of pottery is all polished and dry, a design is painted on it. They never make a mistake, nor do they make a pattern try-out. They use yucca brushes and some designs are beautiful. Each design painted usually has some symbol or meaning to the Indian."[2]

The philosophy of the pueblo designer, and one adhered to by Margaret and her husband, is well expressed by a quotation of a Laguna potter and given to Ruth Bunzel (1929: 52), "I make up all my designs and never copy. I learned this design from my mother. I learned most of my designs from my mother." Margaret regrets that the present generation of Santa Clara potters shows little interest in either learning the meaning of the designs or reproducing them accurately. This in spite of the fact that they have all the necessary skills.

There have been many studies of pueblo designs and their meanings such as those of Wade and McChesney (1981), Chapman (1938 and 1970), Bunzel (1929), Spinden (1911), and Fewkes (1898 and 1919). With the exception of LeFree (1975: 91-99), little attention has been given to the designs employed by the potters of Santa Clara. These designs, while having much in common with other pueblos, also have unique characteristics of their own. Animals and foliage were graphically portrayed here beginning in the 1930's, but stylized leaves such as those found on Santo Domingo ware or the birds painted on the pottery of the Zia and Santa Ana were never popular at Santa Clara. Santa Clara designs do not stress a line break or a "spirit path", and one does not notice hatching in their decoration such as is found on Hopi, Zuni or Acoma pottery.

Interestingly, one can find similarities between the designs of the Tewa and those of some Meso-American cultures. "The square angled spirals [that] are the symbols of rain of the Mexican Teotihuacan peoples, whose culture reached a zenith between 300 and 650 A.D." (Chan 1965: 53), bear a strong resemblance to one of the water symbols used by the present day Tewa designers.

One of the most popular designs with Santa Clara artists for many years has been the "Avanyu" or "water serpent". The origin of this symbol is unclear, but it is often claimed that there is a relationship between this and the various serpents of the early Central American Indian cultures. One can see a resemblance between the Avanyu and the "jaguar serpent" of the Teotihuacan people as well as some of Aztec origin.

The Tewa have many designs which symbolize some form of water. These include rain, snow, lightning, storm clouds, and ponds and lakes. Even the Avanyu and the unique bear paw designs are asociated with water. In any form, water is welcome in the dry climate of the Tewa, who formerly depended so much on successful crops for their existence. It is, therefore, strange that symbols for corn, so sacred to the Tewas, are seldom found on their pottery.

Simplistic representations of the Tafoya designs, both carved and painted, are presented in Figure 3-57. Like her pottery shapes, Margaret's designs are not complicated but have a simple beauty characteristic of her art. The placement of the design is accomplished in a manner which does not detract from, but enhances, the shape of her pottery forms.

Drying

Many of the defects found in pueblo pottery are the result of improper drying. Unless a clay body is dried slowly and uniformly, differential shrinkage will occur within the mass which will set up severe strains resulting in the following deficiences:

1. Warping: This is a drying defect produced while the clay is still in the plastic condition. It is caused by strains set up during differential drying. If one part of a piece dries and shrinks and becomes rigid before another, the forces generated may pull the plastic portion out of shape.

2. Cracking: Cracking is caused by strains which exert pressure enough to break the drying body after it becomes too rigid to yield.

3. Checking: This is similar to cracking, the difference being that checks are such small cracks that they are not visible to the naked eye, and the piece may look perfectly sound until it has been fired. Checking usually appears near the surface and is caused by rapid shrinkage of clay near the surface.

Safe drying, to avoid rapid shrinkage, is best carried out under conditions of high humidity. It has often been observed that many native American potters, to hasten the process of drying, will place the ware in an oven or out in the hot sunlight. This is poor practice and should not be followed until the ware has completed its initial drying shrinkage. An experienced potter such as Margaret dries her pottery slowly over a long period of time and usually under conditions as humid as possible. One of Sara Fina's descendants who produces beautifully carved pieces, dries her ware in her bathroom—a drying enclosure with almost ideal humidity conditions. It naturally follows that the larger the piece, the slower and more carefully it should be dried.

Once drying shrinkage is complete, it is then beneficial to warm the ware in an oven, or in front of a burning fireplace for the larger pieces, before firing, This not only accelerates drying, but has a second advantage of minimizing thermal shock created if the warm ware is taken immediately from its warming source and placed on the fire before it cools.

Firing

For the Indian potter working in the traditional manner, firing represents a great moment of truth. It is here that the defects incorporated in the ware during the previous steps of formation, such as sloppy or hastily done work and poor drying practices, are exposed. These may either disfigure or destroy the work and all of the labor put in the piece will have been for naught. If a vessel cracks or breaks prior to this operation, at least the difficult procedure of firing can be avoided, and some of the raw materials can be reclaimed for future use by breaking the ware into small pieces and soaking them in water until they again become a pliable mass. Margaret reuses material of this type and also the dust produced by the sanding process, although she says she avoids mixing this material with fresh clay.

Should a gross defect such as a large gas bubble or piece of organic material be incorporated in the piece during forming, the piece may explode violently during the rapid upcycle of the firing. This often sends projectiles of pottery shards flying in all directions, which may shatter surrounding flawless pieces. Voids containing water vapor or filled with gases generated by burning organic materials may be subjected to tremendous pressures to cause the explosion.

To minimize loss, most Tafoya potters fire only one piece at a time, while others will fire more pieces at once. In the past, when pottery finish was not an important factor, single firing was almost never done. For her very large pieces, Margaret fires singly, but because she is skilled in the art of firing, she may include several of her medium to smaller pieces in one firing.

Building a pottery fire on damp ground is a practice which all agree should be avoided. Through centuries of experience, it has been learned that the presence of excessive moisture not only wastes fuel by requiring the input of more heat to reach the maturing temperature, but it may cause defects such as dull spots on polished surfaces and general discoloration of the ware. To eliminate moisture, firing areas are kept covered, and often the ground is preheated with a small fire which is maintained for the necessary drying time (Figure 3-58 a).

Racks and crude equipment necessary for positioning the pottery within the fire, known to the ceramist as kiln furniture, are built up around the ware before the fuel is added. In the main, this equipment consists of tin cans either saved or collected from the Santa Clara disposal area, metal sheets, metal grates and old metal milk bottle containers which are especially prized. Cans with ridged sides are preferred to those with smooth sides because they better withstand the heat of firing.

The assembling of the kiln furniture used to support the ware begins by placing a grate or milk bottle container over a number of cans standing upright. In the space created by the cans between the grate and the ground, kindling is placed. Preferably, these are small pieces of juniper or cedar which are easily ignited and burn with a hot flame, without giving off the volatile tar of pine that may condense on the pottery surface. The ware is carefully placed on the grate or within the milk bottle container, depending on its size. A larger piece placed on a grate requires sheet metal walls to be built up around it with a piece of sheet metal being used as a protective lid (Figures 3-58 b). The side walls are carefully located so as to give the ware access to circulating heated air during firing.

Margaret states that Sara Fina always stacked her pottery upside down "to cook from the inside out." She also used broken pieces of fired pottery as a cover over pieces in the fire to prevent their contact with debris. (There is an excellent motion picture produced by the National Park Service which shows María Martinez, Clara Montoya (María's sister), and Tony Da (María's grandson) firing inverted pots in the same manner as Sara Fina.)

It is interesting to speculate on the construction of prehistoric and early historic kilns. In all probability, the first pottery was placed directly over a small fire, and the outer walls were heated by adding more fuel to the outside. Later, perhaps the unfired pottery was placed in a small protective stone structure so constructed as to allow the free circulation of the hot air around the piece.

Firing is begun by igniting the kindling, letting it burn for a short time, and then placing the fuel around the built-up furniture. The fuel consists of cut-to-size dried bark portions of lumberyard trimmings commonly called "barks" (Figure 3-58 c). These are stacked either vertically or horizontally

Fig. 3-57 A few of the almost infinite variations of Tafoya Avanyu designs.

1. *Plate, Red-on-red Avanyu, ca. 1940.*
2. *Variations in Avanyu head designs: a. Bowl, Black-on-black, ca. 1950. b. Plate, Black-on-black, ca. 1935. c. Plate, polychrome, ca. 1930-1935. d. Wedding vase, Black-on-black, ca. 1960.*
3. *Variations in Avanyu fin designs: a. Jar, carved, ca. 1970. b. Plate, Black-on-black, ca. 1935. c. Wedding vase, Black-on-black, ca. 1960. d. Plate, polychrome, ca. 1930-1935.*
4. *Variations in Avanyu tail designs: a. Plate, Black-on-black, ca. 1935. b. Plate, Black-on-black, ca. 1935. c. Plate, polychrome, ca. 1930-1935.*

Other Tafoya designs and their interpretations.

5. *Tadpole or lizard. Bowl, Black-on-black, orange outline, ca. 1930.*
6. *Small pond or swampy area. Bowl, Black-on-black outlined in orange. ca. 1930.*
7. *Storm designs: a. Sun emerging after thunderstorm. Bowl, Black-on-black outlined in orange. ca. 1932. b. Rain drawn in pencil by Margaret Tafoya 1983. c. Rainbow after a thunderstorm. Corn meal box, polychrome by Margaret Tafoya. ca. 1930. d. Snow storm drawn in pencil by Margaret 1983.*
8. *Tableta for early summer dance. Wedding vase, carved ca. 1950.*
9. *Kiva steps: a. Vase, carved, 1974. b. Corn meal box, Red-on-red outlined in white. ca. 1928-1930.*
10. *Lightning. Wedding vase, Manuel Tafoya polychrome. ca. 1930.*
11. *a. and b. Clear sky symbols. All forms of decoration found on a range of different shapes made by the Tafoyas from the early 1900's to date.*
12. *Mountains: a. Jar, polychrome. ca. 1935. b. Design drawn by Margaret 1983.*
13. *Prayer feather stick. Bowl, carved 1980.*
14. *Masked face. Bowl, Black-on-black outlined in orange. ca. 1930.*
15. *Buffalo head. Plate, polychrome. ca. 1930.*
16. *a. and b. Water symbols. Usually carved decoration found on all forms of pottery. ca. 1925 to date.*
17. *Mask and tableta used for rain ceremony. Wedding vase, polychrome design by Manuel Tafoya. ca. 1930.*
18. *a. through c. Feather designs drawn by Margaret Tafoya 1983.*
19. *Animal horns: a. Elk or deer horns. Plate, carved ca. 1925-1930. b. Mountain sheep horns. Plate, carved ca. 1950-1960. c. Buffalo horns. Plate, polychrome ca. 1930.*
20. *Bear paws. All shapes, usually impressed or carved ca. 1920's to date. (Margaret's forebears have been using the bear paw design since about 1865.)*

depending on the size of the structure to be heated. The wood slabs, like the metal, must be carefully placed to allow for proper ventilation and to leave a sight hole through which a portion of the pottery may be viewed during the heating process. In the past, Margaret remembers using dried cottonwood limbs before the availablity of lumberyard slabs.

In prehistoric times, it is probable that most, if not all, pottery fires were fueled with wood. It is possible that dried manure from wild animals could have been used, although its availability must have been strictly limited. The use of coal as a fuel was restricted to those with nearby deposits such as the Hopi and the Tewa who moved to Hopi First Mesa. Examination of pottery shards at Awatovi Ruin on the Hopi reservation shows them to be highly vitrified, indicating that the ware was fired at much higher temperatures such as those obtained from the burning of coal, and surface coal seams are abundant in that area. None seems to have been available to the Tewa of the Pajarito Plateau or the Rio Grande Valley.

The colonizing Spaniards brought with them domesticated animals, so it is probable that the large-scale use of manure as a pottery firing fuel occurred shortly after the establishment of the first Spanish farming settlements. The fuel took the form of dried chips and briquettes made by forming moist manure into disc-like shapes. In their paintings, pueblo artists of the early 20th century show the use of this form of fuel as do early photographs taken during that time.

In 1931, an observer noted not only the collection and use of cow chips for firing, but also the use of sheep manure.[2] Dockstader (1972: 24) and Guthe (1925: 26) indicate widespread use of sheep dung briquettes at Santa Clara, but Margaret claims that this was not sheep dung. However, the formation of cow and horse manure briquettes is remembered by some of her daughters as childhood chores assigned by either Sara Fina or Margaret, and definitely not their favorite form of work (Figure 3-59).

Presently, Santa Clara potters use wood as a fuel almost exclusively and dry, powdered manure is reserved as a smothering agent for the production of the beautiful black ware. This is not altogether true for the potters of the neighboring pueblo of San Ildefonso, many of whom use manure both as a fuel and a smothering agent (usually cow manure to fire and horse manure to smother).

Green wood, when burned, gives off volatile gases which often condense on the ware and cause characteristic spotting on the polished surface. Most potters destroy such pieces and will not offer them for sale. However, at a recent Indian Market in Santa Fe, one piece was sold which had this defect. The maker claimed that this was a secret and artistic process which he had discovered rather than admitting to the fact that it was simply produced by firing with green wood.

Once the firing has started, the potter pays careful attention to the surface of the pottery which has been exposed for sighting purposes. Firing is terminated when this surface emits the desired color. As Margaret explains, "When it looks real pink and shiny, then it's ready to take out. That's the way we go about it in baking." The experienced eye of the potter is her pyrometer, and the skilled eye can insure that firing temperatures are remarkably uniform from one fire to another.

When the piece emits the bright cherry red color, it has reached its maximum firing temperature. It is at this point that the firing processes for producing red and black ware differ (Figure 3-58 d). The temperature for red ware is reduced by removing the fuel and allowing the vessel to cool in the open air. Black ware is produced by smothering the fire with fine dry horse or cow manure at this point (Figure 3-58 e). According to Margaret, "When the pot looks real red, then it is ready for manure. [That's why] the black is harder for me. I have to run here and there with a shovel [covering the areas which begin to emit smoke], and sometimes the wind gets me. I have to hurry to the side where the wind is strong so we don't overbake the pottery. It's hard." Air cannot be allowed to penetrate the smothering cover, or the surface of the ware will begin to oxidize, and spotting of the surface will occur. Like wood, the manure must be dried or it too will cause surface spotting.

Once the fire has been completely smothered and smoke no longer is seen coming from the pile, it is allowed to stand for at least a half hour or more, depending on the size of the vessel. The longer it stands, the less the possibility of cracking due to sudden cooling. When enough time has elapsed, the pile is opened and the ware removed (Figure 3-58 f).

Pots and other vessels are removed from the firing area with a stick, while plates which are too hot to handle are allowed to stay in place until they can be moved by gloved hands. When completely cool, the pieces are dusted, given a quick bath in a mild detergent, dried, examined carefully for defects, and then perhaps rubbed with some grease or fat to bring out the luster.

Larger pieces are more difficult to fire than smaller ones. Margaret's large black polished storage jar which won the Best of Show Award at the 1979 Santa Fe Indian Market is an excellent example of this, and the following description of the work involved may aid in an appreciation of the value of the final product.

After Margaret's skillful work of forming, carving, drying, and smoothing, six members of her immediate family were involved in the final steps of the procedure. First came the polishing which

Fig. 3-58 Clarence and Donald Fulton photographers, 1951 or 1952. a. Margaret carefully watching her preliminary warming fire built under an elevated grate. Dry unfired pottery awaits placement on top of the grate. b. Margaret placing metal protectors around the ware. A void is deliberately created through which she can watch the heated pottery to determine when it is properly fired. c. Tree "barks" are stacked vertically around the fire. The viewing gap is continued through the vertically stacked wood. d. Ware is observed through viewing space. When it omits the proper red color it is either removed from the fire as red ware or the fire is smothered with powdered manure to produce black ware. e. To produce black pottery the powdered dried manure is quickly shovelled on the fire. Skilled teamwork is required for this step of the procedure, especially for large pieces. The pile is carefully monitored to check for areas that are burning through, which are indicated by smoke escaping and are quickly covered with additional powder. Burn throughs will cause firing discoloration on the ware. See Figure 2-9. f. Some beautiful black bowls emerge from a firing. The ware is examined in bright sunlight, which makes minute cracks visible to the trained eye. At this point imperfect pottery is broken.

Fig. 3-59 Museum of the American Indian, Heye Foundation, New York, Neg. No. 31757. "Woman firing pottery, ca. 1910, Pueblo Santa Clara, New Mexico." Margaret identified the lady as Sara Fina who is preparing to fire pottery with formed manure disks.

required the efforts not only of Margaret, but also of a daughter and a grandson. These three continuously polished for a period of nearly five and a half hours. Prior to firing, the piece was warmed on Margaret's fireplace hearth for several more hours, being rotated approximately 120 degrees each hour to insure uniform preheating prior to firing.

In the meantime, the ground was prepared by keeping a fire burning on the firing spot for about four hours, and the kiln furniture was assembled in the back yard. A sturdy grate was set on top of eight supporting cans four and a half inches in height. Metal sheets were strategically located so that they could be quickly placed in their final position for firing.

Next, the warmed jar was placed on a carrying cloth, requiring three people to carefully move it to the grate which was to support it during firing. At this point, the weight of the piece was estimated to be sixty pounds.

After placement on the grate and insuring its stability, the metal shields were put in place and the kindling wood which was already located was ignited. This small kindling fire was kept burning for about one half hour to gradually increase the temperature of the pot.

As soon as the preheating period had expired, 36-inch long, pre-cut barks were placed around the shield in an upright position completely surrounding the metallic shields. These were ignited by the already burning kindling and allowed to burn until the previously described bright cherry red color was sighted from the vessel. Approximately two hours were required for this to occur.

At a point which was deemed proper by Margaret, the fire was smothered with the dry powdered manure. A volume of manure powder which would fill 330 one gallon containers or a half ton pick-up truck was required to complete this step. Six adults, including Margaret, put forth hard physical labor for two additional hours in building up the smudge pile and covering areas which constantly had a tendency to burn through. Total firing time was two and a half hours because it was such a large vessel.

With the above information in mind, one is led to speculate on how the Ka'po Grey and Black pieces were smudge-fired at a time when manure could not have been a readily available commodity. Perhaps the answer to this was provided by Sara Fina, who remembered her grandmother telling of the use of mulched pine needles which were dried for this purpose. Margaret had her doubts that the "pinon leaves" would work, and so she experimented with this peat-like substance. "I didn't believe it until I saw it myself, but when I did it, it came out good."

Another form of material that has been used, both as a smothering agent and as a fuel, is sawdust. Again, this must be well dried or it will produce the same surface defects as green wood or moist manure. At least one contemporary potter has experimented with this material at Santa Clara, but its use is more common with the Indian potters of the southeastern United States and western Canada.

Recently, firing practices have been developed which are said to allow the production of both a• brown and black color from the same slip during the same fire. This type of heat treatment is known as "resist firing". It is claimed that this is accomplished by covering the area which is to remain brown with a piece of foil or thin aluminum metal. Areas thus protected are usually used as a background for incised decoration which may be applied either before or after the ware is fired. An effect similar to the one produced by resist fire is created by reheating a portion of the black surface in the oxidizing portion of a hot flame such as that produced by a blowtorch. These non-traditional procedures are claimed by the artists to be secret processes.

Firing is generally done during the early hours of the day when there is less likelihood of wind. Wind is one of the biggest threats to a successful firing. It not only causes severe thermal gradients within the firing pile, but may also result in excessive fire marks which detract from the value of the piece (Figure 3-60).

Barriers of various kinds are erected around the firing area to eliminate the wind effects not only during firing, but also during the cooling and removal periods. "You have to be careful in getting it out of the fire. If it's not windy you can get it out, but if it's windy it's just like glass. You break the pot."

In any consideration of firing, the use of commercially available kilns by the Indian merits discussion. More and more Indian potters are turning to this easily available guarantee of successful firing, some honestly and some with deceit. Kiln firing is being taught on some reservations by well meaning non-Indian instructors who do not realize that in reality they are doing much to destroy the Indian's artistic heritage.

Kiln fired pottery is uniform in color and often dull and flat looking when compared to those fired by the traditional methods. Color penetration is uniform from the surface down and scratching a small section of the piece if the resultant damage is not too great, will reveal this uniformity.

Fire marks are absent from ware that has been kiln fired. Prior to the introduction of the white man's kilns, a uniformly colored piece was more highly prized by the collector; but in today's market, with the exception of black ware, a piece which is slightly fire marked is often of more value, particularly Hopi pottery. One should not demand fire markings on all pottery, however, because skilled potters are capable of producing completely uniform colored pieces by using traditional firing techniques. To them, a fire marked vessel is one of which they are not proud and such work is often destroyed or sold at a lower price.

Margaret and her immediate family all fire by the traditional methods and bitterly resent any Indian potter who fires in a commercial kiln but won't admit it. "I don't even know how a kiln looks, how they bake...With us, we just watch our fires." When the lights dim within the Santa Clara Pueblo, it is half-jokingly remarked that some potter has just turned on his or her electric kiln.

Losses during traditional firing may be staggering. It is not uncommon for a good Tewa potter to lose fifty percent of the ware in firing, with the percentage even higher for larger pieces. In addition to exposing all of the defects built into the ware during forming, improper firing can cause a perfectly formed piece to break. Should a portion of the surface of the ware be heated or cooled too rapidly, that part will expand or contract in relation to the rest of the mass and build up enormous strains. The result of this is often either complete or hairline cracking, and it is not uncommon to have a piece completely fracture into small sections. The invisible or hairline cracks may further expand simply by standing over a period of time. Humidity also will increase the development of cracking.

It is remarkable how well the Tewa potter can accept her losses. Shows of emotion are rare. One of Margaret's daughters will work off her frustrations after a very disappointing fire by scrubbing the floor of her kitchen. Most members of the family feel that losses are the "will of Mother Clay" and quietly go on to new work.

From the standpoint of the buyer, no large or expensive piece of pottery can be too thoroughly examined for defects at the time of acquisition, especially for traces of spalling (surface pitting which generally occurs after firing) and almost invisible cracking. Unfortunately, spalling may not become noticeable until a short time (two to six weeks) after the ware has been fired. This defect is seldom, if ever, found in Santa Clara ware. However, "hot out of the oven" pottery from Acoma whose clay has a tendency to spall, make even the best of potters suspect. Should one question the possibility of cracking, the smallest crack can be made visible by applying water to the surface with a paint brush or damp rag. When contemplating purchase, pottery should be examined in the brightest possible light, if a faultless finish is desired. In the past this was not considered a necessity, but Anglo tastes have demanded perfection of polish.

In the sunlight, Margaret and her descendants carefully scrutinize all of their pieces after firing. If the ware is distinctly visibly damaged, it is immediately broken. Should the defect be barely noticeable, the ware may be saved and presented to a close friend or relative as a gift. It is never sold.

Only the largest of the broken pieces may find use as firing shields, and the remainder are discarded. Other pueblos such as Zuni and Acoma grind shards for grog, but this is not the practice at Santa Clara. When Margaret was young, she was advised to dispose of broken ware and today, she and her family simply bury it. "For our part, we were advised never to leave the broken pieces around. Take it to the river."

Marketing

Long gone are the days when potters and their families were required to carefully pack their ware on burros or in horse-drawn wagons and transport it over long distances to barter for the necessities of life or wholesale it to sometimes shrewd traders.

Beginning in 1922 at the Sante Fe Fiesta and in 1923 at the Gallup, New Mexico Inter-Tribal Indian Ceremonial, the potter had the first opportunity to sell directly to the market and receive a fair price for her work. A few years earlier in 1918, Edgar Hewett had begun to educate the public about the beauty of Tewa pottery and its value as an art form by encouraging and publicizing the work of María Martinez. Public awareness was further broadened by Charles Faris, of the Santa Fe Indian School, who arranged to send an exhibition of María's work to the 1933 World's Fair in Chicago (Peterson 1977: 78).

In spite of the fact that they participated in the early Fiestas and Ceremonials, Margaret and her mother generally shunned publicity and were more preoccupied with family and pueblo affairs. As a result, recognition and easy sales did not come to Margaret until several decades later. As late as the 1950's, she was bringing large pieces to dealers which she sold for approximately twenty five dollars. Finally, by the middle 1960's, she had won numerous awards and was showing pieces of such size and beauty that her output was in strong

Fig. 3-61b Photographer L. Blair. Red-on-red bowl from Colorado University collection. Signed "Margarita". #25049, 10" height, 12½" diameter.

demand. At present, she cannot keep up with this demand and her work sells at a premium. In 1983, she attended a reception in her honor given at the Wheelwright Museum in Santa Fe, opening an exhibition of her pottery. She also agreed to attend a similar function at the Denver Museum of Natural History and a private gallery reception in Scottsdale, Arizona, but an unfortunate illness prevented her attending these two functions.

Presently, dealers come to Margaret's house. She prefers that they make an appointment since she does not like to be interrupted while she is working on pottery or in preparation for a ceremonial. These dealers are, for the most part, old business associates with whom a mutual loyalty has developed. She almost never will accept an order for a specific shape, decoration, or sized piece, and the dealers now accept any of her output. Should some of her pieces be uncommitted, which is rare, she will sell to the collector who happens to visit her home at precisely the right moment—a highly unlikely possibility.

Although not referring to the work of any one particular potter, the words of Chapman (1970: 131) aptly describe the pottery of Margaret Tafoya. "Wares so perfectly formed and so beautifully finished that they cast suspicion upon themselves, for one must watch every process in their production to be convinced that they are really handmade, from the first mixing of the clay to the final polishing, decorating and firing...Thus, of all of the ancient pottery making tribes within the United States, the pueblos alone carry one, quite appropriately, the craft which their ancestral potters won such distinction, countless centuries before Europeans appeared to change the whole fabric of Indian life."

Fig. 3-61a Unknown photographer. Margaret Tafoya, 1930 to 1940. With two unidentified children (probably Toni and Leo). Note extreme left bowl which is identical to that shown in figure 3-61b of preceeding page. Collection of Rick Dillingham.

Chapter 4
The Descendents

1925

"I don't want this pottery to die."
Margaret Tafoya[1]

They should not forget the old things unless they learn something better——. It is a bad business to forget the good old ways, especially when there are substituted for them new and worse ways——.

James (1970: 172, 173)—enlarging on the comments of a
Spanish acquaintance from the Santa Clara area.

The above advice of James meets with Margaret's full approval and has been heeded by her offspring. In order not to change the old ways, her children and grandchildren have been known to travel for up to 900 miles from their present homes to return to the pueblo to obtain the venerable raw materials or to transport their unfired works to Santa Clara ground for the traditional firing treatments used by their ancestors.

Spurred by increasing national and international recognition of Santa Clara pottery as a beautiful art form and the accompanying rewards available to the outstanding ceramic artists, the production of pottery at the pueblo seems to be expanding. At the Southwest Association on Indian Affairs Market in Santa Fe each August, pottery booths are second only to jewelry and many of the pottery stands are populated by Santa Clara artists. The competing Tafoya booths which may be found widely separated around the plaza are always surrounded by friends and eager, often aggressive, buyers endeavoring to obtain the few prize pieces which are available.

Though proud to be a Tafoya, a state of rivalry exists between some members of the family, Margaret's children and grandchildren each vying with the other for recognition. Competition is rigorous as each trusts that their ware will outdo others including those of their siblings. This is particularly true during the mid-summer to early fall Indian art competitions. Many of the Tafoya potters will hold back what they consider to be their best works to exhibit at these times—especially at Indian Market—and will sometimes forego quick and profitable sales with the hope that these works will earn the coveted and prestigious blue ribbon awards. A highly polished red or black Santa Clara pottery piece is often enhanced in the eyes of a prospective buyer if a prize ribbon is attached. In addition to the increased value, there is the recognition bestowed by a ribbon. The maker may also be eligible to receive ever increasing amounts of prize money which accompany the awards.

Of his family's pottery making ability, Margaret's grandson Nathan Youngblood states, "We are very fortunate in that we can use the things around us that the spirits have given us to make an income. It is not ours—it is just that we are allowed to use them to go on living."

A gratifying trend in recent years is the increase in the number of male potters, true of all pueblos including Santa Clara, which is well represented by Tafoya family members. The making of pottery in the past was traditionally an Indian woman's responsibility and she was given the credit, although some men did form pottery, or make a significant contribution to the finished work. Considering the work involved, one realizes that men must always have made substantial but unrecognized contributions to the art. It was not until pottery became considered a true art form and Chapman (1970: 26) encouraged María and Julian Martinez to co-sign their pottery beginning in the early 1920's, that men began to be considered true pottery artists. Perhaps the breakdown of sexual barriers in all areas of endeavor was in part responsible. In any case, male potters and the men who help their women are now given full credit, though some still remain reluctant to add their signatures.

Children growing up in pottery making families of the pueblos cannot help but learn the techniques of pottery production—it is a way of life. They are included in the process from the digging of the clay to the marketing of the finished works. Often they are proud to be the best salesmen of the family. As they grow older they are assigned the more difficult tasks of pottery making such as sanding, polishing and gathering and preparation of the fuel for the fires. They soon come to understand the economics involved, whether the derived income is the sole means of support for the family or is used to purchase extras to improve their standard of living. Often the children, because of their selling experience, give advice to other family members as to pricing and different marketing techniques to improve income from sales. The Tafoyas are classic examples of children brought up in this tradition. As in the case of most Tewa families, all hands were required to help and many times Margaret's children will relate that they were asked to assist with the clay gathering, the blending of the clay with the

Fig. 4-1 Walton Youngblood collection. Mary Fredenburgh photographer. Margaret Tafoya and her pottery producing children attending the Eight Northern Pueblo Council Artists and Craftsman show held at San Ildefonso Pueblo, N.M. on June 16, 1977. **Left to right:** *Lee Tafoya, Virginia Ebelacker, Jennie Trammel, Mela Youngblood, Margaret, Toni Roller, Mary Esther Archuleta, Shirley Tafoya, and standing in for Lu Ann was Nancy Youngblood Cutler.*

temper or were handed pieces of formed pottery to either sand, polish, or to place decorative borders on the already painted designs. Naturally the tasks assigned depended on the child's age and ability.

Margaret and Alcario instilled in their children the desire for education and an understanding of the rewards of hard and well executed work. Like many parents, what was not available to them, they wanted for their children. By example and their own abilities, they taught the work ethic. In addition to the chores of pottery making, the children, including the girls, under the supervision of their father, planted, cultivated, weeded and irrigated crops and tended to the animals as after school chores. This work ethic has continued with the now adult children sharing the land and labors needed to support their many families. After 80 years of age, Margaret and Alcario still work with their grandchildren teaching them the skills of farming and pottery making.

The children of Margaret and Alcario have grown into handsome adults (Figure 4-1); most of them are parents and some grandparents. With maternal advice and because of the close pueblo relationships as a result of a limited Santa Clara population,

most married outside of the pueblo with a predominance of Anglo spouses. Tewa custom forbids marriages between distant cousins, in spite of the fact that the same marriages would be sanctioned by the Roman Catholic Church.

Although their children hold widely differing Christian religious beliefs, their sense of Indianness and their sense of responsibility to their Santa Clara and Tewa way of life remains strong. They assist not only in Tewa ceremonials but also in the dances which are offered for public view. In family emergencies concerning their parents they assist not only in running their parents' household, but also in pious Indian prayer for the return to normal health and way of life.

With the training and inherited pottery producing ability, the Tafoya children and grandchildren have never had problems selling their work at an acceptable price. This is due not only to the fact that they are Margaret's descendants, but also to an increasing appreciation of good Indian art by the public as well as the knowledge that they are all accomplished traditional Tewa potters. Though they all grew up in an outstanding pottery producing atmosphere, they usually did not enter the field seriously until after marriage and the arrival of children. Margaret's children agree almost completely on pottery making procedures, with each contributing only slight modifications to a few of the steps.

On one point, the family is in universal agreement: no matter what the circumstance, the clay does not always mold to the potter's wish and there is no point in fighting it. The vessel envisaged is often quite different from the final result. There is nothing one can do but to follow the guidance of one who knows best—Mother Clay. In Margaret's words, "If you feel like working with clay, Mother Clay is always willing to help you. If you don't feel like working with it, Mother Clay knows it—what is in your heart—that today you don't feel like doing the work and so it won't work. It won't come out good. Every time you gonna take the clay you have to talk to Mother Clay [and think] how she has carried our people from so many many years back."

Since this writing has spread over a period of years, the peoples' lives which are covered and their relationships with one another have been constantly changing—particularly the younger Tafoyas. For this reason the authors apologize if the information about the various individuals is not as current as they would wish. The children will be discussed in chronological sequence.

Virginia Ebelacker—loosely translated Tewa name "Snowflakes"—more literally translated "Hoarfrost" Born 1925

The first child of Margaret and Alcario Tafoya, Virginia, spent the first eight or nine years of her life in the home of her grandparents Sara Fina and Geronimo Tafoya. Catastrophic events of her early childhood which included falling against a hot stove while learning to walk and surviving spinal meningitis at the age of three, left permanent physical damage including impaired eyesight and hearing. In spite of this, Virginia indulges in no self pity and has more than compensated for her problems probably due to her inherited Tafoya drive.

Virginia grew up with her first cousin Mary Cain (another Santa Clara potter of repute) who also spent her early years with Sara Fina and Geronimo. She has early memories of pleasant times at Mary Cain's home with Mary's parents, Victor and Christina Tafoya Naranjo, (Margaret's sister and a well established potter at the time). The two children were treated to the generous hospitality of Mary's parents who, they remember, often took them to the movies at Española. Both Mary Cain and Virginia are excellent sources of information concerning their grandparents and other Tafoya relatives.

Mary, Virginia and Teresita Naranjo, (still another accomplished Tafoya family potter) as children helped Christina polish pottery birds and animals which were sold for ten cents apiece,, good training for these three future potters. The first pottery that Virginia made without help was this type of animal form which was sold from her uncle Manuel's house. Manuel, Alcario, Margaret and others cleaned an old storage room and used this as a display and sales area where tourists and dealers could come to select purchases during the 1930's. This room was later converted into living space and is now part of the home of yet another outstanding Tafoya potter and artist, Grace Medicine Flower. In addition to this outlet for her work, Virginia also met the Fred Harvey buses where she sold her wares and those made by other members of the family.

Through the sixth grade, Virginia attended school in Española where one of her teachers was the same Clara True who had taught Margaret at the Santa Clara Day School which by then had been abandoned. Miss True, as with Margaret, took special interest in Virginia, giving her much encouragement with her art and music. Apparently the spinster teacher, whom Margaret remembers as wearing "mannish clothes", was a close friend of the family for many years before she retired and moved to Oklahoma. When, as a remnant of the Summer—Winter dispute, Margaret and Alcario were having problems locating a site for a home, it was Clara True who helped them obtain legal assistance and eventually prevail in locating their home on the land of their choice.

After sixth grade, Virginia continued her education through High School in Española. Between the tenth and eleventh grades, Margaret's cousin Felario (son of Tomas Tafoya) found a summer job for Virginia at the Cliff House in Manitou Springs, Colorado. Here she prepared salads and desserts for the tourists staying at the resort. Although homesick at first, she soon found this to be a pleasant break from pueblo life and decided to return the next summer. The second season proved to be so much to her liking that she remained at her work and missed the opening of school in the fall. Determined that she should have the education that he missed, Alcario sent a letter to her saying that if she did not return to school immediately he would come to the hotel to get her. She returned post haste to finish her schooling.

Virginia was married in 1945 to Robert E. Ebelacker who was employed at the Scientific Laboratory in Los Alamos. She left Santa Clara to live at Los Alamos where she found employment. Her work has continued for over 30 years at the Laboratories where she has served in various capacities including quality inspector and metallographic laboratory technician.

During this time in Los Alamos, she studied and worked at silversmithing, painting, and leather work, but it was not until 1968, after the couple had returned to Santa Clara to raise their family of two boys, that she decided to pursue pottery making as both a hobby and adjunct to her career. Heading the long past teachings of her mother and grandmother, she began to concentrate on pottery making. The payoff came quickly—for the next year at the New Mexico State Fair she won her first ribbon.

Of all of the steps required to produce a piece of pottery, Virginia enjoys the forming most and states that her large pieces are the most rewarding (Figure 4-2). Lacking a ceramic puki, she has used a basket as a starting form exactly as her ancient Tewa ancestors had done long before the development of the ceramic supports.

The piece that stands out in her memory was probably the largest she has made to date and one that has won the most awards for her. This masterpiece exceeds 19 inches in its smallest dimension. The most difficult forms for her to make are those which are flat on top (Figure 4-3) or those that require fitting lids. Maintaining her reputation, she won the award for excellence, technique and creativity in traditional pottery revival at Indian Market, 1985.

When time permits, perhaps after she retires from her Los Alamos position, she plans to experiment and improvise with different forms and designs. She also has as one of her goals, producing by traditional methods, a pot that will hold water. In addition, she aspires to collect an example of pottery from every member of her family and is not sure how far into the family past this collection will extend.

Her own words best summarize her philosophy concerning her pottery endeavors: "When I was young, my folks paid to teach me how to play the piano. I would sit there, and I can read notes, but I am not musically minded and no matter what, it was not there. If it's there, you can show people what you can do.—Smart can be different ways.—I was born at the right time because I have seen the old, old ways and I have seen the best of the new. I am not smart but I can do with my hands and I know the difference.—I've always inspected [at the Scientific Laboratories]. We have to do everything precisely, every step is important, and that is the way I feel about making my pottery."

Richard Ebelacker—Tewa name "Beaver Falls" named after his father's home town of Beaver Falls, Pennsylvania Born 1946

James Ebelacker—Tewa name "High Hawk" Born 1960

As children of working parents, Richard and James spent much of their early years with their grandparents Margaret and Alcario and still consider

the Tafoya's their second home. When possible they were included in the summer work activities at Royal Gorge, Colorado, as part of the dance group. Looking back, Richard still is very impressed by the fact that the Tafoyas were able to manage the group in the summer, maintain the crops and livestock at Santa Clara and at the same time produce a limited amount of pottery.

On the advice of Virginia, both boys started to make pottery about 1968. Their mother had convinced them that this would provide a good source of extra income while at the same time providing an activity which both would enjoy.

Richard served in the U.S. Marines, returning from Vietnam in 1966. In 1976 he married Yvonne Ortiz. They have two boys, Jerome (Tewa name "Rising Mist"—born 1977) and Jayson (Tewa name "White Cloud"—born 1980). In their father's words, Jerome is the family "honkie" and his brother Jayson is the family "Tewa". Richard is employed as a fireman in Los Alamos and also holds down a part time job in the stockrooms of the Scientific Laboratories. He would prefer raising livestock and making pottery in the fashion of his grandparents but respects the security provided by his Los Alamos work.

Lacking the time, Richard does not produce much pottery and is content if he can produce one major piece a year (Figure 4-4). The forming of the ware is the most enjoyable part of the process while sanding is the least enjoyable due to his allergies to dust. Figurines or animal pottery forms are difficult for him and therefore he avoids making them. He studies older pottery forms and the works of his mother and grandmother for inspiration and intends to produce only pieces which fall within traditional Tewa standards. He feels rewarded if he successfully forms vessel lips on larger pieces. With more time, he hopes to develop an ability for making miniature works.

Probably the most motivating and exciting time of Richard's pottery making career (up to 1984) came in August of 1981 at the Santa Fe Indian Market where he won a First Prize and a ribbon for Best of Division for a traditionally carved large pot. For this he is grateful for his grandmother Margaret's expert advice and help with the project. While thinking about this work, Richard commented, "I don't make that many, but whatever I make I like to say that this is something I think is pretty."

About his maternal grandparents whom he likes to visit early in the mornings on his days off from work, Richard has said, "She makes damned good pottery. She does OK in religion or anything. I can go down there, that's my second mother. When they ask for help, we'll go down there and brand calves, stuff like that. Any kind of crisis comes up, Grandma's there. She will back you up."

At the time of this writing, James Ebelacker is in

military service, stationed at San Antonio, Texas, and the authors regret not having had the opportunity of interviewing him. When on leave, we are told he helps with the pottery chores such as the digging and mixing of the clay. With the limited time he has at home, he only produces one or two pieces a year, however these are of high quality (Figure 4-5). There is some competition between the two brothers, especially when it comes to pottery making, each trying to produce something a little bigger or better than the other. If one uses the other's clay there is a strict rule that it must be replaced.

Lee Tafoya—Tewa name "Standing Snow" or "Snowdrift" Born 1926

As a young boy, Lee was constantly exposed to pottery making simply by being a Tafoya and helping his mother. He also developed a love of and respect for the soil and enjoyed helping his father with the farming and ranching work. Being the oldest boy, he was often given the responsibility for organizing work parties for himself and the others. The girls fondly remember these as they were always pleasant occasions. He could turn a wood gathering expedition up the Santa Clara Canyon into an enjoyable day's outing for all who were recruited. In his late teens he worked during the summer months at Los Alamos where he apprenticed as an iron monger, a career which he pursued for over four years.

In his last year of high school, Lee was drafted into the Army and had to leave home before being awarded his diploma which Margaret obtained for him in absentia. About his leaving for military duty, Margaret remembers, "The worst thing that hurt me, when his clothes were returned to me." Lee endeared himself to his family while in service by sending his pay to his parents to use for the younger children's school needs. During part of this time Alcario was governor of the pueblo, at that time a non-paying position, and Lee's pay was of great help in providing for the other children.

After completing army service, Lee first attended school in Berkeley, California, and later transferred to the Baptist Bible Institute in Florida where he matriculated. During his studies at the Bible Institute, he met and married Betty Barber in 1953.

About 1963, after returning to the pueblo, Lee and Betty started to work with Margaret on pottery and shortly thereafter began to produce works on their own. Betty was the only white woman involved in producing Santa Clara pottery (Anon. 1974: 63). From the start, Lee was capable of making rather large pieces (a skill attributed to some Santa Clara men) and won a prize for a water jar the first year in which he competed at the New Mexico State Fair in 1964. They worked as a team, with Lee forming and carving the vessels, while Betty smoothed and polished them. They later became well known for their large black plates carved usually with a "bear paw" decoration and particularly difficult to form and fire. Plates have a tendency to explode or crack during firing and for most makers the breakage rate during this step in the process is well above average.

It is unfortunate that neither Lee nor Betty have been well enough physically to produce much pottery in recent times. The traditional Santa Clara pottery pieces which they have made are illustrated in Figures 4-6 and 4-7.

Lee presently, and only on occasion, will assist other members of the family with their pottery work. He is considered an expert in the firing process. Occasionally he will form a piece which others finish but these are almost never signed. Lee remembers helping his mother fire one huge black storage jar that required 15 large laundry tubs of manure.

The Lee Tafoyas have four children, three of whom have taken up pottery making at least part time.

Phillis—Tewa name "Medicine Flower" Born 1955
Melvin—Tewa name "Shaking Flower" Born 1957
Allen Scott—Tewa name "White Medicine" Born 1960
Lynda—Tewa name "Blue Water Lake" Born 1962

Lee and Betty's oldest child, Phillis, remembers that she did her first pottery making when she was in junior high school, learning the rudiments from her grandmother Margaret. She has worked with her brother Melvin and both signed the work (Figure 4-8/top). She has one child, Shanda (Tewa name "Blue Cloud") born in 1975.

Melvin Tafoya prefers a shortened version of his name, Mel, and signs his pottery that way. He gives credit to his father for instilling in him his interest in pottery when he was about eight years old.

After attending college for a time, he returned to his home land and worked full time for an engineering company out of Santa Fe, New Mexico. In spite of the time required by this occupation, he makes a surprising number of pieces which he sells out of his father's home or through the local dealers. His work to date is almost exclusively limited to smaller pieces which he sometimes co-signs with one of his sisters. He is strongly motivated and wishes to become more involved with pottery making.

Allen Scott was away at school when this was written and the authors again regret not having had the opportunity of interviewing him. Other

Fig. 4-2 Ebelacker collection. Black polished storage jar with bear paw design, signed Virginia Ebelacker. ca. 1980. 19¾" height, 18" diameter. Very much in the Tafoya family tradition. Compare to those in Figure 3-39. Virginia periodically produces large masterpieces.

Fig. 4-3 Heard Museum, Phoenix, Az. #10-34. Black carved and polished jar, signed Virginia Ebelacker. 1974. 14½" diameter, 7¾" height. Beautifully proportioned as well as a difficult shape to form because of its horizontal top.

Fig. 4-4 V. Ebelacker collection. Red carved and polished jar with Avanyu design, signed Richard Ebelacker. ca. 1980. 12½" height, 11¾" diameter. Though this piece is cracked, a similar one won a first prize and Best of Division at the 1981 Southwest Association on Indian Affairs Market in Santa Fe, N.M.

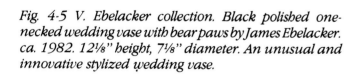

Fig. 4-5 V. Ebelacker collection. Black polished one-necked wedding vase with bear paws by James Ebelacker. ca. 1982. 12⅛" height, 7⅛" diameter. An unusual and innovative stylized wedding vase.

Fig. 4-6 Private collection. Black carved and polished jar by Lee and Betty Tafoya. ca. 1977. 7½" height, 7" diameter. Typical of their work, which is always traditional and often massive.

Fig. 4-7 Mrs. J.B. Jobe collection. Black polished vase by Betty and Lee Tafoya. ca. 1975. 3¾" height, 4" diameter.

Fig. 4-8 **Top:** *Private collection. Black carved and polished bowl signed Mel and Phillis Tafoya. 1981. 3⅞" diameter, 1⅞" height. Mel formed and carved this piece and Phillis polished it.*

Center: *Black carved and polished Avanyu bowl signed Mel and Lynda Tafoya. 1981. 4½" diameter, 2⅞" height. As with the piece shown above, Mel formed and carved and Lynda polished it.*

Bottom: *Black carved and polished bowl signed Tafoya-Oyenque. 1984. 3⅛" diameter, 2½" height. A well executed piece with a non-traditional stylized paw design and one small turquoise stone added. Lynda probably formed and polished while Oyenque (a San Juan), did the decorating.*

members of the family say that he has all of the know-how of pottery making and could produce works of his own.

The youngest of Lee's children, Lynda, has done more with pottery work than her brothers or sister. She too credits her father for teaching her most of what she knows about pottery. Her early work that was sold, was done in conjunction with her brother Mel. She, like the older sister, polished the pieces which Mel formed and co-signed them with him (Figure 4-8 center).

In 1983 Lynda started co-producing well formed pottery with a San Juan signed "Tafoya-Oyenque". This pottery (Figure 4-8 bottom) indicates that there is potential for the making of fine pottery works in the future. She has one child, born in 1984.

Jennie Trammel—Tewa name "Hidden Lake" Born 1929

The authors regret not having been allowed to have an opportunity of interviewing this shy and retiring lady. Her reclusive nature may be the result of many personal tragedies which she has experienced during her life.

Jennie makes her pottery by traditional techniques producing both red and black ware with usually carved designs (Figure 4-9). She is well known for both her traditional and unusual and innovative shapes. Among the many oddly shaped pieces made by Jennie, members of her family recall her production of a large number of Black-on-black decorated turtles. In addition to other unusual shapes such as droll animals, her unusual candlesticks may be found in many collections. Among others, she was awarded a Blue Ribbon Prize at the 1981 Inter-Tribal Ceremonial for a beautifully carved and polished pottery canoe (Figure 4-10).

Jennie was married to Charles Trammel and bore him two children, Karen and Gordon.

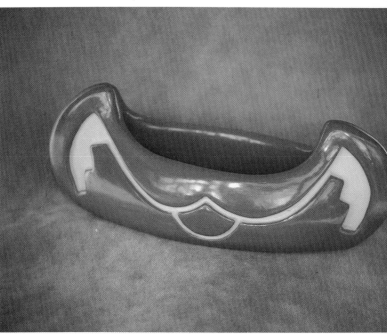

Fig. 4-9 Private collection. Black bowl all-over polished with bear paw carved inside bottom and diagonally carved melon design on the outside. Signed Jennie Trammel. 1974. 9" diameter, 3" height. A distinct and beautiful piece—simple and traditional.

Fig. 4-10 Private collection. Red carved and polished canoe signed Jennie Trammel. 1981. 9" long, 3¼" height. Well executed work with an exquisite polish.

Fig. 4-11 Private collection. Black polished duck signed Karen Davis. 1982. 3½" height. Following in her mother's footsteps, Karen seems to like making animal forms.

Karen—Tewa name and date of birth unknown
Gordon—Tewa name "Sea Shell" Born 1948

Karen Davis Beloris has three children, Cynthia, Elizabeth and Charles. Their dates of birth and Tewa names, if bestowed, are unknown. Karen occasionally produces black polished animals similar to those of her mother (Figure 4-11).

Gordon was involved in a tragic automobile accident which left him seriously handicapped. Following the accident, he moved to Jennie's home where he gives whatever assistance possible to his mother. He is the father of two children, Tara and Kelley, whose dates of birth and Tewa names are undetermined. There is no evidence of any pottery making activities of either Gordon or his children.

Fig. 4-12 Private collection. L. Blair photographer. Black carved and polished plate signed Mela Youngblood. 1983. 11" diameter. One of a series of uniquely different and gracefully decorated plates which Mela occasionally makes for fun.

Mela Youngblood—Tewa name "Yellow Mistletoe" Born 1931

As a child, Mela was much more into being a tomboy than entertaining serious thoughts about becoming a well known Santa Clara potter. She hoed the garden with more enthusiasm than most men and because required, she painted white outlines around pottery designs on polished pots for her parents. She remembers that her attitude changed when she and her sister Jennie sold their own small pieces to tourists in the Santa Clara plaza and she was able to enjoy the pocket money from these sales.

The tomboy grew into a very attractive woman who like many of her siblings left the pueblo to pursue a career. She obtained a nurses aid position at the Penrose Hospital in Colorado Springs, Colorado. She was married in 1953 and spent several years of her life as a military wife, moving from coast to coast and spending three years abroad in Holland. Her two children, Nancy and Nathan, were born during this period. When her husband, Walton Youngblood, was sent to Vietnam in 1968, Mela returned to Santa Clara to live near her family and bring up her children.

At this point in her life while contemplating becoming a potter, Mela had the following thoughts:

"Being an Indian and believing as I do—if I am going to work with clay, I must really search myself and understand myself first. My children were in school—so I was searching for something else that I could do and I could enjoy. Is this what I want to do? Am I going to be doing this just for fun or as a hobby, or is this going to be my life?"[2]

Fig. 4-13 Private collection. Black carved and polished Avanyu vase signed Mela Youngblood. 1976. 11½" height, 9" diameter. This large beautiful work came through the fire with a slight blemish which could not be detected by most observers. Following her policy, she refused to sell it, but gave it to a friend, otherwise it would have been destroyed.

Fig. 4-14 Mrs. J.B. Jobe collection. Black carved and polished melon bowls. **Left:** a signed Nathan Youngblood swirled melon bowl. 1976. 6" diameter, 5⅞" height. **Right:** by Mela Youngblood. 1976. 7⅞" diameter, 5⅞" height. *Also see Figure 4-18 by Nancy Youngblood Cutler.* Examples of meticulous polishing by the Youngblood family, which is one of the characteristics of their melon bowls.

Though she learned the skills of pottery making from her mother many years earlier, she credits her uncle Camilio with placing her thoughts into perspective which finally led to her decision to take pottery making seriously. By 1974 she entered 18 works at the Gallup Inter-Tribal Ceremonial and won 17 awards.

With much hard work Mela feels that anyone can become a potter, but it is also certain that with much hard work most do not have the capabilities of becoming a pottery artist such as Mela.

Mela is sentimental about many of her works and those of her family. She retains these in her personal collection and refuses to offer them for sale. Included in this group are a set of differently decorated plates to which she continues to add (Figure 4-12) and the first large storage jar she ever made, 25½ inches in diameter (Figure 3-39).

This storage jar was one of six which she formed and one of only three which made it to the final firing step. Two of these exploded during firing, a subject not discussed in the family for at least two weeks. When the only survivor of the original six pieces was safely recovered, she burst into tears and immediately called her mother probably feeling that she had finally earned the right to be considered a master Tewa potter. She doesn't waste tears on failures.

Mela is a perfectionist about her work, being more critical of her pieces than anyone judging a well recognized competition. With even the most minute imperfection Mela will discard the work as a second, either destroying it or giving it to a close friend. She can find the tiniest of flaws in her work, flaws which would be missed by most experts. (Figure 4-13)

Mela forms larger pieces which in a few instances may be plain but are generally beautifully carved. Her carving is described by her children as having a "soft boldness". Her daughter Nancy states, "It has strength, and yet it has a feminine touch about it." Because of an allergy to red slip, Mela produces only black pieces. She enjoys polishing and often will completely polish a surface eight times at one sitting to achieve the perfect finish. Removing entrapped air during the coiling process is the most difficult for her and it is not uncommon for her to lose seven out of ten of her pieces during firing because of air pockets.

Nathan and Nancy appreciate the meticulous habits of their mother, not only with her pottery, but also with her other endeavors. Mela is an excellent seamstress and embroiderer. Her children remember the delicate animal shaped pancakes which she used to make for them when they were young.

Both of her children agree that she never forced them into pottery making but rather by her example is responsible for the high standards which they set for themselves—they being every bit as meticulous about their art as is their mother. Mela in turn is justly proud of their accomplishments, but takes no credit. "My two, they just see me working. That's what they wanted to do and that is what they do. The motive is all theirs."

Fig. 4-15 Private collection. **Left:** *Red and tan Tesuque water jar with fluted rim. Maker unknown. 1920. 5¾" height, 6" diameter. This was the inspiration for* **right:** *black polished water jar with fluted rim signed Nathan Youngblood and Mela Youngblood (Mela's polishing) 1983. 5⅜" height, 5½" diameter.*

Nathan Youngblood—Tewa name "Deer Path" or "Deer Track" Born 1954

Nancy Youngblood Cutler—Tewa name "Yellow Aspen" Born 1955

It is of note that Nathan and Nancy were born out of the Santa Clara environment, spent their formative years (until they were 13 and 14) moving about in the mainstream of American life and even living abroad, yet are now the only ones of their generation who wholly support themselves with their pottery art. They both feel that their earlier childhood experiences outside of the pueblo have helped them in promoting and marketing their work because they have learned to be adaptable to many situations.

They began producing ceramic pieces about 1970 when their father gave them twenty dollars apiece on the condition that they would each make a piece of pottery for him. Nathan's first work he describes as "a tiny bowl which looked like a thimble." In turn, Nancy describes her piece as "a base with one coil and a serpent scratched on it." Their father entered each as a juvenile entry at the Gallup Inter-Tribal Ceremonial and each won a second place ribbon, providing great encourage-

ment to them. Both have almost continuously been winning prestigious awards for their work since that time.

In 1975, Nathan decided that he was more committed to making pottery than in continuing his education after his high school diploma. As a school boy he had made combination wood, leather and ceramic peace pipes for which he gained a reputation (Anon. 1974: 62) but he grew to making larger pieces.

For a few months between year's end 1976 and the beginning of 1977, he lived with Grandma Margaret and credits her with answering all of his questions and problems which he was encountering learning his art. He attests to her reputation as an exacting master but he is continually grateful to her for the skills which she taught him and the confidence which she instilled in him.

Fig. 4-16 Private collection. Plain black polished wedding jar signed Nathan Youngblood. 1976. 9½" height, 6¼" diameter. The slant of his wedding jar necks is similar to his great grandmother's, Sara Fina. Although unsigned, the lustrous polish on this piece was performed by his mother, Mela.

Fig. 4-17 Private collection. L. Blair photographer. Red and unslipped vase by Nathan Youngblood. 15" height, 11½" diameter. This shows Nathan's originality of design. The unslipped portion is referred to as "natural polish" by the potters.

Fig. 4-18 Private collection. One of Nancy Youngblood Cutler's swirled melon bowls, 2" high, coming out of a demonstration firing at Denver Museum of Natural History, Denver, Co. Nov. 12, 1983. The dull surface is the result of soot settling on the work during firing. When the ware has cooled, the soot will be washed and wiped off gently to reveal a brilliant polish beneath.

Nathan most enjoys and excels in the forming of a vessel. In his words, "I think that anybody can put a design on a pot but the essence of a true potter is shape and form. That is how I feel. Carving is a thing that helps to improve the appearance of my pottery once in a while, but it is not the total thing. Long, tall, curvaceous shapes are hard to make, large storage jars are hard to make and small intricate miniature shapes are hard to make. It is the shape that is hard to make, not putting the design on it. If you've got good tools and imagination, you can put a design on—but you're not a potter, you are a decorative artist. I want to be a great potter." In addition to the forms discussed above, he understandably considers the impressed (not carved) gourd or melon as being a very difficult form to make.

Most of the melon forms made by Nathan, his mother and his sister, are carved with the grooves as well as the ridges being polished, a Tafoya family practice. (Figure 4-14 and 4-18)

Nathan is fascinated by the older Tewa and prehistoric Indian pottery forms and is challenged to do a stylized reproduction of them adding his own variations (Figure 4-15).

The step of pottery making which Nathan cares for least is that of polishing. His early works were often not up to the Tafoya standards of polishing. When polishing he has learned to discipline himself to achieve a fine finish—a job he considers to be most tedious.

With time, Nathan has well mastered the firing step of the pottery making process and is respected by his immediate family for this skill. He is an excellent judge of firing times and is the first to blame himself when something goes wrong. His philosophy is that after all of the long, hard work that goes into the making of a piece, it is senseless to rush during the firing and better to take the time and do it correctly.

The variety of Nathan's output is surprising. He constantly produces new and beautiful shape variations, many of which are reminiscent of the older forms of his great grandmother Sara Fina (Figure 4-16), while others bear unique designs. (Figure 4-17).

Creative and independent, Nancy Youngblood Cutler always knew what she wanted and that was to create with her hands. While atending McCurdy High School in Española, she devoted much of her time to painting and sketching. She tried commercial art school in San Francisco but soon decided that it was not right for her and returned to Santa Clara. Living alone at the pueblo for a while, she prides herself in the fact that she became a self-taught "trial and error" potter, although she had watched her mother and grandmother work and had helped Mela with her polishing.

Fig. 4-19 Private collection. Black carved and polished necklace signed Nancy Youngblood Cutler. 1979. Seven miniature pottery shapes (from 1½" to 2½" long) that are produced at Santa Clara. The backs are hollowed out to lay flat. Ceramic beads between and strung on leather. This was such a difficult item to make and required so many firings that Nancy has refused to duplicate it.

A financial loan from her father saw her through a period of near starvation. This was a time of hard work and learning, but she gradually produced work which could be sold and provide her with food and clothing.

After the turning point with her pottery sales, she married her long time sweetheart, Paul Cutler. Nancy, her mother and her Tafoya grandparents graced the occasion by dressing in their beautiful native fashions. (Figure 2-54)

After their marriage, Nancy and Paul moved to Albuquerque, New Mexico, where Paul attended undergraduate and graduate medical schools after which they moved to Kansas where, at this writing, Paul is in his third year of internship. Nancy has provided much of their support by selling pottery. She knows that the day will come when she will have complete financial freedom and will be able to explore her limits in creating ceramic beauty.

Early on, Nancy decided that quality should take precedence over quantity and this path has led her to being awarded many prizes and honors for her work. She has gained a reputation for her miniature ceramic "gems". Perhaps due to maternal influence she is a perfectionist, often spending several hours polishing one small section of a tiny work of art. She always feels ill at ease when polishing for fear that she is not producing her best. She has learned that a lesser proportion of sand or temper to clay in her mix produces a better finish since the sand particles tend to float to the surface when polishing tiny, thin-walled vessels. Designing and carving are her favorite steps in pottery making, with great attention being given to minute detail. She considers sanding to be the most tedious step.

Nancy is most anxious for prospective buyers and the general public to understand how time consuming and exacting the making of true art pottery is and also wants them to understand the economics involved. She is determined to maintain her reputation and stresses this in her statement, "You are only as good as your last blue ribbon." Nancy, contrary to what she feels, is far past the stage where blue ribbons will have any effect on her excellent reputation.

Her pottery is much in demand and she has a waiting list of customers. In spite of this, she continues to set aside her outstanding work for the various southwest Indian art competitions. At these she often has a difficult time in limiting her sales to one per buyer but she strictly adheres to this policy. She is probably best known for her intricately carved and polished melon jars (Figure 4-18), although she produces an infinite variety of other pieces, each having a unique charm of its own (Figures 4-19 and 4-20).

Fig. 4-20 Private collection. Red and tan carved and polished miniature jar signed Nancy "Yellow Aspen" Youngblood. 1977. 1½" height, 2⅛" diameter. A meticulous potter, Nancy fired this piece four times before she was satisfied with the final results.

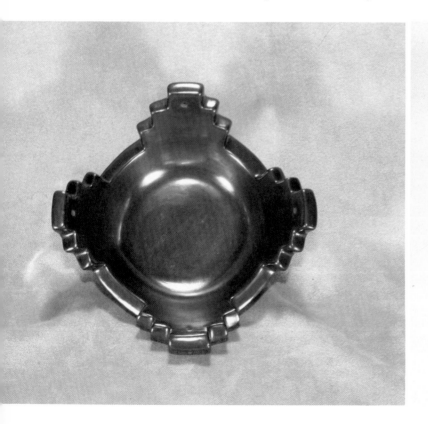

Fig. 4-21 Private collection. Black polished kiva step bowl signed Toni Roller. 1974. 7" diameter, 2¾" height. One of the many of this type on which Toni has built her reputation.

Fig. 4-22 Rick Dillingham collection. Black carved and polished jar signed Toni Roller. 1978. 7⅜" diameter, 4¼" height. A good example of Toni's nicely executed and delicately carved pottery, which shows her mastery of producing a difficult shape.

Fig. 4-23 **Left:** *Susan Whittington collection and photo. Red polished bowl with shallow paw carved design, 1984. 10" diameter, 6" height. This is an example of her more recent and larger pieces.*

Right: *Clifford Roller collection. L. Blair photo. 1984. Black polished jar with two carved bear paws opposite each other by Clifford Roller. 6¾" height, 5¾" diameter.*

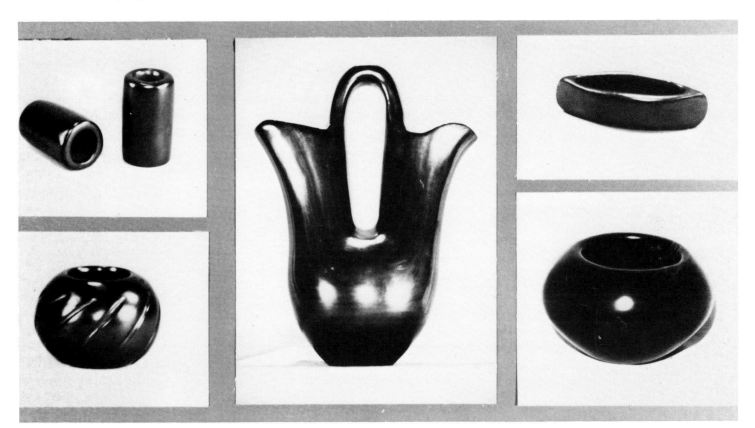

Fig. 4-24 Private collection. **Upper left:** *A pair of black polished candlesticks signed Charlie Lewis. 1983. 3" height. 1¼" diameter. Polished and fired by his grandmother Toni Roller, these are two of the three first pieces formed by a great-grandchild of Margaret Tafoya's.*

Center: *Plain black polished wedding vase by Deborah Roller Lucia Vaughn and signed "Morning Star" Roller. 1982. 7½" height, 5½" diameter. Living so far from the pueblo and busy raising a family, it is difficult for Debbie to produce much pottery.*

Lower left: *Black carved and polished bowl signed Tim Roller. 1983. 2½" diameter, 1¾" height. The slightly swirled diagonally carved lines give the impression of a melon pot.*

Lower right: *Plain black polished jar signed Jeff Roller. 1985. 8" height, 6" diameter. Jeff's pots have been increasing in size.*

Upper right: *Black polished canoe signed B.J. Roller. 1983. 4¼" long, 1½" wide. Polished and fired by his mother Toni, this is one of his first attempts which was probably inspired by two museum exhibitions of his grandmother Margaret Tafoya's work.*

Fig. 4-26 Lu Ann Tafoya collection. Black polished jar with bear paw design signed Lu Ann Tafoya. ca. 1982. 11½" diameter, 11⅛" height. Lu Ann's pottery, both red and black, is increasing in size and quality.

Fig. 4-25 Lu Ann Tafoya collection. Red carved and polished wedding vase signed Lu Ann Tafoya. ca. 1982. 17" height, 9⅞" diameter. The shapes, particularly the vertical necks on Lu Ann's wedding vases, bear a close resemblance to her mother's work. Even the carved design on this piece could be mistakenly thought of as Margaret's or Alcario's. Beautifully polished.

Fig. 4-27 Private collection. Black polished miniature gourd pot signed Michelle Tapia. 1976. 1" height, 1¼" diameter. Being one of her first, this piece is nicely done. Michelle's present production is much larger in size and more sophisticated.

Fig. 4-28 Private collection. Red and tan carved and polished vase signed Mary E. Archuleta. 1974. 8½" height, 6½" diameter. This photo does not do justice to the beautiful red luster of Mary Esther's work, but does show her ability to form graceful shapes and highly polish slipped and unslipped areas.

Fig. 4-29 Private collection. Red polished bowl with incised mica wash. ca. 1980. 4½" height, 5¼" diameter. An interesting combination of Santa Clara and San Juan pottery which is unique to Mary Esther. The light portion is unslipped, incised, and mica washed.

Fig. 4-30 Private collection. Red carved and polished bowl signed Sheila Archuleta. 1979. 3" diameter, 2⅛" height. Grandmother Margaret supervised the making of this bowl—one of Sheila's first. Though time is scarce, Sheila continues to produce promising pieces.

Fig. 4-31 Private collection. Black polished miniature wedding jar with carved bear paw design signed Shirley "Cactus Flower" Tafoya. 1974. 2¼" height, 1½" diameter. One of Shirley's earlier pieces, very well done. She continues to produce dainty miniatures well executed with an occasional larger one.

Fig. 4-32 Shirley Tafoya collection. Black polished miniature water jar with double rainbow bands by Shirley Tafoya. 1983. 1¾" height, 3" diameter. With its rather squat appearance, the proportions of this piece are reminiscent of her grandmother's work (Sara Fina). (Figure 2-13)

Nancy's signatures have changed since her marriage. Prior to 1979, she inscribed her signature delicately "Nancy Yellow Aspen Youngblood" followed by a date. She has changed this to "Nancy Youngblood Cutler" followed by a date, adding "Yellow Aspen" when space permits. Usually the area on which the signature is placed is so small that there is no room for more and one wonders how these inscriptions could be done without the use of a strong magnifying glass—it often requires a magnifying glass to read them.

Her feelings about her work and that of her contemporaries: "I think of my pots as my little children, each one a little creation...I have that feeling about other people's pottery, too...I think that the personality of the person making the pot rubs off. A lot of times it shows very little and sometimes it shows a lot. That person's personality is in that pot." Proving her point, Nancy won the award for most creative design in any classification at Indian Market, 1985.

Nathan and Nancy are traditional in their approach to their work. They respect Mother Clay, observe the traditional amenities in digging clay, and try to be in the proper frame of mind when working with clay. Occasionally each departs from tradition to keep the work distinct and vibrant. They both produce black, red and tan pieces which are either plain or more often carved.

Toni Roller—Tewa name "Green Leaves" Born 1935

Early in the morning of the 29th of May, 1935, as Margaret was shoveling manure to smother her pottery fire, she received a signal which told her that her next baby was about to arrive. Alcario, who was helping with the firing, ran to get Sara Fina, and young Virginia who was observing the firing procedure was left to finish the operation. So, unexpectedly Toni arrived on the scene. No one remembers how the pottery fared.

Toni, like Mela, grew up as a tomboy during the depression years. As her first pottery making project she remembers making clay marbles since there was little money for the purchase of these or any other toys. When a firing was in progress, she would throw her hand formed marbles into the flame to harden them. Eventually she became such a marble enthusiast that she lost two of her fingernails playing the game. When a little older, she made what she calls small unpolished "thunderbirds" but they were never sold. She, like the others, grew up surrounded by pottery.

Toni and Mela are probably the two most extroverted people in the family. As an outgoing person Toni remembers resenting being left at home while her parents visited surrounding towns to sell their pottery. She claims that she never saw the city of Santa Fe (some 20 miles from the pueblo) until she was 16 years old and that visit was occasioned by her need to have her McCurdy High School graduation pictures taken.

Immediately after graduation, when Mela was in nurses training school and the rest of the family was preparing to move to Royal Gorge for the summer, Toni decided to follow Mela and applied for admittance to the fall term of the same nursing school. In order to keep busy until school opened, she took a part time job. It was during this time that she met Ted Roller, who was stationed at the army installation of Fort Carson near "The Springs".

When invited to the pueblo to meet Toni's parents, she teased Ted into believing that Indian etiquette demanded that one should take trade goods or money when visiting any Indian reservation. He survived the joke, and Ted and Toni were married at Santa Clara in 1954 amidst the wonderful Santa Clara celebrations and feasts, most of which were provided by Margaret and Alcario. From the beginning, Ted has felt great admiration and respect for both Margaret and Alcario.

After finishing his military service, Ted found work in Albuquerque and the couple lived there for 12 years, visiting Santa Clara on weekends. Toni would often take some of Margaret's pots home to Albuquerque to polish and return them the following weekend, but this was the extent of her pottery making at that time. Toni relates, "A story that is told through the grandparents and great grandparents—when you're an Indian, you are going to go back to your home base." Following this tradition, the Roller family returned to Santa Clara following a pattern set by the preceding Tafoya children.

Back at the pueblo Toni observed, "Everywhere we went someone was working on pottery—why not do that too." She remembers her grandmother Sara Fina working with clay but states that her mother is the one responsible for her becoming a serious potter. This did not happen until 1968 when most of her children were finally in school and she had the time to begin working in earnest. By 1973, she began competing in shows and winning ribbons for her work.

One damp year, Toni spent much time and effort in preparing her pottery for Indian Market. She postponed firing as long as she could in hopes that the ground would dry, but finally was forced to proceed with the operation. Her worst fears were realized when she lost most of her work because of moisture damage and had very little to show for all of her efforts. It was then that she decided that she would always have a dry firing location. Ted built a shallow cement pit for her which she always keeps covered along with all of her firing materials. Following these precautions and using portable home made wood wind screens, she is now able to fire safely most days of the year.

Toni seems to enjoy demonstrations because she is confident about her subject and wants the public to know how much work goes into a piece of pottery. Her outgoing and hospitable nature welcomes questions and spectators while she works, but understandably she would rather not have "help" either from her family or well meaning bystanders when she is firing.

Toni specializes in traditional black polished and carved pieces and is best known for her kiva step ceremonial bowls (Figure 4-21). She works hard at keeping the walls of her vessels as thin as possible and thus her carving is narrow and shallow as compared to the deeper trenched work of others in her family. Her favorite designs are the Avanyu, bear paws, kiva steps, sun symbols and feathers. Her feather designs are distinctive, with each feather having an extra curl at the tip. Her most beautiful creations are her small mouthed bowls whose flattened tops are delicately carved (Figure 4-22).

Now that her children are grown, like her mother, Toni often manages to have grandchildren around, but she still manages to devote time to her work and can produce many delicate pieces.

Susan—Tewa name "Rose by the Water" Born 1955
William—Tewa name "Rocky Mountain" Born 1956
Deborah—Tewa name "Morning Star" Born 1957
Timothy—Tewa name "White Rain" Born 1959
Clifford—Tewa name "Tobacco Flower" Born 1961
Jeffrey—Tewa name "Valley of Flowers" Born 1963
Brandon Jayson—Tewa name "Painted Quiver" Born 1970

All of Ted and Toni's children have made small pieces of pottery but none have pursued it seriously as a profession until recently.

Susan is married to James Whittington and is a professional photographer in Española, New Mexico. The dainty pots which Susan has produced were not usually sold but were given to friends as gifts on special occasions. She has admitted that she never enjoyed making pottery until recently. Inspired by Grandma Margaret's pottery show at the Denver Museum of Natural History in 1983, she tried making larger vessels and these larger pieces are giving her much satisfaction. (Figure 4-23)

Susan's son by a former marriage, Charlie Lewis, surprised his family in the fall of 1983 by making a couple of small pottery pieces which were placed on exhibit with the pottery of Margaret and her family in Denver (Figure 4-24). This was the first pottery work to be made by a grandchild of Toni and a great grandchild of Margaret.

Deborah Lucia Vaughn has one child and lives in California. She visits the pueblo during the summer and likes to work on pottery at these times. Her pottery usually takes the form of small or miniature works (Figure 4-24).

William, Timothy, Clifford and Jeffrey Roller have learned the processes of pottery making but, until lately, have shown no inclination to make a career of Santa Clara ceramics. (Figures 4-23 and 4-24)

Brandon Jayson, called B.J. by his family, is in school and lives at home with his mother and father. He has recently produced a few small pottery pieces. (Figure 4-24)

Perhaps some day one or more of Toni's offspring will understand Toni's feelings for pottery making and follow in her footsteps. "Like a dressmaker, nobody's pushing you, something inside of you kind of says, 'come on'."

Leo—Tewa name "Red Fox" Born 1936

Margaret's seventh child, Leo, has never produced pottery but has assisted his mother in her work for as long as he can remember. Leo has a very pleasant and agreeable personality and a thin, wiry build like his mother, He farms and raises livestock at the pueblo and also is of great help to his father and brother Lee in their agricultural activities. Leo has never married.

Lu Ann—Tewa name "Corn Silk" Born 1938

Lu Ann spent her childhood at the pueblo attending the day school and assisting with the hoeing of the fields, household chores and helping her mother polish and fire pottery. As a child she particularly remembers dealers coming to the Tafoya house to buy Margaret's pottery, usually on Fridays. Lu Ann finished high school just outside Española at McCurdy School. Following graduation she attended a trade school in Santa Fe.

Following her trade school training, she married and moved to Colorado, first to Denver and then to Colorado Springs where she now resides. Her occupation is that of a quality control inspector for a large tool manufacturing company. She has worked steadily at this job for a number of years. Lu Ann is looking forward to retiring in the future and to making pottery a full time career.

While vacationing at Santa Clara, she made her first successful pieces of pottery. This group consisted of some small bowls and a cookie jar with a lid.

Most of her vacations and other free times are spent at the pueblo where she digs clay with the family, helps members of the family (particularly her mother) with polishing, and assists with all of the extra chores involved with feast days and other family social functions.

Lu Ann brings her raw materials such as the slip materials, clays and temper from the pueblo to her home in Colorado Springs where she forms and finishes her pottery up to the firing stage. Her polishing ranks with the best in the family. When the pottery is finished, she brings it back to the pueblo for firing at her mother's home.

At the time of interview, Lu Ann found it possible to make only six to twelve pottery pieces per year. Most of these are marketed from her parents' home but she does withhold some of her better work which she enters in various competitions. Coiling is the most difficult operation for her, particularly in the formation of wedding vases and plates. Polishing is the most enjoyable part of her potting.

Lu Ann's pottery art has improved to such an extent and she has been so influenced by her mother that it is sometimes difficult to distinguish her work from Margaret's when their medium sized vessels are compared. (Figure 4-25 and 4-26) She is recognized as a premium artist in spite of the limit of her output and was awarded the Jack Hoover award for Santa Clara pottery at Indian Market 1985. Before her divorce she signed her work "Lulu Tapia or L. Tapia", but her more recent pieces are signed "Lu Ann Tafoya". She is a very shy, modest person who until recently had the feeling that she was not involved enough with pottery making to seriously enter the various competitions, in spite of the fact that she had already been awarded several ribbons.

Lu Ann is the mother of two grown children.

Michelle Tapia—Tewa name "Wood Blossom" Born 1960
Daryl Whitegeese—Tewa name "White Geese"— Daryl has legally adopted his Tewa name as his surname. Born 1964

Michelle has her mothers shy and modest characteristics. She lives and works at the Pojoaque Pueblo with her small daughter Mindy June (Tewa name "Yellow Bird"). In 1976, she began to produce small pottery pieces (Figure 4-27) but she has been inspired by exhibitions of her grandmother's work and is now forming larger works.

Lu Ann's son Daryl is more interested in following a career in electronics rather than pottery making. In 1983, he married Yvette Powless. The couple have one child and now make their home in Colorado Springs. In attendance at their wedding were at least twenty well known Santa Clara potters, again illustrating the fact that on occasions such as this all differences are put aside and the Tewa show their remarkable ability to unite. Should a collector have but one work from all of the potters present at that wedding, he would possess a remarkable Santa Clara collection of much value.

Mary Esther—Tewa name "Standing Red Flower" literally translated "Indian Paint Brush" Born 1942

Mary Esther's memories of her youth include little of her grandmother Sara Fina except for the large storage jars that were in use at their home. She vaguely recalls the business of their home during the days when her father was Governor, but vividly remembers the fact that her mother was (and still is) always in motion—darting about the house doing chores, cooking, making pottery, preparing for feasts and other special ocassions and caring for her family. As a child she resented her mother's perfectionist ideas regarding the proper method of polishing a piece of pottery. She now realizes that it was her youthful impatience rather than the fastidiousness of her mother that created her problems.

Beyond a few insignificant bowls, Mary Esther remembers little of her youthful pottery making endeavors. Gradually, by watching and asking questions of her mother and father, her pottery making skills developed. In spite of this, she gave little thought to becoming a serious potter until several years after her marriage.

Mary Esther and Anselmo (Pop) Archuleta were married in 1967 and made their home in his home pueblo of San Juan. Shortly thereafter, children started to arrive and there was little time for pottery making. At first she made a small number of red or black carved pieces typical of her home pueblo of Santa Clara and she particularly remembers her "swan ashtrays" which resembled bowls with long necks and tails.

Mary Esther has always admired the San Juan type pottery, particularly the incised type[3] made by her new neighbors and with Margaret's urging she began to experiment. "She [Margaret] gave me the idea. I was looking through some old photographs of some San Juan pots and she asked me, 'Why don't you try some? There are a lot of potters around here but mostly they are not doing the incising the way they used to'—they were coming out with carving— and [I thought] if I just take the time I could do that. She [Margaret] told me, I'll tell you how to design it, I'll give you ideas on those geometric designs like they used to do.' The time when she used to stay up here [Margaret's early days when she spent time with her brother Juan Isidro and his family], she remembers people up here from the times that she used to stay or visit.—She remembers those pots. My mom can remember more things than anyone else about certain things."

With Margaret and Alcario's encouragement, experimentation led to a beautiful and unique style of Mary's own, a blending of the designs of both Santa Clara and San Juan. "A lot of times I would sit there—not knowing what would look good on this pot and she [Margaret] always suggested things. My dad too, the same way—'cause they know design work. Then I would go from there with my own designs.—After a while you already know how it is going to look when it is finished."

Mary Esther's pottery is usually red with a carved design, often highlighted with the tan produced from polishing the natural unslipped clay (Figure 4-28). Sometimes the decoration will consist partly of San Juan incised design with a mica wash being applied to the incising before firing (Figure 4-29).

Mary Esther returns to Santa Clara to dig clay with her family (she is not encouraged to use the clay available to the San Juan people) and to fire her pottery at the home of her family at Santa Clara. Her home at San Juan is located atop a small hill which is constantly windy and therefore is a poor location for firing. She also enjoys working with her sisters on this step of the process. Although perfectly capable, she finds that she must force herself to make black pottery and admits that it is nice not to have to think about having manure on hand for firing. She has become a master in polishing red slip which dries faster than that applied to a pot which is to be black, so she has developed a fast working skill.

She enjoys using her imagination in making the design fit the shape of the formed piece. Sanding is the least liked part of the operation and the formation of wedding jars and plates seems to be difficult for her. Ingeniously, she has been able to make some fairly large jars using an ordinary terracotta flower pot holder for her puki. She aspires to produce huge pots and admires the skill necessary to make handled vessels such as those of her mother and grandmother. She rightfully resents jealous remarks that her pots resemble her mother's too closely (which they do not), with the accompanying inferences that perhaps Margaret, and not she, made them.

Since 1972 she has been entering and winning pottery competitions. Margaret asked for her help in polishing a huge red storage jar which won the Best of Division and Best of Show at the 1978 Indian Market. Mary was timid about undertaking such a monumental task but consented. When the piece was so widely praised, it gave her the confidence needed to seriously enter all competitions.

Mary Esther believes in close family relationships, is a competent hairdresser, and an avid collector of the pottery works of her family. The Archuleta children are:

Sheila—Tewa name "Rain Water Lake" Born 1967
Barry—Tewa name "White Lightning" Born 1969
Bryan—Tewa name "Falling Blossom" Born 1973

Of the three school aged children, only Sheila has shown an interest in pottery making to date. Sheila attends school in Española and works on her pottery as time permits, often under the guidance of her grandmother Margaret. To date she has produced some beautifully polished small pieces. History often repeats itself. When questioned about one piece of her work (Figure 4-30), she admitted that Margaret had forced her reluctant granddaughter to repolish the work eight times before it was accepted for firing. Mary Esther says that, like herself, Sheila has to learn Tewa patience when making pottery.

Roger—Tewa name "Flower Bird" Born 1944

Very little is known about Roger Tafoya, the last born son of Margaret and Alcario. As a young boy he was a principal dancer with his family at Royal Gorge where he became a favorite of Mr. Wann, proprietor of the resort and also a director of the Denver and Rio Grande Railroad. With this connection Roger often was given free railroad rides with his brothers and cousins.

He was married to Ruth Gutierrez and lived in California for a period of years, returning in 1982 when Alcario became very ill. To the authors' knowledge, he has remained at Santa Clara. Roger's children are:

Bernadette, Patricia, Rena, and *Rogers,*—Tewa names unknown. Dates of births unknown.

As far as is known to date, none of Roger's children have shown an interest in pottery making. Possibly, like so many others in the family, they will develop into potters at a later stage in their lives.

Shirley—Tewa name "Cactus Blossom" Born 1947

Shirley, youngest in the family, is nicknamed "Berda". A family picnic in Santa Clara Canyon had been planned for Mother's Day 1947, but this occasion developed into Shirley's birthday rather than an outing. Occasionally, to this day Shirley is reminded by one of her sisters that "Berda spoiled the picnic."

Like her siblings, part of her environment as a child was spent in the presence of pottery making and playing with the clay as a toy. She ocassionally was able to sell a few pieces to keep herself in bubble gum. She admits that these were no more than lumps of pliable clay into which she had pushed her thumb to form a mass which somewhat resembled a crude miniature bowl.[4]

Shirley was part of the Tafoya family that performed at Royal Gorge in the summertime and the older members of the family recall "Berda's tiny moccasins" on which Margaret spent so much time keeping them in repair for the dances.

About 1964 or 1965, Shirley won her first prize for pottery at the New Mexico State Fair. This award was given to an eight-inch tall lamp base. However, it was not until the fall of 1973 that she began to give serious consideration to making a full time career out of pottery.

In the meantime, she had prepared for a career as a medical assistant, working full time at the Española Hospital. Her pottery making finally became so important to her that she is now following this endeavor as a full time occupation.

Shirley is a meticulous potter who excels in miniature works, likes to carve, and enjoys competing and winning in the various judged pottery events. In spite of the fact that she enjoys the competitions she does not care for the pressure involved in getting ready for them. She feels obligated to have a certain number of pieces ready for each show and until these are made she does not feel that she should compete.

She produces both red and black works but claims, with too much modesty, that she cannot make larger pieces. Her polishing is outstanding, so good in fact that her work is often difficult to photograph (Figures 4-31 and 4-32).

When preparing to decorate or carve a piece she establishes the boundaries within which the design will be contained in a unique manner. A pencil is rested on a stack of poker chips, (certainly not traditional Tewa tools) and the ware is rotated against the pencil point so that the bottom border is inscribed. She then adds additional chips until the desired top height is established and she repeats the process. Shirley does not take the credit for developing this unusual method but will quickly give the credit to her nephew, Nathan Youngblood. Shirley always is quick to give credit where credit is due.

Her most severe competitor has been her niece, Nancy Youngblood Cutler. Since there is only eight years difference in their age and they have strong facial resemblances, Nancy has been thought to be a younger sister rather than a niece. They worked closely together from 1973 until the time that Nancy moved to Kansas in 1982. They have long since agreed not to conflict but to cooperate. Leaving personalities out of their pottery discussions, each has the ability to criticize and accept criticism from the other in a positive and constructive manner. The sole object of the discussions is an attempt to produce perfect pottery pieces.

Although usually quiet and shy in the presence of strangers, Berda has a subtle sense of humor and is an accomplished mimic. She contributes much to the family welfare and unity, assisting with the work of any who ask and acting as a chauffeur for those who do not drive. She is an avid student on the history of the Tewa and whenever the opportunity presents itself, she memorizes the shapes and designs of the pottery of her ancestors.

Berda, like her mother and sisters, devotes much time and thought to her personal appearance at the various markets and shows. The Tafoyas are always splendid at these events, dressing in long skirts with plain blouses which show to perfection the classic native American jewelry which they are all fond of wearing. When possible, the final touch is their footwear—the white moccasins of their people.

Of all of the daughters, Shirley most resembles her mother in appearance. This is most striking when early photographs of Margaret are compared to the present ones of Berda. Her philosophy of pottery making is also similar to Margaret's, "You have to put your heart into it."

It is said of Margaret that she always wants children around her. By the time that Berda arrived she was already a grandmother. After giving birth to twelve children (two of whom passed away within a year of their birth) she, following Tewa custom, adopted three boys who needed a mother. Phillip and Kenneth were the sons of her deceased niece Cecelia and Wayne was a grandchild of Margaret's older sister Dolorita. None of these boys are potters, although Wayne assists Margaret when needed. The tragic and untimely death of Kenneth in 1982 was deeply felt by both Alcario and Margaret.

There are often children in the home of the elder Tafoyas and Margaret enjoys their presence in spite of the mischief and problems involved. Margaret never uses the expression "when I die" but always says, "if I die." She and those who know her expect that she will be here forever, raising children and instructing them and commissioning them with the responsibility of carrying on and passing on the traditions of Tewa pottery making skills until the end of time.

"We're not pretty but we're good workers. The children, I'm proud of them because they like to do this pottery. Long time ago my mother used to worry. She said, 'We're the ones used to do a lot of pottery—and I don't want this pottery to die.—When your children grow old enough to handle this clay, make them work.'—So that's how [they come to be] doing it today."

Footnotes

Chapter One

[1] The "small house country" is located some forty miles northwest of the present pueblo of San Juan, beginning where the Rio Chama is joined by the Rio Gallina. Above the juncture, both rivers flow through deep canyons, and it is on the mesa above these canyons that the ruins are to be found.

[2] Research indicates that Fray Marcos was a man of questionable integrity and bravery, who was responsible for the fable of untold wealth among the pueblos and the incursions of ruthless treasure-seekers who blazed paths of destruction throughout the pueblo world.

[3] Terrell (1968) covers the history of this remarkable man.

[4] An excellent and informative account of the explorations of Coronado and his men is given by Horgan (1954: 109-153).

[5] Similar pottery was discovered by Kidder during his excavations of Pecos (Kidder and Shepard 1936).

[6] This and the second site are described by Harrington (1916:246-247) and are illustrated on fig. 1-2 as sites one and two. Evidence of the existence of these locations continues to be found as the Santa Clarans dig foundations for new homes, trenches for new utilities, and roadbeds. Site One appears to have been abandoned before the arrival of the Spanish, and Site Two was probably where the pueblo was located when visited by Castaño.

[7] At present, all that remains to remind the traveller of the existence of San Gabriel are historical markers one and one-half miles east of the actual site on State Highway 68, and a permanent monument on the site itself. The old capital is now a vague pile of rubble.

[8] Hackett (1942, xxii-xxiv) covers this event and gives a complete description of the Revolt and the events that immediately preceeded it. Simmons (1980: 11-15) also gives an excellent summary of the causes of the revolt.

[9] It is doubtful that the decision to move was sudden; apparently, negotiations had been going on with the Hopi for a long time, possibly as long as six years. There are two versions of the exact motivation: the Hopi claim that the Tewa requested asylum and desired to become Hopi; the Tewa claim that they were invited to Hopiland to act as defenders against the Spanish and the nomadic raiders and that one of the conditions was that they keep their own identity (Yava 1978: 26-33; Dozier 1966: 17-19).

[10] Had the Spanish not returned when they did, it is possible that some of the pueblo civilizations known today would have passed from existence.

[11] Pueblo land grants, eventually validated by the United States government in 1858 (fig. 1-6), were made by the Spanish Crown three years before the Spanish reestablished themselves in the Rio Grande Valley. The original grants, whose parallel boundaries were established by measuring one league in each of the cardinal directions from the large cross located in each pueblo's church cemetery, should have encompassed 17,741.96 acres; the grant registered in the name of the Santa Clara people totals only 17,368.52 acres (Kessell 1979: 429). The fact that such rights were recognized at the highest governmental levels did not deter Governor de Vargas from creating a Spanish settlement at Santa Cruz, well inside the boundaries set aside for the Santa Clarans. Documentation of most original pueblo grants was in existence at the time of their final validation by the U.S.; however, that for Santa Clara could not be located. Could this be connected in any way with de Vargas' seemingly illegal actions?

[12] Today, long lines of pilgrims may be seen travelling the road to the shrine during Easter holy season, led by the Archbishop of Sante Fe. Members of Margaret's family have participated in this annual procession.

[13] Records of participation in these sacraments were kept in the mother church and provided the primary basis for researching the Tafoya genealogy. Records go back to shortly after the Spanish returned to the area.

[14] One of the first art forms developed by the padres consisted of paintings on tanned hides which depicted saints and various scenes from the Bible. Many of these paintings were located at the church at Santa Cruz while others were displayed in the surrounding pueblos' missions. Information on this art form was supplied by Captain John G. Bourke, aide to Indian Affairs in 1881. While on a visit to Santa Cruz he purchased one of these almost extinct hide paintings upon which he commented, "The account that the Indians give of it is that it was formerly the altar piece of one of their churches, Nambe, I think, and that about a century ago (1780) one of their Archbishops directed that all pictures of that class should be replaced by more pretentious works upon muslin or canvas. This decree banished to the retirement of a private house the efforts upon which some pious priest concentrated all of his artistic skills for weeks, or perhaps months" (Bloom 1936: 24).

[15] Title to various pieces of land was often in doubt. As a consequence, disputes have continued throughout the years; much of the land in question has gradually been returned to the Santa Clarans through a series of long and costly legal wrangles. The land grab, which grew to alarming proportions during the time of

Mexican control, did not end with the annexation of the river province by the U.S., but has continued until recently, when, with the passage of new legislation and with the native Americans becoming increasingly aware of their rights and how to preserve them, property is reverting to Tewa control.

[16] It is possible that a few, and possibly all, of the Montoyas associated with the revolt were Margaret Tafoya's ancestors. Fortunately, the Santa Cruz church records and Hill's enquiries (1982: 363-374) allow the tracing of ancestors to a point where both grandmothers' names are revealed: Candelaria Tafoya Gutierrez (b. circa 1815) and Tomacita Montoya (b. circa 1820). Since the names Tafoya and Gutierrez are common in Santa Clara and Montoya is not, but *is* found at Taos, it is possible that there is a relationship between the Tafoyas and the Montoyas. Though Margaret is unclear as to the exact connection, she is certain that one exists at Taos.

[17] This magnificent piece, with its many mends and patches, is part of the collection of the Philbrook Art Center in Tulsa, Oklahoma.

[18] Sprague (1957) discusses the Anglo duplicity and greed that stripped the Ute of their land and wealth.

[19] Traces of many of these relationships, established well over half a century ago, exist to this day, and are the prime reason why many fine museum and private collections of Santa Clara pottery are extant, particularly throughout the state of Colorado.

[20] Although the time tables indicated that the train was due to pass Santa Clara at eleven A.M. it was, almost without exception, late. The lack of determination to run the train on time is witnessed by Edith Warner's memories of the train crews dropping off ice for use in her tea room and who would often tarry to have a cold drink on a hot day or to have a meal in the tiny dining room of her establishment (Church 1959: 40).

[21] During its last three years, the Chili Line was the backdrop for two motion pictures: *The Texas Rangers* (filmed on location in Españ in 1938) and *The Light that Failed*. The latter and more spectacular, required the water level of the Rio Grande to be raised by several feet through temporary damming; for filming purposes, the Rio Grande became the Nile River, some six hundred Tewa became Africans, and pieces of rolling stock were altered to resemble Egyptian rail equipment.

[22] Inspiration for much of the epic *Ben Hur* came to Lew Wallace while he studied and worked in the Santa Cruz rectory. It is also claimed that the same is true for Puccini while composing portions of his *Girl of the Golden West.*

Chapter Two

[1] As with almost all groups of native Americans, in a manner alien to a majority of non-Indian people, the Tewa is capable of sustaining complete faith in seemingly opposite doctrines. Thus, Geronimo and Sara Fina, their parents before them, and their ancestors before that could live easily with Spanish Catholicism and also with the equally strict Tewa way of life. This is accomplished without stress or mental conflict.

[2] Most male children were given the first name of either Juan or José at that time, a tradition that began with the Spanish priests who often selected the names for those they baptized. Similarly, most females were given the first name of María. These names were often discarded, either as a matter of preference or simply to avoid confusion.

[3] Because of the early death of the mother, an absence of information about the father, and the dearth of church records related to both Sara Fina's family and the Taos church, little is known about the Taos branch. Efforts to interview older people living at Taos met with little success. It is also unfortunate that Sara Fina's and Geronimo's marriage record was not located in the archives, since marriage records in particular provide much valuable side information.

[4] Unpublished notes made between 1931 and 1935 of Blanche Fulton, courtesy of her son, Donald Fulton, written up in the 1940's.

[5] In researching this book, two fine storage jars, each approximately fifteen inches in height and sixteen inches in diameter were found in the Philbrook Art Center in Tulsa, Oklahoma. One was red and the other black, and both were signed Eloisa Povijua. They were collected at San Juan Pueblo by Clark Field, dated about 1920, and donated to the Philbrook. Povijua or Proviqua ("Dragging Blossom") is the Tewa surname of Margaret's family and is said to have been used by Juan Isidro during his residence at San Juan. Either of these jars could be easily mistaken for Santa Clara work. It is not the intent here to relate these vessels directly to the Tafoyas of Santa Clara. It is interesting to note that just as the ceramic heritage of the two pueblos is similar, their Tewa inheritance could produce duplication in names. Potters have always traded ceramic ideas from one pueblo to another, and the identification of Indian pottery can often be misleading.

[6] It was not until recently that the Indian's concept of himself as an artist began to be emphasized. This probably was the result of Anglo encouragement: the publicizing of Nampeyo's work by Keam, Stephen and Fewkes; Hewett's sponsorship of María Martinez: and Susie Peter's and sister Oliva's promotion of a group of artists known as the Kiowa Five. These early native American artists, at first, were not encouraged to exhibit in the United States, but their first public recognition came from Czechoslovakia in 1927 and from France in 1929.

[7] Santa Fe business directories list the Seligmans as operating a dry goods store in 1905, and later that James Seligmen was a postmaster and store owner in 1915. The store was located near the southeast corner of the Santa Fe Plaza. In 1930 and 1931, he was listed as president of a business known as the Old Santa Fe Trading Post located at 321 Hillside Avenue. (Information courtesy of R. Dillingham). In the early 1870s, records show that members of the Seligmen family were licensed traders to the Indians, including the Hopi and Navajo tribes. (McNitt 1962: 110-112).

[8] The conservative pueblo Indian was, and remains, a member of one of the lowest paid and hardest working groups of people in the United States. The exception to this is the modern Indian artist (potter, painter, weaver or carver) who, if recognized, is being fairly compensated.

[9] They may have been introduced to Colorado by José Filario Tafoya who, in 1920, married Petra Suazo in a public ceremony at Manitou Springs, Colorado. From then on, he is said to have commuted between there and the Santa Clara Pueblo. (Sandow: 53-59 and Poley 1920:74, 75)

[10] Brief autobiographies of each potter were collected and edited by R. Dillingham for a phamphlet for the exhibition.

Chapter Three

[1] The only other manual pottery forming process practiced by native Americans is the stone anvil and wooden paddle technique. This method is practiced by the Papago Indians of Arizona who inherited it from their Hohokam ancestors (Tanner 1976: 95). This method is also practiced by the Cherokees.

[2] From unpublished notes about Margaret Tafoya's family and the Santa Clara Pueblo made from 1929 to 1935 by Blanche Fulton, Albuquerque, New Mexico. Courtesy of her son, Donald Fulton.

[3] Information provided by María Martinez, San Ildefonso Pueblo, to the authors, October 5th, 1977.

[4] This identification was made at the Laboratory of Anthropology, Museum of New Mexico, Santa Fe on February 9th, 1981 in the presence of the then curator of collections, Marina Ochoa, R. Dillingham, authority on Southwest Indian Pottery, Margaret's daughters Mela Youngblood, Mary Ester Archuleta, and Shirley Tafoya and the authors.

[5] One is led to speculate that a study of shapes and cross-sections of old Tewa family pukis would assist in the identification of the maker of many older, unsigned pieces. If nothing else, the family source of the ware might be revealed.

[6] Information obtained from conversations with, and observations of, the working of Daisy Nampeyo Hooee, Tewa granddaughter of Nampeyo of Hano (Tewa Village of Hopi First Mesa).

[7] Information courtesy of Toni Roller.

[8] Excellent collections of these pottery types may be seen in the Anthropological Museum located at Guadalajara, Jalisco, Mexico and at Mexico City.

[9] Information courtesy of Maurine Grammer, Albuquerque, New Mexico.

[10] Information courtesy of Dr. Phillip Solis Olguin, Curator of Aztec Collections, National Anthropological Museum, Mexico City.

[11] This set was donated to the Wheelwright Museum of the American Indian, Santa Fe, New Mexico in 1984.

[12] Two of these combined impressed carved decorated vessels are located at the Denver, Colorado, Art Museum, one at the Anthropological Laboratories, Museum of New Mexico, Santa Fe, one at the Maxwell Museum, University of New Mexico, Albuquerque, New Mexico and two in private collections.

[13] María Martinez's and Andreita Baca's birth records were located in the Baptism and Birth Records of 1887 of the Holy Cross Catholic Church, Santa Cruz, New Mexico.

[14] Many informants state that this slip was discovered by Monica Silva, a distant relative of Alcario Tafoya. She married Santiago Lovato and moved to his pueblo of Santa Domingo. Presently, this slip is sold by her descendants.

[15] Information courtesy of Lu Ann Tafoya and Mary Esther Archuleta.

[16] This quote from a Dewy-Kofron Gallery leaflet issued for a pueblo pottery exhibition and gathering of Indian pottery artists, October 8th, 1977.

[17] Information courtesy of Mela Youngblood.

[18] Information courtesy of Nancy Youngblood Cutler.

[19] Information courtesy of Nathan Youngblood.

[20] Any discussion concerning ceramic processes other than hers or other technical items is obtained from the authors background or research, and in no way involves Margaret Tafoya.

[21] Smithsonian Institution specimen #361866 and New York Museum of Natural History specimen #29.0/560. Synthetic analine dyes are derived from coal. They were discovered in 1856 by Sir W.H. Perkin and were first sold by white merchants in the Rio Grande area as textile dyes.

[22] A suspect color, resembling chrome green was analyzed by the Colorado School of Mines and proved to be just that, rather than plant sap, as was claimed by the potter.

Chapter Four

[1] Margaret Tafoya quoting her mother Sara Fina.

[2] This quote and other information was obtained from a tape made by Edna Norton when interviewing Mela Youngblood.

[3] Modern San Juan incised decoration began as a revival about 1930. It's use has declined since 1960. It was inspired by the fifteenth century Potsuwi'i. Incised type produced in the lower Chama Valley and the Parajito Plateau regions by the ancestors of the Tewa now living at San Juan. Though the shapes differ, the technique of a mica filled geometric scratched design is essentially the same (Harlow 1973: 37, 43, 207).

[4] One of these early pieces was found in an Indian art gallery in Missoula, Montana.

Appendix 2—Slip Casting

[1] Information courtesy of A. E. Anthony, Jr., Adobe Gallery, Albuquerque, New Mexico.

[2] Information courtesy of Edna Norton, Albuquerque, New Mexico and Carl Schlosser, Taos, New Mexico.

Appendix 1
The Evolution of Santa Clara Pottery

B.C. Coiled pottery was produced in South and Central America.

B.C. 1000-A.D. 700 Small bands of desert people migrated north through Mexico, some up the Rio Grande Valley, and as farth north as the upper San Juan Basin.

B.C. 300 Hohokam and Mogollon cultures in today's New Mexico and Arizona produced the first pottery in the southwest United States.

A.D. 200-300 Anasazi people in the Four Corners region showed evidence of crude pottery in the form of mud-lined sun-dried baskets.

A.D. 400-700 Upper San Juan Brownwares showed possible Mogollon influence from the south and west. Plain utilitarian bowls and jars for gathering and storing food were rough, later *stone polished,* and were *oxidized fired* with smudged interiors.

A.D. 500-750 Rio Grande Anasazi pottery was probably influenced by San Juan Basin Brownware although gray in color and *reduced fired.* Agricultural villages in the upper Rio Grande area made *utilitarian vessels,* some micaseous.

A.D. 600-950 *Painted* black-on-white wares were first imported into the Rio Grande region from the north and west, and influenced the Rio Grande white wares that followed. By 725 A.d. polished *slip* was used on bowl interiors and jar exteriors. Sand or crushed sherd was the temper, and black designs were painted with *mineral paint.*

A.D. 750-1400 *Rio Grande white* wares showed inheritance from the Four Corners area and the Mimbres culture. Volcanic *tuff tempered,* pottery showed the first use of *vegetable paint* about 1225 A.D. and was probably brought by people who were continually migrating to the area from the north and west.

A.D. 850-1700 *Corrugated* wares were produced in all pueblo areas following basket patterns in design and varying in temper and color. Some were micaseous, later types were painted. After 1300 A.D. corrugation became increasingly smooth.

A.D. 1000 *Red slip* (with oxidizing fire) developed in the lower San Juan Basin. Possibly of Mogollon influence, this led to the development of bichromes (two colors), the forerunners of polychromes (more than two colors).

A.D. 1275-1350 The Four Corners area was deserted. Wandering bands of people drifted south and east. *Tewa villages* developed along the Chama River and the tributaries of the Rio Grande. People came together in larger units which produced a blending of varied ideas including pottery, and giving rise to expanding cultures.

A.D. 1375 La Bajada Hill (south of present day Santa Fe) marked the boundary between northern and southern Tewa ceramics in the Rio Grande Valley. Glaze-paint pottery introduced south of this point, from the west, developed into polychrome wares. Tewas north of La Bajada continued in the black-on-white (vegetable paints) utilitarian traditions.

A.D. pre-1400-1650 Prehistoric Tewa plainwares may have evolved from corrugation with early examples showing underbody coils. Occurring in the lower Chama Valley, on the Pajarito Plateau, and later in the Rio Grande Valley; it was generally hard bodied, tuff tempered, oxidized to reduced fired, and with some micaseous ware. *Incised* decoration, usually believed to be an eastern tribal influence,[*] occurred about 1450 in this area. More jars than bowls were produced, later examples were well polished. About 1550 pottery shows the first use of *pukis* (concave rather than convex bases). Shapes were similar to the contemporaneous Biscuit Ware.

A.D. 1375-1600 Tewa Prehistoric Biscuit Wares were an extension of the earlier Rio Grande black-on-white types. Consisting of a soft clay body and tuff temper, they were decorated with vegetable paint and oxidized fired. Occurring in the upper Rio Grande region and the Rio Grande Valley, there were more bowls than jars produced, some polished inside and out. Designs were simple, such as steps and circles.

The first identified Tewa *Avanyu design* was used about 1425.

A.D. 1450-1550 *Puyé Cliffs* were inhabited by the Santa Clarans' ancestors as were other ruins on the Pajarito Plateau which predate it. About

A.D. 1525 Tewas gradually started moving from the Plateau and the Chama River Valley to the Rio Grande Valley which was already occupied by other Indian people. The first *Santa Clara Pueblo* location was established.

A.D. 1598 The end of the Prehistoric era. Spanish colonization began in the Rio Grande region. The pueblos revolted against the Spanish in 1680, the Spanish reconquered them in 1692. They brought new agriculture, animals, metal products, and disease. It was a time of unrest, community disruption, and forced Catholicism under Spanish rule. Raids by Indian tribes from the north and east forced pueblo people into larger groups for protection. Indian religion went underground and the arts, including pottery, declined.

A.D. 1600-1850 Rio Grande polychromes, of possible glaze-paint influence, were more important to the pueblos south of Santa Clara except in the development of shapes. Tewa Polychrome types (1650-1730) established the classic bowl and jar shapes that were to be perpetuated at Santa Clara. Feather design decoration appeared. The latter part of this period saw an emphasis on painted designs and a decline in shape toward the globular at most other Rio Grande pueblos.

A.D. 1650-present Rio Grande plainwares:

1650-1725 Ka'po (Tewa name for Santa Clara) Gray was a continuation of Prehistoric Tewa plainware. It was hard, thin-walled, unslipped, stone polished inside and out, and reduced fired with a predominance of jars showing concave bases. Concave under-bodies, bulging mid-bodies, somewhat abrupt shoulders, gradually sloping jar necks terminating in out-flaring rims reflect the classic Tewa Poychrome form.

1650-1750 Posuge Red was similar to Ka'po Gray with the addition of a slip that fired red in an oxidized fire. Emphasis was on bowls with concave upper walls, an abrupt joining at the shoulder to the underbody, and with usually concave bases. This was the fore-runner of Santa Clara Red and Polychrome, Nambe Red, and San Juan Red-on-tan types.

1720-1800 Ka'po Black retained the Tewa Polychrome shapes and was made pre-dominantly at Santa Clara with more jars than bowls. It was thin-walled, hard and utilitarian, and was slipped two-thirds down from the rim (to the same line as red based contemporaneous polychromes), all-over polished, and reduced fired.

1760-1930 Santa Clara Black (with a few produced at San Juan) was very like Ka'po Black, slightly thicker walled, and utilitarian. Perpetuating the Tewa Polychrome shapes, bowls were slipped inside and all-over polished, and jars were slipped and polished outside and in over the lip. Some micaceous pieces, all were reduced fired.

A.D. 1800-1841 There was much confusion in all the Rio Grande pueblos, partly due to continuing raids by tribes from the north and east. Mexican independence from Spain intensified controversy over land grants. The Santa Fe Trail brought Anglo influences and goods. Each pueblo withdrew into itself and began producing pueblo pottery specializations.

A.D. 1841-1920 New Mexico Territory was established under the United States, raiding was abolished, and schools established. Logging and mining operations provided jobs outside the pueblos. Railroads brought goods, tourists, and anthropologists. There was less emphasis on utilitarian pottery, though some micaceous ware was produced at Santa Clara even after 1920. Impressed designs appeared on Santa Clara Black, also rainbow bands on water jar shoulders, bear paws, wedding jars, and huge storage jars. Diverse styles were tourist oriented, and handled vessels and animal forms increased.

A.D. 1920's-present Santa Clara Red and Santa Clara Polychrome, descendants of Posuge Red, had been perpetuated mainly at San Juan and Nambe Pueblos. Outlining in white on redware became popular at Santa Clara. Excavations and institutions began sponsoring interest in Indian pottery, collections were begun, and Indian traders began to sponsor art and craft shows. Black-on-black designs were adopted at Santa Clara due to their success at San Ildefonso. Impressed designs developed into carved designs.

A.D. 1930's were Depression years. Tourists were welcome at the pueblos for pottery sales. Santa Clara pottery became thicker walled, probably due to the loss of some of their clay deposits. A dull unpolished slip was applied in the carved depressions of both red and black wares to emphasize the design. A Polychrome-on-buff pottery appeared.

A.D. 1940's Some realistic painting on polychrome pottery was done at Santa Clara with the addition of pink, tan and gray. World War II took a high percentage of pueblo men in the military, and museums and institutions ceased functioning. The Scientific Labs at nearby Los Alamos provided good paying jobs for pueblo people, so pottery production was severely curtailed.

A.D. 1950's Post World War II. There was renewed interest in art, particularly Indian art in the Southwest. The U.S. government, through the Bureau of Indian Affairs, established educational programs, on-the-job vocational programs, and Public Health Services at the pueblos.

A.D. 1960's Indian youth became interested in their inheritance. The All Indian Pueblo Council was formed to preserve ancient culture and stabilize modern government in the developing pueblos. Potters became artists, antique pottery became scarce, and interest spurred more shows and competitions in pottery. Resist firing and grafitto were introduced at the Tewa pueblos.

A.D. 1970's and 1980's When the U.S. economy is good, there is a good market for pottery and there is always a demand for quality work. Pueblo Indian pottery is now international art, and Indian managed organizations, museums, and gallery dealers promote interest in all forms of Indian art. Collectors resist the potter's use of commercially produced clay and slip, and also scientific methods of firing in the production of traditional Indian pottery. There is no terminology to distinguish the pottery produced at Santa Clara now from its immediate predecessors. All are called simply Santa Clara Black, Santa Clara Red, and Santa Clara Polychrome. According to some scholars, the type called Santa Clara Black was not made after about 1930. That is true if one distinguishes utilitarian pottery from today's art pottery. The same steps are followed to produce either, and it is a matter of whether vessels are made to be used or are decorative pieces.

Note: This chart is a compilation of facts and averaged dates from the following sources. (Brody 1977, 1979) (Chapman 1970) (Devereau 1966) (Dittert and Plog 1980) (Dutton 1966) (Ellis 1975) (Goddard 1931) (Harlow 1973, 1970, 1977) (Hewett 1909, 1937) (Jeançon 1930, 1931) (Kidder 1915) (LeFree 1975) (Mera 1934, 1939) (Noble 1981) (Ortiz 1979) (Reed 1946, 1949) (Sando 1976) (Tanner 1968, 1976) (Toulouse 1976) (Wormington 1951, 1956) (Underhill 1944)

---

* Incising could also have been a Mexican influence. A prehistoric pot observed in the Field Museum of Natural History in Chicago from Chihuahua was incised. No date was given for this piece, but the caption included the information that this type developed into a highly polished blackware.

Appendix 2
Slip Casting

Were it not for the fact that slip cast ceramics are being sold to the unwary buyer as art pieces made by the Indian using their conventional methods, this process of forming doesn't deserve mention in a discussion of Tewa pottery. This less labor intensive process developed by the white man has been introduced to Indian potters including those of the pueblos and is sometimes adopted by those less skilled as a method of producing well-formed shapes which can be distributed to the market in the lower priced area to buyers desiring Indian crafts but who cannot afford to pay the fine art prices which the coiled work demands.

The technology of this form of casting has reached a point where objects made from molds, obtained from original works of art, are carefully finished and sold as originals.[1]

Slip casting is a method of forming ware from a fluid which contains clay and temper in suspension in water. (McNamara 1939:94—97). Dry mixes suitable for slip casting can be purchased in hobby shops. These contain mixtures of a white burning clay, a clean temper and a dispersing agent such as sodium silicate which, when added to the proper amount of water, result in a workable slip. The dead white color of the fired bodies made from these mixtures signifies that such are not hand coiled works made from the impure Indian clays.

Briefly, a liquid slip is poured into a dry, negative, plaster mold. Because of the high porosity of the mold, water is absorbed from the slip and a semi-plastic body is built up on the interior of the mold. At the interface between the mold and the plastic, the body surface faithfully reproduces the mold surface. The longer the fluid stands in the mold the thicker this plastic layer becomes. The closed mold rests until a desired wall thickness is obtained. As the water is absorbed the slip level drops within the mold and fresh slip must be added to keep the top and bottom wall thicknesses uniform.

When the desired thickness is reached, the excess slip is poured from the mold and allowed to stand until the built up wall becomes hard enough to handle. As the cast piece hardens, it shrinks allowing for easy removal from the mold. The excess slip, which is poured off before standing, can be reused usually requiring the addition of only a small amount of water and dispersant to return it to its original condition.

Once removed from the mold the surface of the piece will be marred by pieces of flashing which form when two sections of mold meet. Flashing is removed by trimming and smoothing with a wet sponge. Across and throughout the body where the flashing occurs, fine particles of clay tend to be preferentially absorbed at mold joints. This selective deposition leaves a permanent mark. These joint surface marks are difficult to detect but are also impossible to remove. Mold marks provide a second means of identifying slip cast work. The most obvious part of the marks occur on the interior of the vessel as slight indentations or valleys which run parallel to the flash marks on the outside, and are most easily detected when viewing the inside surface of the piece.

After carefully drying the ware (usually produced at a hobby shop) a decision to sell the ware as is or to fire it in the shop's kilns is made. Purchasing unfired bodies allows the Indian to apply his own slips over the outer surfaces, further disguising the method of manufacture.

While fired pieces are more expensive than the raw or green articles, they are less apt to break and eliminate the firing step which is difficult for some. As with the green ware the fired pieces may be further decorated and refired. Firing is usually done in commercial kilns which are heated electrically adding to the dull white effect of slip cast ware. The artistic effect produced by firing marks is never found.

It is obvious that, with the exception of decoration, the native American has contributed little to the making of the work. The amount of artistry and skill involved is minimal and anyone can form a piece in this manner. The most blatant peddlers of slip cast work are members of the following pueblos or groups: Zuni who have made fetish bowls, the Chemeheuvi who make delicate miniatures, the Zia pots whose surfaces are sometimes covered with rather excellent oil paintings, various shaped vessels from Isleta and Acoma and a few Hopi-Tewa pieces often modeled after the traditional shapes and designs which are sometimes signed with counterfeit signatures!

To the authors' knowledge, only one rash of slip cast Santa Clara work has been produced to date. These pieces are all the more interesting since the body was not clay, but plaster of Paris. A slip of this material and water had been poured into a rubber mold that showed no mold marks. When set and removed, the objects were spray painted, usually with a Santa Clara-like black color. They were so well executed that they temporarily deceived some reputable Indian art dealers with years of experience.[2] Fortunately, this type of counterfeit or cheap substitute can, in most instances, be detected when closely studied. In summary, slip cast products have the following distinctive characteristics:

1. Wall thicknesses are *very* uniform and thin, much thinner than the finest coiled ware.
2. Due to air trapped within the viscous slip and the use of some materials with a low specific gravity, the ware feels lighter in weight than traditionally made pottery with the same average wall thickness.
3. The entrapped air in the slip forms tiny round cavities which are dispersed throughout the body with high concentrations at the mold contact surfaces.
4. The body is usually a uniform dead white color.
5. The difficult to remove mold marks are characteristic of slip cast items. These are caused by small particle sized and lower specific gravity materials being drawn together by the more rapid water removal at the mold joints.

Appendix 3
Genealogy

In order to better understand and report on the life of an artist such as Margaret Tafoya, the authors are convinced that in addition to studying the history of the subject and her people, other important areas must be investigated. The reporters should immerse themselves as deeply as possible in the environment of the artist, and also learn as much as practical about the subject's personal heritage.

To understand the pueblo environment would mean to live within its boundaries, (a situation which is virtually impossible for a non-Indian in a Tewa community) and locating and studying the sites which are or were of importance to the people of that community. Such activities as visiting the prehistoric ruins of people who had produced influencing pottery types, locating the original Santa Cruz Valley home of Margaret's Tewa-Hopi relatives, or locating and tracing the remains of the "Chile Line" railroad bed all helped to a better understanding of Margaret's background.

Margaret's pottery heritage and her contributions to the artists of the generations which follow her are enhanced by studying her genealogy and diagraming the relationships. It was this study that was not only one of the most enjoyable, but also a very productive part of the research.

The collecting of information for the following charts began with extensive interviews with Margaret which, at times, must have stretched her patience although she sat for hours, at our request, often reviewing ground that had been previously covered many times. For example, we asked for the English translation of the Tewa name of her brother Juan Isidro. To our untrained ears the answer came back, "White Whistle."

"White Whistle," we asked, "do you mean White Thistle?"

"No, White Whistle."

"White Whistle—we do not understand. That's an unusual name."

"White Whistle—the small animal that changes its color to white in winter."

With much relief, "Oh, you mean White Weasel."

"Yes." Thus, Juan Isidro's given Tewa name was established and recorded.

It was during these discussions of Margaret's little known brother and his San Juan in-laws that it was learned where her understanding and skill in forming San Juan pottery types had originated. Other sessions concerning other people in her life who had long since passed away, served to refresh her very accurate memory, and facts were brought out which Margaret had not thought about for years.

Interviews with Margaret and some of her near relatives revealed the names of her parents, grandparents, siblings, children, and most of her aunts and uncles. With this information a rough genealogical framework was constructed which could be made almost complete by working with available birth, marriage and death records, extracting pertinent information from the literature, and using a few other sources of obtainable raw data.

It was soon realized that it would be almost impossible to trace Margaret's ancestors prior to the return of the Spanish to the region in 1692. During the great Revolt of 1680, the Tewa completely destroyed everything that reminded them of the oppressive Spanish rule including shedding their Christian names and destroying all Catholic Church records. Although there is a remote possibility that records exist in archives located either in Mexico City or in Spain which could refer to Margaret's ancestors, especially if they were involved in the Inquisition, it would be impossible to locate them without knowing the names to research. It must be remembered that the surname Tafoya was not introduced to the Santa Clara people until after 1706, and that most Indian family names used before that time are unknown.

The fact that the Rio Grande Indians were given Spanish names by Catholic Church officials after the second occupation allows one to trace Santa Clara families back for several generations. Conversely, the method by which these names were bestowed on the Tewa people created a great mass of confusion, making it difficult to separate various individuals and families.

At Santa Clara the Tafoyas and Naranjos illustrate

this point. All Indian people who were forced to labor on the lands of Juan Tafoya or his Spanish relatives were given the Tafoya surname in spite of the fact that they might not be remotely related by blood. So today, a Tafoya may marry a Tafoya who is of no blood relationship, and a large number of the same situations exist with the Naranjos and other well known Santa Clara surnames. To further complicate the picture, non-related infants were often given the same first and middle names depending on the day that they were baptised. The priests, rather than the parents, often bestowed the names of the saints whose feast dates were being celebrated on that date. Thus, eleven José A. Tafoyas and twelve José A. Naranjos have been found in the records, all born within a time span of a century. To further complicate the situation the same person may be found in different records as either José, José A., José Antonio, or Antonio depending on how the entry was made on a particular occasion. There are countless José and María Tafoyas and Naranjos in the records of the Santa Clara people.

The mission church of Santa Clara where many of the baptisms, weddings and burial ceremonies were conducted was, until recently, located within the parish of Santa Cruz de la Cañada where the mother church, the Church of the Holy Cross, is located near the town of Española. These extensive records of the Santa Clara people, held both at the mission church and at the Holy Cross Church were stored in the archives of the Holy Cross Church. It was here that inquiry was made about the possibility of studying these records to obtain data which could be used to further piece together Margaret's genealogy.

The reception to this request was overwhelming. The cooperation of the people in charge of running the business of the rectory, Mr. Rubin Martinez and Mrs. Alice Pacheco, was much appreciated. Above all, the guidance, assistance, and friendship of Father José Cubells, long time resident priest at the Holy Cross Church, provided some of the most memorable and pleasant experiences encountered during the preparation of the manuscript. This priest, scholar, historian, author, scientist, and humorist not only assisted us with the deciphering and understanding of the old records, but also provided many priests to minister to the Spanish archaeology, and geology of the area in which Margaret has spent most of her life. Through the kindness of Fr. Cubells we were provided a pleasant place in which to work in the church rectory.

Father Cubells is a member of the Order of the Sons of the Holy Family, based in Spain which has proved many priests to minister to the Spanish speaking communities served by the Church of the Holy Cross. The first of this group arrived at the Española railroad station on August 15th, 1920.

It was there that they learned that the bridge over the Rio Grande River, which they must cross before they could reach their new home, had been destroyed by flood so part of the remaining journey was made by boat to cross the river. A few years after the arrival of the first group, Fr. Cubells migrated from the Old World to Santa Cruz where he has ministered for well over half a century spending much time with the Tewa speaking people.

Shortly after completing our study of the Holy Cross Church records we learned that the older ones had been removed to the Archdiocese of Santa Fe Archives in Albuquerque. These records and those of other Rio Grande villages have been microfilmed and can be studied at the New Mexico State Archives in Santa Fe. Unfortunately, they are not complete. For example, the Taos records which might have provided information on some of Sara Fina's ancestors could not be located. Without the assistance of Fr. Cubells, deciphering the microfilmed records became much more difficult and far less enjoyable.

Following the collection of information from Santa Cruz, a rather extensive family tree for Margaret was constructed, but several gaps remained. Information on the younger generations proved more difficult to obtain than was first imagined. With the coming of different Christian missions to Santa Clara and nearby Española, the percentage of records housed at the Santa Cruz Church began to diminish. The decrease was further accelerated by military enlistments from Santa Clara beginning with World War I in 1917. Increasing numbers of Santa Clara people were married or born at bases far distant from the pueblo. The second World War was responsible for an even greater increase in the move away from Santa Clara, and this involved many of Margaret's relatives. Therefore, completing the later portions of her genealogy required interviewing available members of the family. Because of time limitations and relevance, the extent of these interviews diminished as relationship to Margaret became more distant.

In addition to church records and personal interviews, other sources of information were utilized. These included data from the literature as well as studying grave and descanso markers located within the pueblo.

Pioneering in pueblo pottery genealogy was Rick Dillingham, who went from house to house gathering information to be used in a catalog for a pottery exhibition featuring the works of seven famous pueblo pottery making families. This was published in 1974 (Anon). The only other known publication which provides genealogical information on Santa Clara people, including the Tafoyas, is that of Hill (1982: 353-374). Although Hill began collecting genealogical data much before Dillingham, his untimely death prevented its publication until several years later. Not only was Hill unable to complete his research, but he did not have the time to check its accuracy. For example, Tomacita, Margaret's oldest sister is presented as being a member of a younger generation than Margaret, and Tomacita's daughter, Eva, is shown as being her sister. Had Hill been allowed to complete his work and make the necessary corrections, this would have been a landmark source of information.

Other sources of raw data used in the construction of the genealogical charts were found on crosses in the Santa Clara graveyard and on the descanso markers on Santa Clara land. (Descanso is a Spanish word meaning "a resting place along the way." It is here that the pallbearers stop to rest as they carry the remains of the deceased to the final burial place.) Descanso sites in that area of New Mexico are marked by small shrines beside the roads, but those at Santa Clara are marked with crosses usually inscribed with the name, birth, and death dates of those whose remains were rested there. The most valuable data obtained from these and the grave markers are the dates of death, since few of these were found in the Holy Cross Church archives. It should be emphasized that the information on cemetery and descanso markers is limited to the recent past. Both are exposed to the elements. It was not until recently that the graveyard was protected by either a wall or a fence, and factors such as children at play or grazing animals have taken their toll.

There are many possible sources of error located in the data used to establish the genealogy of the Tafoya family. These would include: 1. Duplication of peoples names whose birthdates are within a few years of each other resulting in the confusion of the exact identity of an individual. 2. Errors arising from difficulties of communication. 3. Errors in transcription. All of the Holy Cross Church entries were handwritten. In a few instances the hand writing was practically illegible or almost impossible to decipher. 4. Errors in recording. For example, it was found in a few cases that information taken from descanso markers differed from that found on the cemetery marker for the same person.

To those whose names we may have omitted or to those whose information we have not properly recorded, we apologize. These errors were not intended. The authors have simply used the available information to the best of their abilities.

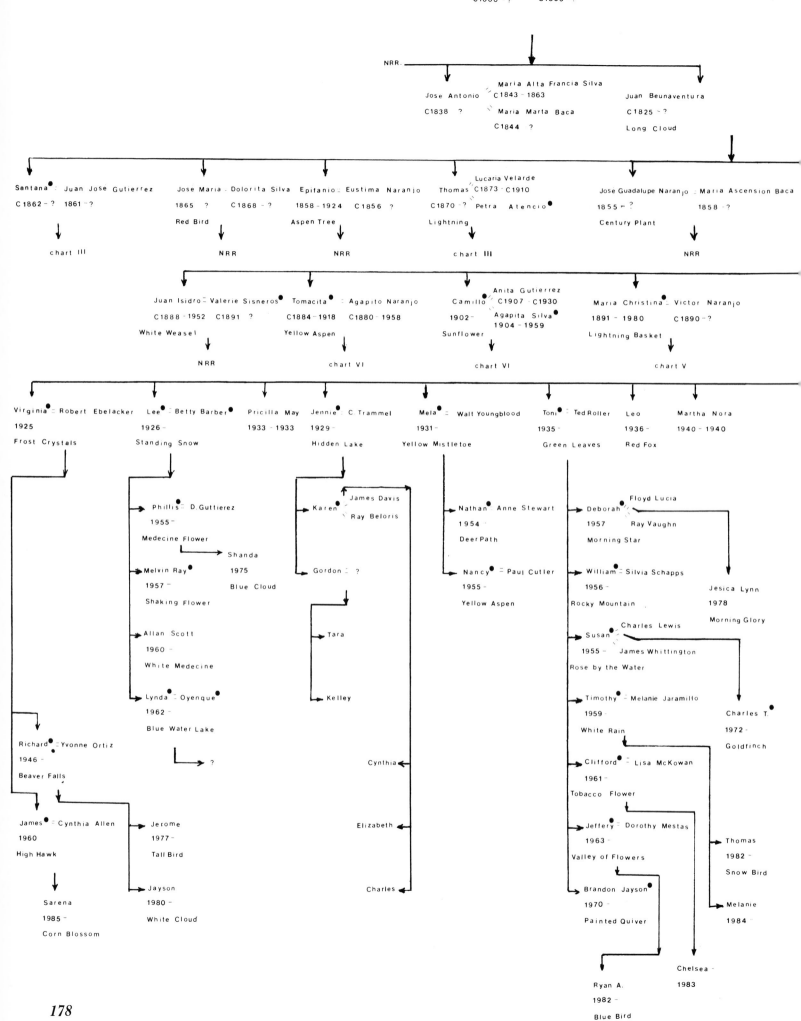

Jose Tafoya   Maria Romulda Garcia
C1800 -?   C1805 -?

NRR

Jose Antonio   Maria Alta Francia Silva   Juan Beunaventura
C1838 ?   C1843 - 1863   C1825 ~?
                Maria Marta Baca   Long Cloud
                C1844 ?

Santana ● = Juan Jose Gutierrez   Jose Maria = Dolorita Silva   Epifanio = Eustima Naranjo   Thomas C1873 - C1910 Lucaria Velarde   Jose Guadalupe Naranjo = Maria Ascension Baca
C1862 - ? 1861 -?   1865   ?   C1868 - ?   1858 -1924 C1856 ?   C1870 -? Petra Atencio ●   1855 ~ ?   1858 -?

                                   Red Bird   Aspen Tree   Lightning   Century Plant

chart III   NRR   NRR   chart III   NRR

Juan Isidro = Valerie Sisneros ●   Tomacita = Agapito Naranjo   Camillo Anita Gutierrez   Maria Christina = Victor Naranjo
C1888 -1952 C1891 ?   C1884 -1918 C1880 -1958   1902 -   C1907 - C1930   1891 - 1980   C1890 -?
                                                                          Agapita Silva
White Weasel   Yellow Aspen   1904 - 1959   Lightning Basket
                                                                   Sunflower
NRR   chart VI   chart VI   chart V

Virginia ● = Robert Ebelacker   Lee ● = Betty Barber ●   Pricilla May   Jennie ● = C.Trammel   Mela ● = Walt Youngblood   Toni ● = Ted Roller   Leo   Martha Nora
1925   1926 -   1933 - 1933   1929 -   1931 -   1935 -   1936 - 1940 - 1940

Frost Crystals   Standing Snow   Hidden Lake   Yellow Mistletoe   Green Leaves   Red Fox

                                                                                                                                        Floyd Lucia
                                Phillis ● = D.Guttierez   Karen ═ James Davis   Nathan ● = Anne Stewart   Deborah =
                                1955 -   Ray Beloris   1954   1957   Ray Vaughn
                                Medecine Flower   Deer Path   Morning Star

                                         Shanda   William = Silvia Schapps
                                Melvin Ray ●   1975   Gordon = ?   Nancy ● = Paul Cutler   1956 -   Jesica Lynn
                                1957 -   Blue Cloud   1955 -   Rocky Mountain   1978
                                Shaking Flower   Yellow Aspen   Morning Glory

                                                                          Tara   Charles Lewis
                                Allan Scott   Susan ●
                                1960 -   1955 -   James Whittington
                                White Medecine   Rose by the Water

                                Lynda ● = Oyenque ●   Kelley   Timothy ● = Melanie Jaramillo
                                1962 -   1959 -   Charles T. ●
                                Blue Water Lake   White Rain   1972 -
                                                                                                                                                               Goldfinch
                                        ═ ?
Richard ● = Yvonne Ortiz   Clifford ● = Lisa McKowan
1946 -   Cynthia   1961 -
Beaver Falls   Tobacco Flower

James ● = Cynthia Allen   Jerome   Jeffery = Dorothy Mestas
1960   1977 -   Elizabeth   1963 -   Thomas
High Hawk   Tall Bird   Valley of Flowers   1982 -
                                                                                                                                                               Snow Bird
         Jayson   Brandon Jayson ●
Sarena   1980 -   Charles   1970 -   Melanie
1985 -   White Cloud   Painted Quiver   1984
Corn Blossom

                                                                                                                          Ryan A.   Chelsea -
                                                                                                                          1982 -   1983
                                                                                                                          Blue Bird

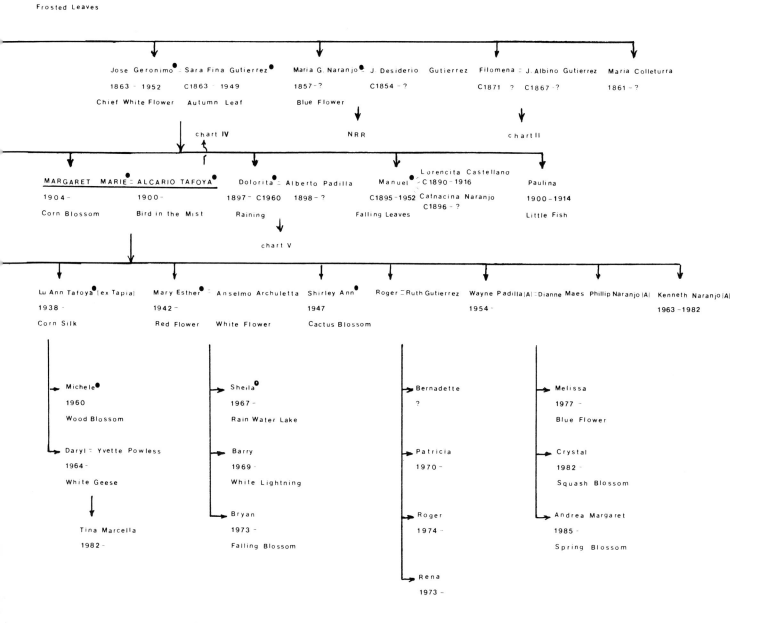

Leandro Naranjo = Ascension Cajete

C1805 - ?   C1810 - ?

Maria Nestora Naranjo

C 1830 - ?

Frosted Leaves

Jose Geronimo = Sara Fina Gutierrez	Maria G. Naranjo = J. Desiderio Gutierrez	Filomena = J. Albino Gutierrez	Maria Colleturra
1863 - 1952 C1863 - 1949	1857 - ? C1854 - ?	C1871 ? C1867 - ?	1861 - ?
Chief White Flower Autumn Leaf	Blue Flower		
chart IV	NRR	chart II	

MARGARET MARIE = ALCARIO TAFOYA	Dolorita = Alberto Padilla	Manuel Lorencita Castellano	Paulina
1904 - 1900 -	1897 - C1960 1898 - ?	C1895 -1952 C 1890 - 1916	1900 - 1914
Corn Blossom Bird in the Mist	Raining	Catnacina Naranjo C1896 - ?	Little Fish
	chart V	Falling Leaves	

Lu Ann Tafoya (ex Tapia)	Mary Esther = Anselmo Archuletta	Shirley Ann	Roger = Ruth Gutierrez	Wayne Padilla (A) = Dianne Maes	Phillip Naranjo (A)	Kenneth Naranjo (A)
1938 -	1942 -	1947		1954 -		1963 - 1982
Corn Silk	Red Flower White Flower	Cactus Blossom				

Michele
1960
Wood Blossom

Daryl = Yvette Powless
1964 -
White Geese

Tina Marcella
1982 -

Sheila
1967 -
Rain Water Lake

Barry
1969 -
White Lightning

Bryan
1973 -
Falling Blossom

Bernadette
?

Patricia
1970 -

Roger
1974 -

Rena
1973 -

Melissa
1977 -
Blue Flower

Crystal
1982 -
Squash Blossom

Andrea Margaret
1985 -
Spring Blossom

TAFOYA FAMILY GENEALOGY - CHART I

LEGEND

Chistian Name

Date of Birth - Date of Death

Tewa Name

● Known to Have Made Pottery   C   Circa

x   Known Artist   M   Year of Marriage

|A| Adopted   NRR Either not Researched or

                                           not Relevant

                                      ☼ utilizing data available as of 3/11/1985

179

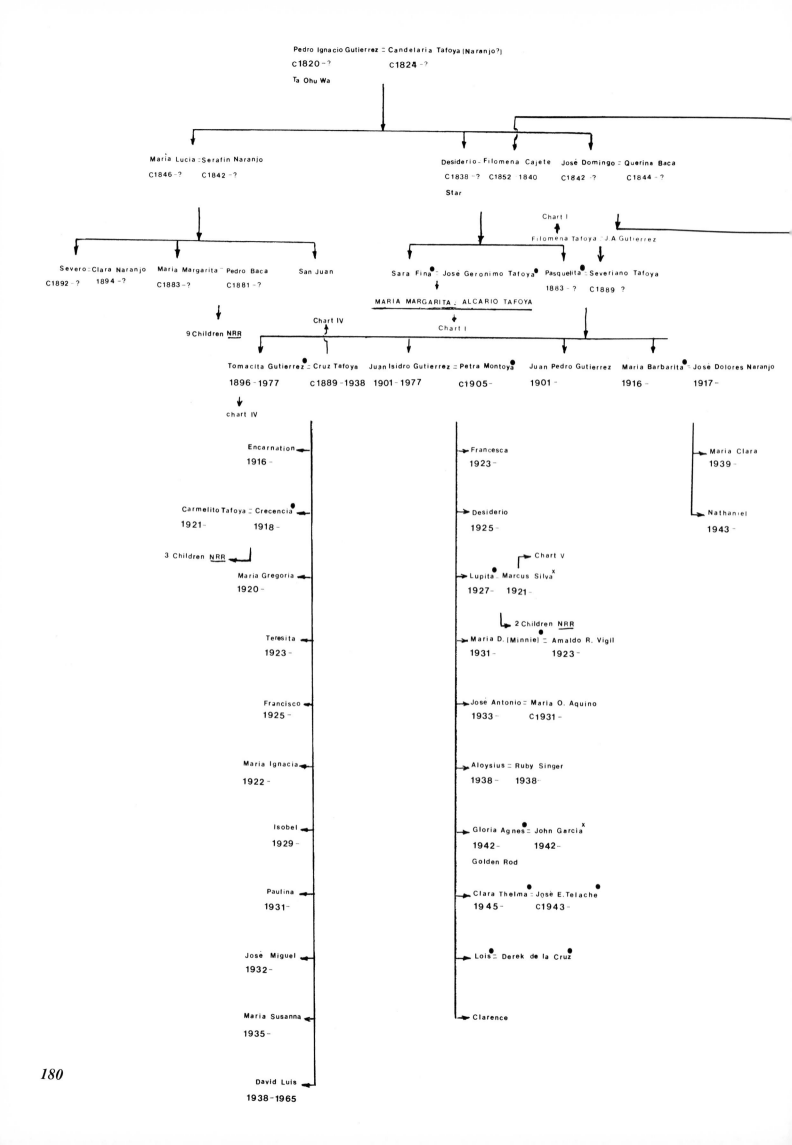

Pedro Ignacio Gutierrez = Candelaria Tafoya (Naranjo?)

c1820 -?   C1824 -?

Ta Ohu Wa

Maria Lucia = Serafin Naranjo

C1846 -?   C1842 -?

Desiderio = Filomena Cajete   José Domingo = Querina Baca

C1838 -?   C1852   1840   C1842 -?   C1844 -?

Star

Chart I

Filomena Tafoya = J.A Gutierrez

Severo = Clara Naranjo   Maria Margarita = Pedro Baca   San Juan

C1892 -?   1894 -?   C1883 -?   C1881 -?

Sara Fina = José Geronimo Tafoya   Pasquelita = Severiano Tafoya

1883 -?   C1889 ?

MARIA MARGARITA = ALCARIO TAFOYA

9 Children NRR

Chart IV

Chart I

Tomacita Gutierrez = Cruz Tafoya   Juan Isidro Gutierrez = Petra Montoya   Juan Pedro Gutierrez   Maria Barbarita = José Dolores Naranjo

1896 - 1977   C1889 - 1938   1901 - 1977   C1905 -   1901 -   1916 -   1917 -

chart IV

Encarnation   Francesca   Maria Clara

1916 -   1923 -   1939 -

Carmelito Tafoya = Crecencia   Desiderio   Nathaniel

1921 -   1918 -   1925 -   1943 -

3 Children NRR

Maria Gregoria   Chart V

1920 -   Lupita = Marcus Silva[x]

       1927 -   1921 -

2 Children NRR

Teresita   Maria D. (Minnie) = Amaldo R. Vigil

1923 -   1931 -   1923 -

Francisco   José Antonio = Maria O. Aquino

1925 -   1933 -   C1931 -

Maria Ignacia   Aloysius = Ruby Singer

1922 -   1938 -   1938 -

Isobel   Gloria Agnes = John Garcia[x]

1929 -   1942 -   1942 -

Golden Rod

Paulina   Clara Thelma = José E. Telache

1931 -   1945 -   C1943 -

José Miguel   Lois = Derek de la Cruz

1932 -

Maria Susanna   Clarence

1935 -

David Luis

1938 - 1965

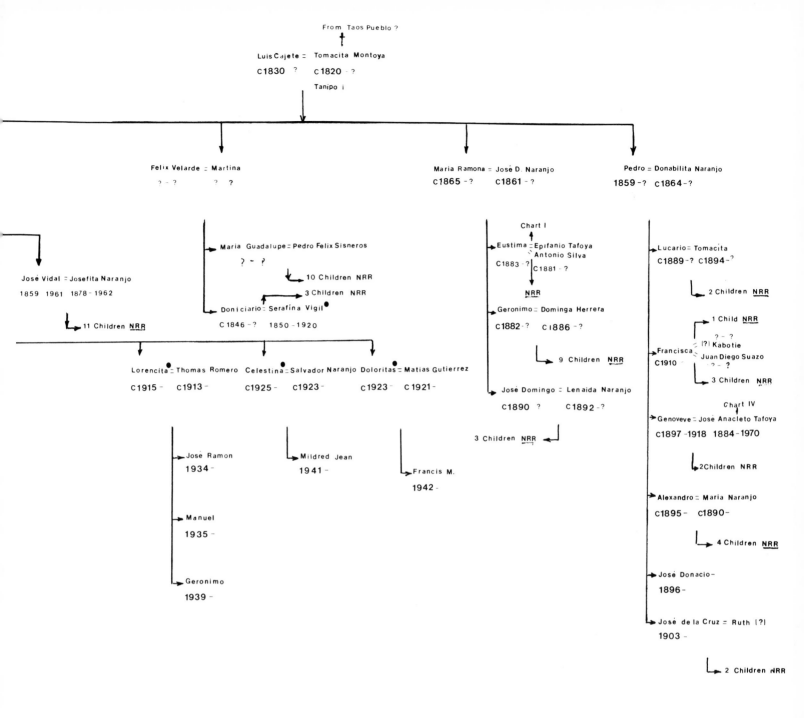

TAFOYA FAMILY GENEALOGY-
GUTIERREZ BRANCH
CHART II

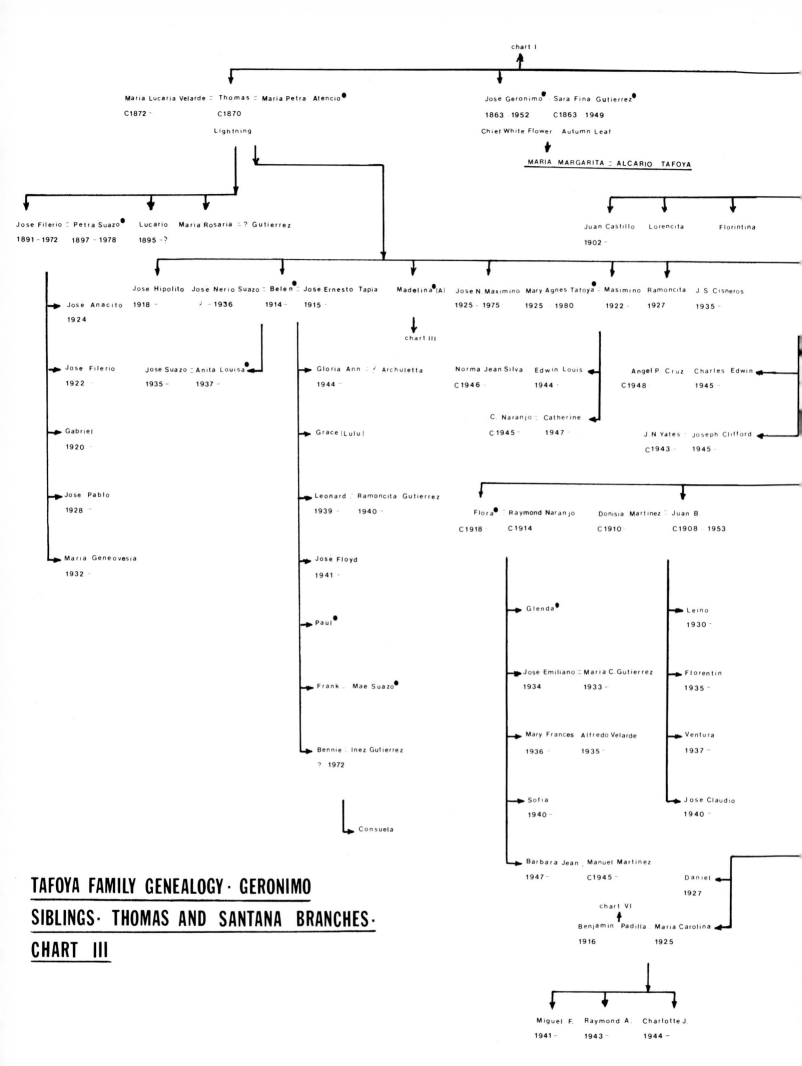

chart I

Maria Lucaria Velarde = Thomas = Maria Petra Atencio●

C1872 –   C1870

Lightning

Jose Geronimo● · Sara Fina Gutierrez●

1863 – 1952   C1863 1949

Chief White Flower   Autumn Leaf

MARIA MARGARITA = ALCARIO TAFOYA

Jose Filerio = Petra Suazo●

1891 – 1972   1897 – 1978

Lucario

1895 – ?

Maria Rosaria = ? Gutierrez

Juan Castillo   Lorencita   Florintina

1902 –

Jose Anacito

1924

Jose Hipolito

1918 –

Jose Nerio Suazo = Belen●

? – 1936   1914 –

Jose Ernesto Tapia

1915

Madelina (A)

chart III

Jose N. Maximino

1925 – 1975

Mary Agnes Tafoya● = Masimino

1925 – 1980   1922 –

Ramoncita

1927

J.S Cisneros

1935 –

Jose Filerio

1922 –

Jose Suazo = Anita Louisa●

1935 –   1937 –

Gloria Ann = ? Archuletta

1944 –

Norma Jean Silva

C1946 –

Edwin Louis

1944 –

Angel P. Cruz

C1948 –

Charles Edwin

1945 –

Gabriel

1920

Grace (Lulu)

C. Naranjo = Catherine

C1945 –   1947 –

J.N. Yates = Joseph Clifford

C1943 –   1945 –

Jose Pablo

1928 –

Leonard = Ramoncita Gutierrez

1939 –   1940 –

Flora● = Raymond Naranjo

C1918 –   C1914

Donisia Martinez = Juan B.

C1910 –   C1908 – 1953

Maria Geneovesia

1932 –

Jose Floyd

1941 –

Glenda●

Leino

1930 –

Paul●

Jose Emiliano = Maria C. Gutierrez

1934   1933 –

Florentin

1935 –

Frank = Mae Suazo●

Mary Frances   Alfredo Velarde

1936 –   1935 –

Ventura

1937 –

Bennie = Inez Gutierrez

? 1972

Sofia

1940 –

Jose Claudio

1940 –

Consuela

Barbara Jean = Manuel Martinez

1947 –   C1945 –

Daniel

1927

chart VI

Benjamin Padilla = Maria Carolina

1916   1925

TAFOYA FAMILY GENEALOGY · GERONIMO
SIBLINGS · THOMAS AND SANTANA BRANCHES ·
CHART III

Miguel F.   Raymond A.   Charlotte J.

1941 –   1943 –   1944 –

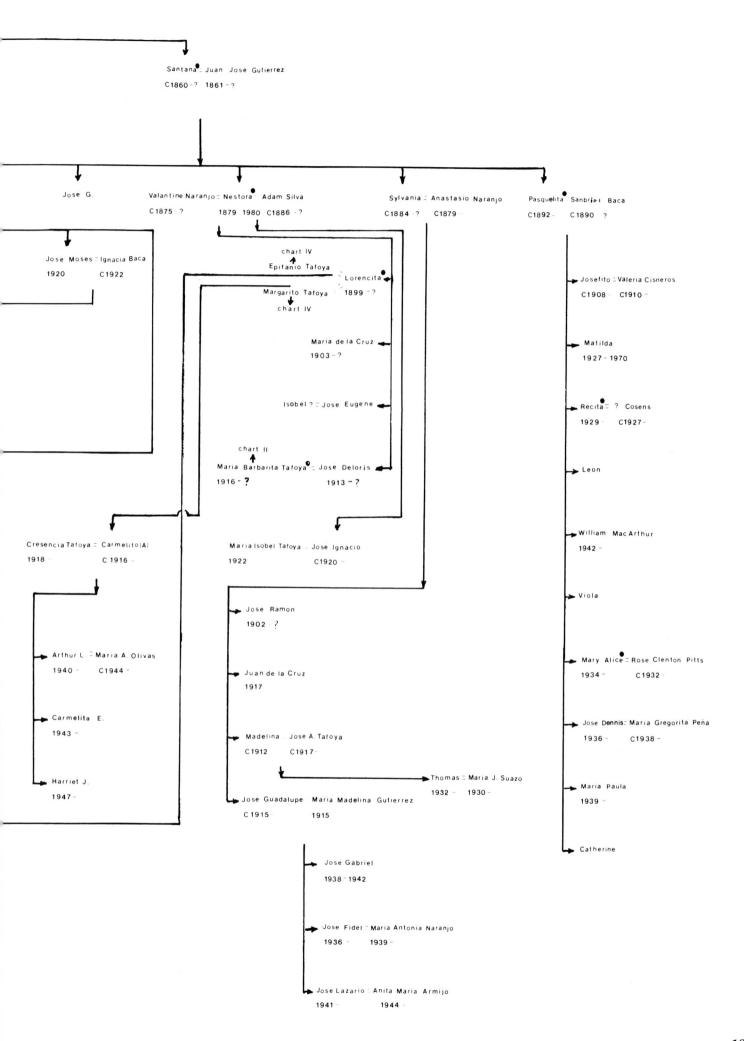

Santana = Juan Jose Gutierrez
C1860-? 1861-?

Jose G.

Valantine Naranjo = Nestora • Adam Silva
C1875 ?   1879 1980 C1886 -?

Sylvania = Anastasio Naranjo
C1884 -?   C1879 -

Pasquelita • Sanbriel Baca
C1892 -   C1890 ?

Jose Moses = Ignacia Baca
1920   C1922

chart IV
Epifanio Tafoya

Lorencita •
1899 -?

Margarito Tafoya
chart IV

Maria de la Cruz
1903 -?

Isobel ? = Jose Eugene

chart II
Maria Barbarita Tafoya ○ = Jose Deloris
1916 - ?   1913 - ?

Josefito = Valeria Cisneros
C1908 -   C1910 -

Matilda
1927 - 1970

Recita = ? Cosens
1929   C1927 -

Leon

William Mac Arthur
1942 -

Cresencia Tafoya = Carmelito (A)
1918 -   C 1916 -

Maria Isobel Tafoya - Jose Ignacio
1922   C1920 -

Viola

Arthur L. = Maria A. Olivas
1940 -   C1944 -

Jose Ramon
1902 - ?

Mary Alice = Rose Clenton Pitts
1934 -   C1932 -

Carmelita E.
1943 -

Juan de la Cruz
1917

Jose Dennis = Maria Gregorita Peña
1936 -   C1938 -

Harriet J.
1947 -

Madelina - Jose A. Tafoya
C1912   C1917 -

Thomas = Maria J. Suazo
1932 -   1930 -

Maria Paula
1939 -

Jose Guadalupe Maria Madelina Gutierrez
C1915 -   1915

Catherine

Jose Gabriel
1938 - 1942

Jose Fidel = Maria Antonia Naranjo
1936 -   1939 -

Jose Lazario = Anita Maria Armijo
1941 -   1944 -

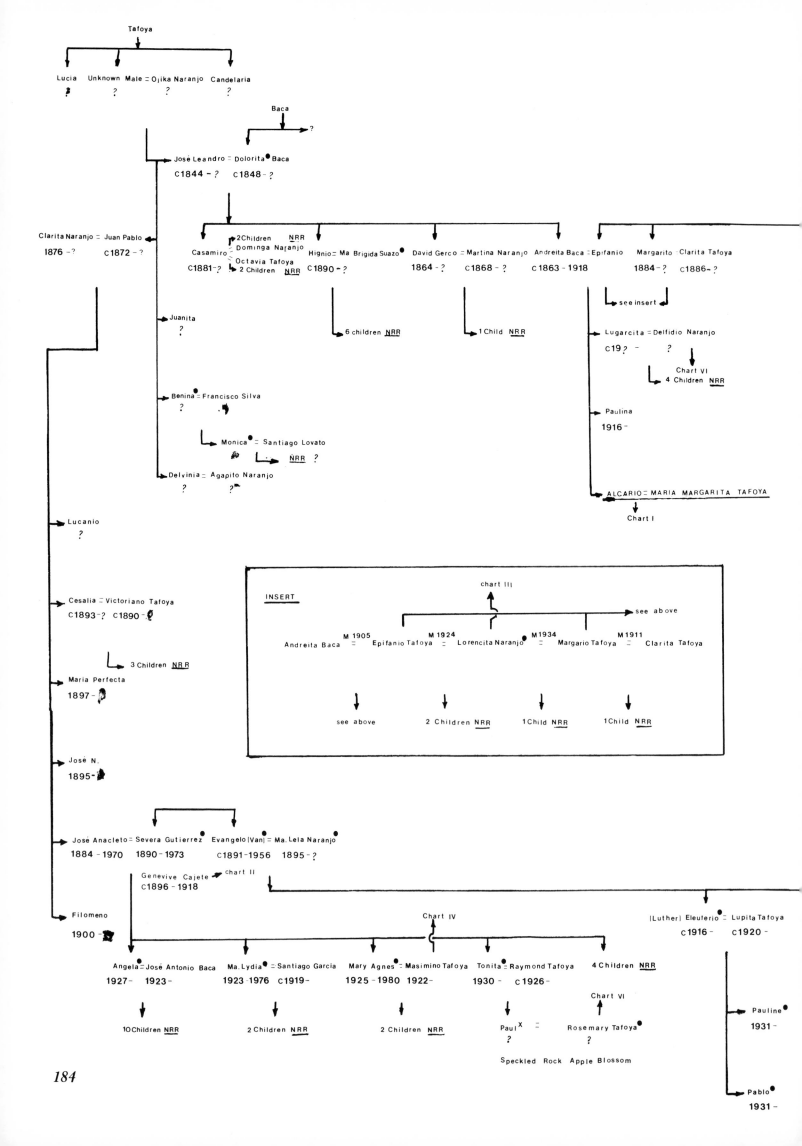

Tafoya

Lucia   Unknown Male = Oȷika Naranjo   Candelaria
?   ?   ?   ?

Baca → ?

José Leandro = Dolorita Baca
C1844 - ?   C1848 - ?

Clarita Naranjo = Juan Pablo
1876 - ?   C1872 - ?

Casamiro   2 Children   NRR
    Dominga Naranjo
    Octavia Tafoya
C1881-?   2 Children   NRR

Hignio = Ma Brigida Suazo
C1890 - ?

David Gerco = Martina Naranjo
1864 - ?   C1868 - ?

Andreita Baca = Epifanio
1863 - 1918

Margarito = Clarita Tafoya
1884 - ?   C1886 - ?

see insert

→ Juanita
?

6 children NRR

1 Child NRR

Lugarcita = Delfidio Naranjo
C19? - ?

Chart VI
4 Children NRR

→ Benina = Francisco Silva
?

Paulina
1916 -

Monica = Santiago Lovato
NRR ?

→ Delvinia = Agapito Naranjo
?   ?

ALCARIO = MARIA MARGARITA TAFOYA

Chart I

→ Lucanio
?

INSERT

chart III

→ see above

Andreita Baca   M 1905   M 1924   M 1934   M 1911
     =   Epifanio Tafoya   =   Lorencita Naranjo   =   Margario Tafoya   =   Clarita Tafoya

→ Cesalia = Victoriano Tafoya
C1893-?   C1890 - ?

see above   2 Children NRR   1 Child NRR   1 Child NRR

3 Children NRR

Maria Perfecta
1897 -

José N.
1895 -

José Anacleto = Severa Gutierrez   Evangelo (Van) = Ma. Lela Naranjo
1884 - 1970   1890 - 1973   C1891 - 1956   1895 - ?

Genevive Cajete → chart II
C1896 - 1918

Chart IV

→ Filomeno
1900 -

(Luther) Eleuterio = Lupita Tafoya
C1916 -   C1920 -

Angela = José Antonio Baca
1927 -   1923 -

Ma. Lydia = Santiago Garcia
1923 - 1976   C1919 -

Mary Agnes = Masimino Tafoya
1925 - 1980   1922 -

Tonita = Raymond Tafoya
1930 -   C1926 -

4 Children NRR

Chart VI

Pauline
1931 -

10 Children NRR

2 Children NRR

2 Children NRR

Paul X =
?

Rosemary Tafoya
?

Speckled Rock   Apple Blossom

Pablo
1931 -

184

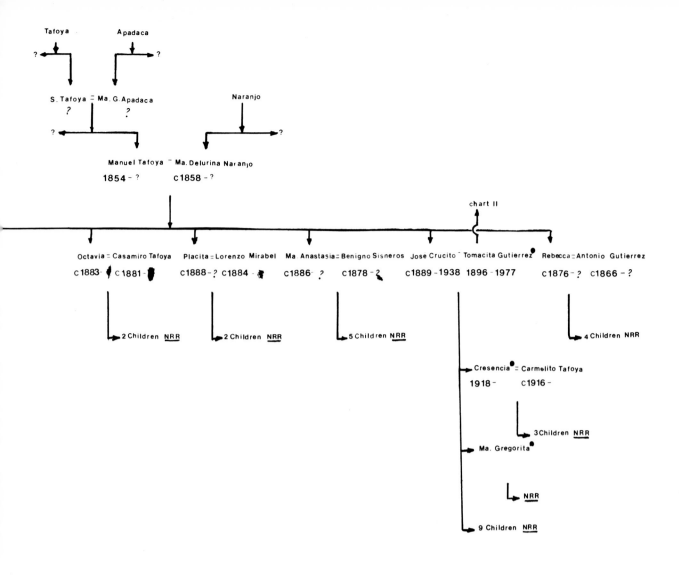

TAFOYA FAMILY GENEALOGY.
ALCARIO BRANCH
CHART IV

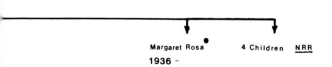

Margaret Rosa
1936 -

4 Children   NRR

Christina ● = José Victor Naranjo

1891 - 1980   1895 - 1942

Lightning Basket

MARIA MARGARITA = ALCARIO TAFOYA

Mary G. ● = Willie Cain   George ●   Teresita ● = Josecito Naranjo   Mary Louise ● = J. O'Brian   Claudio ●

1915 -   Eckberry

Blue Rain   1923 -1976   1917 -   1919 -   1927 -

Apple Blossom

M.Constance (Tina) ● = T.Garcia   Stella ● = Loretto C.Chavarria   Shirley

1946 -   1939 -

Hill Flower

Rosemary ●   Loretta ●   Darlene

1966   1965 -

Marjorie ● = C.Tannin

1936 -   Denise ●   Victor

Autumn Leaves   1960 -

Kieth

1966 -

Two Feathers

Stephen   Joey ●

1968 -   1966 -

Douglas T.   Mildred ● = ? Moore

1942 -

White Flower   1941 -

Linda ● = E.Silva   Kelli ●
            D.Bortz

1949 -

Yellow Corn

Autumn Ray   Adam   Victor

1967 -   1974 -   1946 -   Rick ●

Tammie   Quano

1969 -   1977   Eldon ●

Elzabeth Joy ● = E. Somango

1948 -

Sun Reflection on the Lake   Ernie ●

William ●   Teresa Joy

1950 -   1966 -

White Weasel   Praire Flower

Edward Wm.   Georgia ● = ? Wyasket

1966

Red Bird   1947 -

                                Jayson ●   Roberta ●   Colby ●

Warren = Melinda Archuletta

1951 -

Little Sun

Melony

1974

186

Chart I

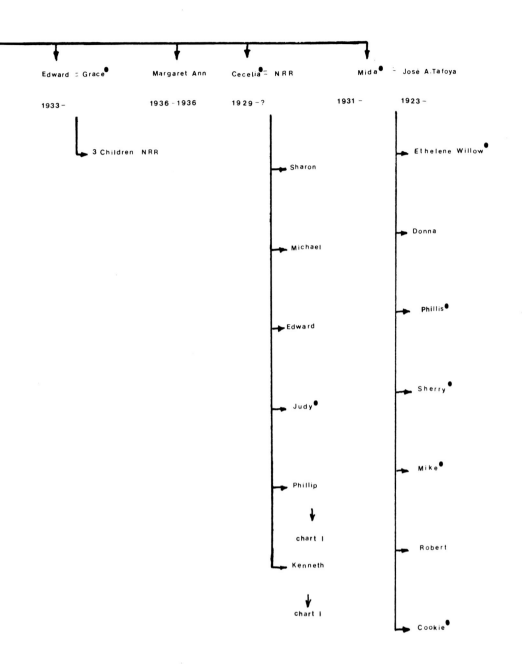

Edward = Grace   Margaret Ann   Cecelia = NRR   Mida = José A.Tafoya

1933 –   1936 - 1936   1929 –?   1931 –   1923 –

3 Children NRR

Sharon

Michael

Edward

Judy

Phillip

chart I

Kenneth

chart I

Ethelene Willow

Donna

Phillis

Sherry

Mike

Robert

Cookie

TAFOYA FAMILY GENEALOGY-
MARGARET'S SIBLINGS-
CHRISTINA BRANCH- CHART V

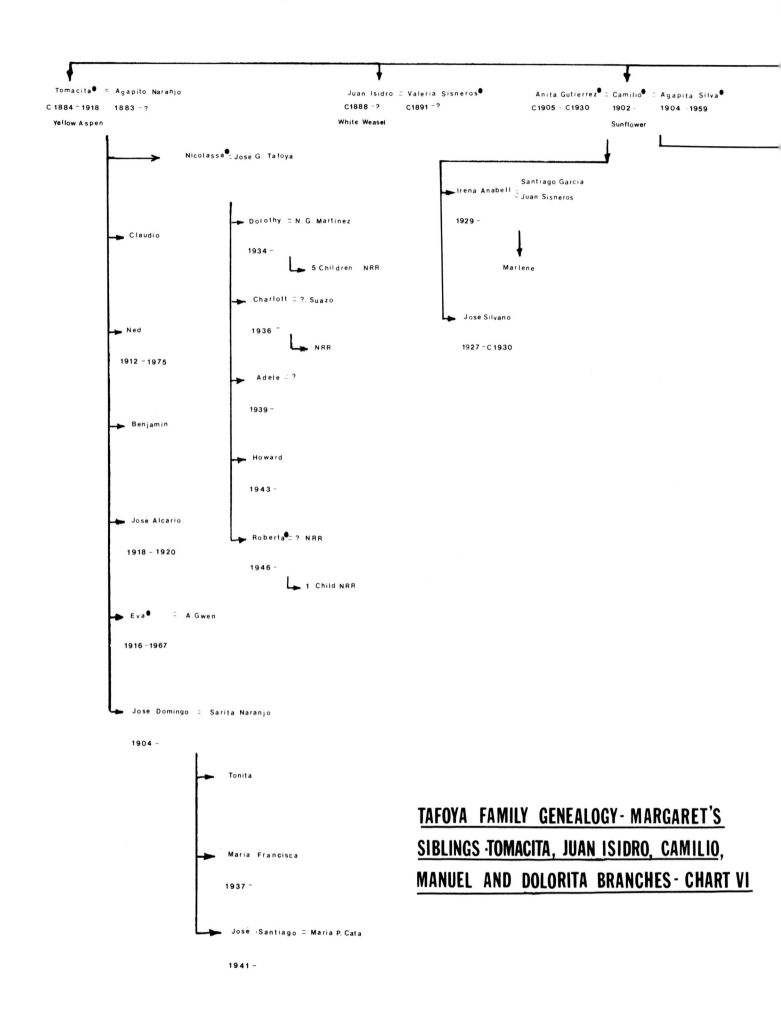

Tomacita● = Agapito Naranjo
C 1884 - 1918   1883 - ?
Yellow Aspen

Juan Isidro = Valeria Sisneros●
C1888 - ?   C1891 - ?
White Weasel

Anita Gutierrez● = Camilio● = Agapita Silva●
C1905 - C1930   1902 -   1904 - 1959
Sunflower

Nicolassa● = Jose G. Tafoya

Irena Anabell   Santiago Garcia
⌐ Juan Sisneros
1929 -

Marlene

José Silvano
1927 - C1930

Claudio

Dorothy = N. G. Martinez
1934 -
5 Children   NRR

Charlott = ?. Suazo
1936 -
NRR

Ned
1912 - 1975

Adele = ?
1939 -

Benjamin

Howard
1943 -

Jose Alcario
1918 - 1920

Roberta● = ? NRR
1946 -
1 Child NRR

Eva● = A. Gwen
1916 - 1967

Jose Domingo = Sarita Naranjo
1904 -

Tonita

Maria Francisca
1937 -

TAFOYA FAMILY GENEALOGY- MARGARET'S
SIBLINGS -TOMACITA, JUAN ISIDRO, CAMILIO,
MANUEL AND DOLORITA BRANCHES- CHART VI

José ·Santiago = Maria P. Cata
1941 -

188

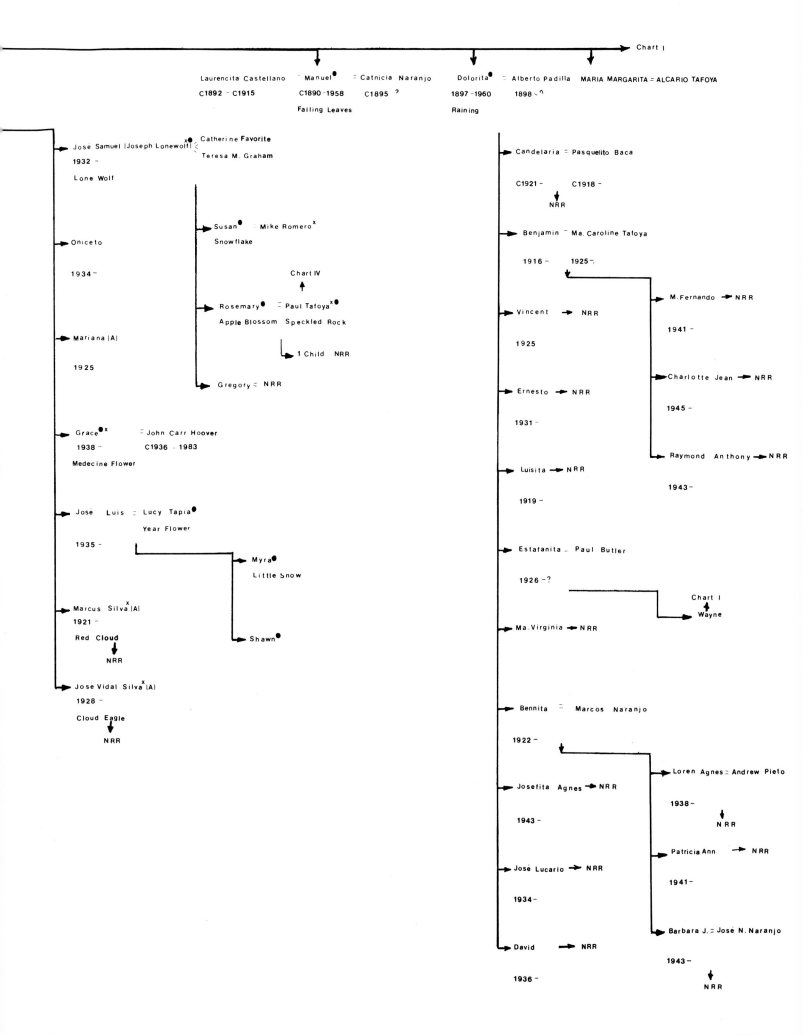

Chart I

Laurencita Castellano   = Manuel ●   = Catnicia Naranjo   Dolorita ●   = Alberto Padilla   MARIA MARGARITA = ALCARIO TAFOYA

C1892 - C1915   C1890 -1958   C1895 ?   1897 -1960   1898 ╲∩

Falling Leaves   Raining

José Samuel (Joseph Lonewolf) ˣ● Catherine **Favorite**

1932 -   Teresa M. Graham

Lone Wolf

Oniceto

1934 ⁻

Mariana (A)

1925

Grace ●ˣ   = John Carr Hoover

1938 -   C1936 - 1983

Medecine Flower

José   Luis   = Lucy Tapia ●

        Year Flower

1935 -

Marcus Silva ˣ (A)

1921 ⁻

Red Cloud

    NRR

José Vidal Silva ˣ (A)

1928 -

Cloud Eagle

    NRR

Susan ●   = Mike Romero ˣ

Snowflake

Chart IV

Rosemary ●   = Paul Tafoya ˣ ●

Apple Blossom   Speckled Rock

     1 Child   NRR

Gregory = NRR

Myra ●

Little Snow

Shawn ●

Candelaria   = Pasquelito Baca

C1921 -   C1918 -

    NRR

Benjamin ⁻ Ma. Caroline Tafoya

1916 -   1925 ⁻.

Vincent →   NRR

1925

Ernesto →   NRR

1931 -

Luisita → NRR

1919 -

Estafanita ₋ Paul Butler

1926 -?

Ma. Virginia →NRR

Bennita   =   Marcos Naranjo

1922 -

Josefita   Agnes →NRR

1943 -

José Lucario →NRR

1934-

David   →   NRR

1936 -

M. Fernando →NRR

1941 -

Charlotte Jean →NRR

1945 -

Raymond Anthony →NRR

1943-

Chart I

Wayne

Loren Agnes = Andrew Pieto

1938-

    NRR

Patricia Ann   →   NRR

1941-

Barbara J. = José N. Naranjo

1943 -

    NRR

References

Adams, E.B. and Fray A. Chavez. 1956. *The Missions of New Mexico, 1776. A Description by Fray Fransisco Atanasio Dominguez with Other Contemporary Documents.* Albuquerque: University of New Mexico Press.

Andrist, R.K. 1964. *The Long Death.* New York: The Macmillan Company.

Anonymous. 1940. "Land Status." *United Pueblo Quarterly Bulletin.* 2. no. 2.

———. 1972 Inter-tribal Indian Ceremonial Program, Gallup, NM.

———. 1974 *Seven Families in Pueblo Pottery.* Maxwell Museum of Anthropology. Albuquerque: University of New Mexico Press.

———. 1977. *Pueblo Pottery Exhibition* (pamphlet). Santa Fe, NM. Dewey-Kofron Gallery.

———. 1979. "Nacimientos." *Pueblo Horizons"* 3, no. 10

———. 1979. *The Quarterly of the Southwestern Association on Indian Affairs.* 14, no. 3.

———. 1982. *El Santuario—Un Alto on the High Road to Taos.* Silver Spring, MD: Sons of the Holy Family.

———. 1983. *La Eglesia de Santa Cruz de la Cañada, 1733-1983.* Sante Fe, N.M.: The Blue Feather Press (Published for the Parish of Santa Cruz by the Meredith Corporation, Albuquerque, NM.

Applegate, F.G. 1929. *Indian Stories from the Pueblos.* Glorieta, NM: The Rio Grande Press.

Arnold, D.L. 1982. "Pueblo Pottery—2,000 Years of Artistry." *National Geographic Magazine.* 162. no. 5.

Austin, M. 1934. *Indian Pottery of the Rio Grande.* Pasadena, CA: Esto Publishing Company.

Bailey, L.R. 1970. *Bosque Redondo.* Pasadena, CA: Socio-Technical Books.

———. 1964. *The Long Walk.* Los Angeles: Western Lore Press.

Bandelier, A.F. 1890-1892. "Final Report of Investigations Among the Indians of the Southwestern United States, Carried on Mainly in the Years from 1880 to 1885." 2 vols. *Papers of the Archaeological Institute of America,* Series 3 and 4. Cambridge, MA: (Archaeological Institute of America.)

Beck, W.A. and Y.D. Haase. 1969. *Historical Atlas of New Mexico.* Norman: University of Oklahoma Press.

Bloom, L.B. 1936. "Bourke on the Southwest, Chapter XIX, 'The Northern Pueblos.'" *New Mexico Historical Review,* 2, no. 3.

Breternitz, D.A., A.H. Rohn Jr., and E.A. Morris. 1974. *Prehistoric Ceramics of the Mesa Verde Region.* Flagstaff, AZ. Museum of Northern Arizona Ceramic Series, 5.

Brody, J.J. 1979. "Southwestern American Indian Pottery," *American Art and Antiques.* 110-117.

———. 1977. *Mimbres Painted Pottery.* Sante Fe, NM: School of American Research.

Brugge, D.M. 1979. "Early 18th Century Spanish-Apachean Relations. Collected Papers in Honor of Bertha Pauline Dutton." *Papers of the Archaeological Society of New Mexico,* 4:103-121.

Bunzel, R.L. 1929. *The Pueblo Potter, A Study of Creative Imagination in Primitive Art.* New York: Dover Publications.

Canfield, K.R. 1975. "Margaret Tafoya's Kitchen," *Kansas City Star.* (June 22 2c). Kansas City, MO.

Cash, J.H. and G.W. Wolff. 1974. *The Comanche People.* Phoenix, AZ: The Indian Tribal Series.

Cervantes, M.A. 1980. *National Anthropological Museum.* Barcelona: Ediciones Grijalbo, S.A.

Chan, R.P. 1965. *A Guide to Mexican Archaeology.* Mexico City: Minuta Mexicana Publishing Company.

Chapman, K.M. 1927. "Post-Spanish Pueblo Pottery," *Art and Archaeology,* no. 23.

———. 1931. *Introduction to American Indian Art—Indian Pottery.* Glorieta, NM: Rio Grande Press.

———. 1977. *The Pottery of Santo Domingo Pueblo; A Detailed Study of Its Decoration.* Albuquerque: School of American Research and University of New Mexico Press.

———. 1977. *The Pottery of San Ildefonso Pueblo.* Albuquerque: School of American Research and University of New Mexico Press.

Chappell, G. 1969. "To Santa Fe by Narrow Gauge: The D and RG's 'Chili Line.'" *Colorado Rail Annual,* no. 7, (3rd printing). Golden.

Chavez, F.A. 1957. *Archives of the Archdiocese of Santa Fe, 1678-1903.* Washington, D.C.: Academy of American Franciscan History.

Collins, J.E., ed. 1977. *Hopi Traditions in Pottery and Painting: Honoring Grace Chapella (1874--).* Signal Hill, CA: G.B. Hammonds Printing Co.

Colton, H.S. 1939. *Archaeological Studies in the La Plata District—Southwest Colorado and Northwest New Mexico.* Washington, D.C.: Carnegie Institution.

Cooke, S.L. 1930. Master's thesis, Albuquerque: University of New Mexico.

Cordell, S. 1979. *Prehistory: Eastern Anasazi,* vol. 9, *Handbook of the North American Indians,* Washington, D.C.: Smithsonian Institution.

Delaney, R.W. 1974. *The Southern Ute People.* Phoenix, AZ: The Indian Tribal Series.

Devereau, D. 1966. "The Relocation of a Pueblo Emergence Shrine," *El Palacio* (Winter 1966).

Dillingham, R., ed.1977. *Indian Autobiographies* (Pueblo Potter Exhibition Program). Santa Fe, NM: Dewey-Kofron Gallery.

Dittert, A.E. Jr. and F. Plog. 1980. *Generations in Clay.* Flagstaff, AZ: Northland Press.

Dobyns, H.F. 1973. *The Mescalero Apache People.* Phoenix, AZ: The Indian Tribal Series.

Dobyns, H.F. and R.C. Euler. 1972. *The Navajo People.* Phoenix, AZ: The Indian Tribal Series.

Dockstader, F.J. 1972 *Naked Clay.* New York: Museum of the American Indian, Heye Foundation.

Douglas, W.B. 1917. "Land of the Small House People," *El Palacio,* 4, no. 2.

———. 1917. "Shrines of the Small House People." *El Palacio* 4, no. 11: 19-29.

Dozier, E.P. 1966. *Hano, A Tewa Indian Community in Arizona.* New York: Holt, Rinehart and Winston, Inc.

Dutton, B.P. 1966. "Pots Pose Problems." *El Palacio,* 73, no. 1: 5-15.

Ellis, F.H. 1975. "Highways to the Past." *New Mexico Magazine,* 53 no. 5.

Faris, C.E. 1954. *Pueblo Governors' Canes.* Albuquerque, NM: United Pueblos Agency.

Fewkes, J.W. 1898. "Sityatki and Its Pottery." Excerpted from Archaeological Expedition to Arizona in 1895. *Report of the Bureau of Ethnology, 1895-1896.* Washington, D.C.: U.S. Government Printing Office. 631-728.

———. 1919. "Designs on Prehistoric Hopi Pottery." *Thirty-Third Annual Report of the Bureau of Ethnology, 1911-1912:* 207-284. Washington, D.C.: U.S. Government Printing Office.

Forrest, E.R. 1979. *Missions and Pueblos of the Old Southwest.* Glorieta, NM: Rio Grande Press.

Frank, L. and F.H. Harlow. 1974. *Historic Pottery of the Pueblo Indians.* Boston: New York Graphic Society.

Goddard, P.E. 1931. *Pottery of the Southwestern Indians.* New York: American Museum of Natural History.

———. 1931. *Indians of the Southwest.* New York: American Museum of Natural History.

Griswold, J. 1946. *Fuels, Combustion and Furnaces.* New York: McGraw-Hill Book Co., Inc.

Guthe, C.E. 1925. *Pueblo Pottery Making, A Study at the Village of San Ildefonso.* New Haven, CT: Yale University Press.

———. 1925. "Pueblo Pottery Making." *Papers of the Phillips Academy Southwest Expedition Number 2.* New Haven, CT: Yale University Press.

Hackett, C.W., ed. 1942. *Revolt of the Pueblo Indians of New Mexico and Ottermin's Attempted Reconquest, 1680-1692.* (2 vols.) Albuquerque: University of New Mexico Press.

Hall, D.J. 1933. *Enchanted Sand: A New Mexican Pilgrimage.* New York: William Morrow and Co.

Hammond, G.P. and R. Agapito. 1945. *Fray Alonso de Benavide's Revised Memorial of 1634.* Albuquerque: University of New Mexico Press.

Harlow, F.H. 1965. "Tewa Indian Ceremonial Pottery." *El Palacio* 72, no. 4:13-23.

———. 1973. *Matte Paint Pottery of the Tewa, Keres, and Zuni Pueblos.* Santa Fe: Museum of New Mexico.

———. 1970. *Historic Pueblo Indian Pottery.* Santa Fe: Museum of New Mexico Press.

———. 1977. *Modern Pueblo Pottery, 1880-1960.* Flagstaff, AZ: Northland Press.

Harrington, J.P. 1909. "A Brief Description of the Tewa Language." *American Anthropologist* 12:497-504.

———. 1916. "Ethnogeography of the Tewa Indians." *Twenty-Ninth Annual Report of the Bureau of Ethnology, 1907-1908:* 29-636. Washington, D.C.: U.S. Government Printing Office.

Harrison, B. 1885. "Espanola and Its Environs, 1885." *Harper's Monthly Magazine* (May 1885). Reprinted by the *Rio Grande Sun* (November 1966), Espanola, NM.

Hawley, F.M. 1936. *Field Manual of Prehistoric Southwestern Pottery Types.* University of New Mexico Bulletin. Albuquerque: University of New Mexico Press.

Henderson, A.C. 1977. *Brothers of Light—Penitenties of the Southwest.* Santa Fe, NM: William Gannon.

Herold, J. 1981. *North American Indian Basketry Basics.* Popular Leaflet, no. three. Colorado: Denver Museum of Natural History.

Hewett, E.L. 1900. "The Archaeology of the Parajito Plateau." *American Anthropologist* 6:629-659.

———. 1904. "A General View of the Archaeology of the Pueblo Region." *Smithsonian Report for 1904:* 583-605. Washington, D.C.: U.S. Government Printing Office.

———. 1909. "The Excavations at Tyuoni, NM, in 1908." *American Anthropologist* 11:334-455.

———. 1909. "The Pajaritan Culture." *American Journal of Archaeology* (2nd series) 13:334-344.

———. 1937. *Indians of the Rio Grande Valley.* Albuquerque: University of New Mexico Press.

———. 1938. *The Pajarito Plateau and Its Ancient People.* Albuquerque: University of New Mexico Press.

Highwater, J. 1976. *Song from the Earth: American Indian Painting.* Boston: New York Graphic Society.

Hill, W.W. 1982. *An Ethnography of Santa Clara Pueblo, New Mexico.* Albuquerque: University of New Mexico Press.

Horgan, P. 1954. *Great River: The Rio Grande in North American History.* 2 vols. New York: Reinhart and Co., Inc.

Hull, D. 1916. "Castaño de Sosa's Expedition to New Mexico in 1590." *Old Santa Fe.*

James, G.W. 1970. *Indian Basketry and How to Make Indian and Other Baskets.* Glorieta, NM: Rio Grande Press.

Jeançon, A.J. 1911. "Explorations in the Chama Basin, New Mexico" *Records of the Past* 10:92-108.

———. 1912. "Ruins at Pesedeuinge." *Records of the Past* 11:28-37.

———. 1916. Unpublished field notes on Santa Clara Pueblo. Colorado: Denver Art Museum.

———. 1930. Santa Clara, An Upper Rio Grande Pueblo. Manuscript 4821, Bureau of American Ethnology. Smithsonian Manuscript Vault, Washington, D.C.

———. 1931. *Santa Clara and San Juan Pottery.* Leaflet no. 35. Colorado: Department of Indian Art, Denver Art Museum.

John, E.A.H. 1975. *Storms Brewed in Other Men's Worlds.* Lincoln: University of Nebraska Press.

Johnson, W. 1925. *Indian Arts Fund Bulletin, no. 1.*

Kelly, L., ed. 1970. *Navajo Roundup. Selected Correspondence of Kit Carson's Expedition Against the Navajo, 1863-1865.* Boulder, CO: Pruett Publishing Company.

Kent, K.P. 1983. *Prehistoric Textiles of the Southwest.* Santa Fe, NM: School of American Research and the University of New Mexico Press.

Kessel, J.L. 1979. *Kiva, Cross and Crown: The Pecos Indians and New Mexico, 1540-1840.* Washington, D.C.: U.S. Department of the Interior, National Park Service.

Kidder, A.V. 1915. "Pottery of the Pajarito Plateau and Some Adjacent Regions in New Mexico." *Memoirs of the Anthropological Association* 2: no. 6:411-461

———. 1962. *An Introduction to the Study of Southwest Archaeology.* New Haven, CT: Yale University Press and Andover, MA: Phillips Academy.

Kidder, A.V. and A.O. Shepard. 1936. "The Pottery of Pecos." *Papers of the Southwest Expedition, 2 vols.* New Haven, CT: Phillips Academy. Yale University Press and Andover, MA.

Lambert, M.F. 1966. *Pueblo Indian Pottery: Materials, Tools and Techniques.* Santa Fe: Museum of New Mexico Press.

LaFree, B. 1975. *Santa Clara Pottery Today.* Santa Fe, NM: School of American Research.

Lister, R.H. and F.C. 1969. *The Earl H. Morris Pottery Collection.* Boulder: University of Colorado Press.

Littlebird, H. 1979. "Margaret Tafoya: Guardian of Mother Clay." *The Quarterly of the Southwestern Association on Indian Affairs* 14, no. 4. Santa Fe, NM.

Mails, T.E. 1983. *The Pueblo Children of the Earth Mother.* 2 vols. Garden City, NY: Doubleday and Company, Inc.

Marden, L. 1936. "Today in the Feathered Serpent's City." *National Geographic Magazine* 70, 110, no. 5:11.

McNamera, E.P. 1939. *Clay Products and Whitewares.* Vol.3, *Ceramics.* State College: Pennsylvania State College Press.

Mera, H.P. 1934. *A Survey of the Biscuit Ware in Northern New Mexico.* Laboratory of Anthropology Technical Series Bulletin, 110, 6.

_____. 1939. *Style Trends of Pueblo Pottery in the Rio Grande and Little Colorado Cultural Areas.* Laboratory of Anthropology, no. 3.

_____. 1940. *Population Changes in the Rio Grande Glaze-Paint Area.* Laboratory of Anthropology Technical Series Bulletin. Santa Fe, NM.

Monthan, G. and D. 1979. *Nacimientos.* Flagstaff, AZ: Northland Press.

Mosley, H. "A Family Tradition." *New Mexico Crafts* 4, no. 1

Muller, F. and B. Hopkins. 1974. *A Guide to Mexican Ceramics.* Mexico, D.F.: Minutiae Mexican, S.A. de C.V.

Noble, D.G. 1981. *Ancient Ruins of the Southwest.* Flagstaff, AZ: Northland Press.

Ortiz, A. 1974. "Farmers and Raiders of the Southwest." *The World of the American Indian.* Washington, D.C.: National Geographic Society.

Ortiz, A., ed. 1979. *Handbook of the North American Indians, Vol. 9, Southwest.* Washington, D.C.: Smithsonian Institution, U.S. Government Printing Office.

_____. 1980. "Popay's Leadership: A Pueblo Perspective." *El Palacio* 86, no. 4.

Parsons, E.C. 1929. "The Social Organization of the Tewa of New Mexico." *Memoirs of the American Anthropology Association* 36.

Pennypacker, S. W. II. 1937. "Friendship as a Functional Motive in Ceramic Types of Eastern North America." *Twenty-fifth Anniversary Studies, Philadelphia Anthropological Society.* Philadelphia: University of Pennsylvania Press.

Peterson, S. 1977. *The Living Tradition of Maria Martinez.* Tokyo, New York, San Francisco: Kodansha Press.

Poley, H.S. 1920. "American Wedding." *El Palacio* 8.

Reed, E.K. 1946. "The Distinctive Features and Distribution of the San Juan Anasazi Culture." *Southwestern Journal of Anthropology* 2, no. 3.

_____. 1949. "Sources of Upper Rio Grande Pueblo Culture and Population." *El Palacio* 56, no. 6:163-183.

Roessel, R., ed. 1973. *Navajo Stories of the Long Walk Period.* Tsalie, AZ: Navajo Community College Press.

Sando, J.S. 1976. *The Pueblo Indians.* San Francisco: The Indian Historian Press.

_____. no date. *Pueblo Indian Biographies.* Albuquerque: University of New Mexico Minority Group Cultural Center, College of Education.

Schroeder, A.H. and D.S. Matson. 1965. *A Colony on the Move: Gaspar Castaño de Sosa's Journal: 1590-1591.* Santa Fe, NM: School of American Research.

Schulman, E. 1956. *Tree Ring Hydrology of the Colorado River Basin.* Tucson: University of Arizona Bulletin 16, no. 4.

Shepard, A. 1965. *Ceramics for the Archaeologist* (publication 609). Washington, D.C.: Carnegie Institute.

Simmons, M. 1974. *Witchcraft in the Southwest.* Flagstaff, AZ: Northland Press.

_____. 1980. "The Pueblo Revolt: Why Did It Happen?" *El Palacio* 86, no. 4.

Sperling, D.M. 1983. "The Chimayo Rebellion." *New Mexico Magazine* 61, no. 11.

Spicer, E.H. 1962. *Cycles of Conquest.* Tucson: University of Arizona Press.

Spinden, H.J. 1911. "The Making of Pottery at San Ildefonso." *The American Museum Journal* 11, no. 6:192-196.

Spivey, R.L. 1979. *Maria.* Flagstaff, AZ: Northland Press.

Sprague, M. 1957. *Massacre: The Tragedy at White River.* Boston: Little, Brown and Co.

Steen, C. 1980. "Prehistory of the Northern Plateau." *Exploration: Annual Bulletin of the School of American Research.* Santa Fe, New Mexico.

Stevenson, J. 1883. "Illustrated Catalogue of the Collections Obtained from the Indians of New Mexico and Arizona in 1880." *Second Annual Report, Bureau of American Ethnology.* Washington, D.C.: Smithsonian Institution.

Stirling, M. 1940. "Indian Tribes of Pueblo Land." *National Geographic Magazine* 78, no. 5:549-596.

Stroup, J.M. 1908. "Earliest Craftsmanship of the United States: Pottery of the Pueblos." *Great Southwest Magazine* 3, no. 4:93-112.

Stubbs, S.A. 1950. *Birds-Eye View of the Pueblos.* Norman: University of Oklahoma Press.

Tanner, C.L. 1968. *Southwest Indian Craft Arts.* Tucson: University of Arizona Press.

_____. 1976. *Prehistoric Southwestern Craft Arts.* Tucson: University of Arizona Press.

Taylor, N., ed. 1936. *The Garden Dictionary.* Cambridge, MA: Houghton Mifflin Co. and the Riverside Press.

Tebble, J. and K. Jennison. 1960. *The American Indian Wars.* New York: Harper and Row and Bonanza Books.

Terrell, J.U. 1968. *Estevanico the Black.* Los Angeles: Western Lore Press.

_____. 1973. *Pueblos, Gods and Spaniards.* New York: Dial Press.

Thomas, D.H. 1978. *The Southwestern Indian Detours.* Phoenix, AZ: Hunter Publishing Co.

Tierney, G. 1976. "Of Pots and Plants." *El Palacio* 82, no. 3.

Toulouse, B. 1976. "Pueblo Pottery Traditions, Ever Constant, Ever Changing." *El Palacio* 82, no. 3.

_____. 1977. *Pueblo Pottery of the New Mexico Indians.* Santa Fe: Museum of New Mexico Press.

Twitchell, R.E. 1914. *The Spanish Archives of New Mexico,* vol. 1. Cedar Rapids, IA: The Torch Press.

Tyler, H.A. 1964. *Pueblo Gods and Myths*. Norman: University of Oklahoma Press.

Underhill, R. 1944. *Pueblo Crafts*. Washington, D.C.: U.S. Department of the Interior, Bureau of Indian Affairs.

Wade, E.L. and L.S. McChesney. 1981. *Historic Hopi Ceramics*. Cambridge, MA: Peabody Museum Press.

Walter, P. A. 1918. "Incorporation of the School of American Research; Dedication of the Art Museum of SAR and Museum of New Mexico." *El Palacio* 5, no. 18.

———. 1920. "The Fiesta of Santa Fe." *Art and Archaeology* 9, no. 1.

Waters, F. 1965. *The Man Who Killed the Deer*. Flagstaff, AZ: Northland Press.

Weber, D.J. 1982. *The Mexican Frontier, 1821-1846: The American Southwest Under Mexico*. Albuquerque: University of New Mexico Press.

Wendorf, F. 1953. *Salvage Archaeology in the Chama Valley, New Mexico*. Santa Fe, NM: Monographs of the School of American Research, no. 17.

Woodbury, R.B. and E.B.W. Zubrow. 1979. "Agricultural Beginnings." *Handbook of the North American Indians, Vol. 9. Southwest*. Washington, D.C.: Smithsonian Institution.

Woods, R.D. and G. Alvarez-Alman. 1978. *Spanish Surnames in the Southwestern United States*. Boston: G.K. Hall and Co.

Wormington, H.M. 1956. *Prehistoric Indians of the Southwest*. Colorado: Denver Museum of Natural History Popular Series, no. 7.

Wormington, H.M. and A. Neal. 1951. *The Story of Pueblo Pottery*. Colorado: Denver Museum of Natural History Popular Series, no. 2.

Wright, B. 1973. *Kachinas: A Hopi Artist's Documentary*. Flagstaff, AZ: Northland Press, and Phoenix, AZ: The Heard Museum.

Yava, A. 1978. *Big Falling Snow*. New York: Crown Publishers.

Young, I. 1983. "Development of the Indo-Hispanic Population in New Mexico." *Pueblo Horizons* 7, no. 3.

Young, J.N. 1975. *The Pottery Jewels of Joseph Lonewolf*. Scottsdale, AZ: Dandic Publications.

Index